T0272610

Changing the Course

Changing the Course

How Charlie Sifford and Stanley Mosk Integrated the PGA

Peter May

ROWMAN & LITTLEFIELD
Lanham · Boulder · New York · London

Published by Rowman & Littlefield
An imprint of The Rowman & Littlefield Publishing Group, Inc.
4501 Forbes Boulevard, Suite 200, Lanham, Maryland 20706
www.rowman.com

86-90 Paul Street, London EC2A 4NE, United Kingdom

Distributed by NATIONAL BOOK NETWORK

British Library Cataloguing in Publication Information Available

Library of Congress Cataloging-in-Publication Data

Names: May, Peter, 1951– author.
Title: Changing the course : how Charlie Sifford and Stanley Mosk
  integrated the PGA / Peter May.
Description: Lanham, MD : Rowman & Littlefield, [2024] | Includes
  bibliographical references and index. | Summary: "The compelling,
  little-known story of Charlie Sifford, the first Black golfer to get his
  PGA card, and Stanley Mosk, a crusading civil rights attorney and
  California Supreme Court justice, who together made history by taking on
  the PGA and the Caucasian Only clause in its bylaws"— Provided by
  publisher.
Identifiers: LCCN 2023026544 (print) | LCCN 2023026545 (ebook) | ISBN
  9781538178010 (cloth) | ISBN 9781538178027 (epub)
Subjects: LCSH: Sifford, Charlie, 1922-2015. | Mosk, Stanley, 1912-2001. |
  Discrimination in sports—United States—History. | Professional
  Golfers' Association of America—History. | African American
  golfers—Biography. | Lawyers—California—Biography. |
  Judges—California—Biography.
Classification: LCC GV964.S53 M39 2024 (print) | LCC GV964.S53 (ebook) |
  DDC 796.352092 [B]—dc23/eng/20230828
LC record available at https://lccn.loc.gov/2023026544
LC ebook record available at https://lccn.loc.gov/2023026545

To the families of Charles L. Sifford and Stanley Mosk

Contents

Foreword

Gary Player

$\mathscr{I}$ have had a lot of honors bestowed on me over the years, but none greater than Charlie Sifford asking me to introduce him when he was inducted into the World Golf Hall of Fame. Me! A white South African! What an honor it was. I met Charlie for the first time when I arrived in America in 1957. I asked him how his round had gone. He said he had not been allowed to play because he was Black. And that hurt me so much, coming from a country with apartheid rule. I tried to make inroads on his behalf and talked to the PGA. I didn't get very far. But I offered him all the support I could and played a lot of practice rounds with him. He became a dear, dear friend. You have to give him so much credit for what he went through. I remember playing with him in one tournament where he was called the N-word and someone kicked his ball into the rough. There were so many other examples. But he never complained. He never was bitter. And it was so rewarding to see the attorney general of California, Stanley Mosk, come to Charlie's defense when the PGA wouldn't let him become a member. I have great admiration for all those who made it happen. I'm so glad Peter May has taken on this task to tell the world about Charlie and Stanley because their story is one that everyone, not just golfers, should know about. Charlie broke barriers and played such an important role and, because of him, we don't have that racist system anymore. But what a price he paid! I hope by reading this book you will come to understand that Charlie's struggle was not just about getting to play golf, but also was one of the great civil rights struggles of the time. And because of his determination, his courage and his perseverance, the PGA is a more welcoming place for Black golfers today. I know he's looking down from heaven with some degree of satisfaction at the role he played in all this.

Prologue: Los Angeles, January 1969

Charlie Sifford had a cold. He spent the first week of January 1969 at his Los Angeles home, resting up to play in the first event of the PGA season, the Los Angeles Open. While trying to shake a persistent cough, Sifford made what, for him, was a dramatic decision: he would forgo his trademark cigar while competing in the tournament. Having a stogie clenched in his jaw as he traversed eighteen holes had been a comfort for the more than two decades that he had been playing professional golf. He often was asked why he played with it, and he said it helped him in two ways. When he made a complete swing, he could tell if he was moving too much because the cigar would move, pointing away from the ball. The other advantage came when he was putting. He focused the end of the cigar on his ball so that he always knew if his head moved too soon.

Now, at forty-six, as he tried to recover, smoking the cigar just made him feel woozy. He would have to do without it for the first start of the 1969 season. Those accustomed to watching him play would be temporarily stunned to see him without his signature stogie.

Sifford reported to the Rancho Park Municipal Golf Course for the first round without his cigars, but with renewed confidence. He was starting his sixth year as a full-time member of the Professional Golf Association, the first Black man ever admitted to an organization that, until 1961, had restricted membership to golfers "of the Caucasian race." It was Sifford, in concert with Stanley Mosk, the attorney general of California, who forced the PGA to eliminate that odious bylaw in its constitution and abandon racial segregation, the last professional sport in the United States to do so.

By the time that happened, Sifford was nearing his fortieth birthday.

Throughout the 1950s, when he was in his prime, Sifford was the dominant Black golfer in the country. He won five consecutive national opens conducted by the United Golf Association, which was where Black golfers were consigned to compete. They played a tournament schedule every summer on hardscrabble courses with little landscaping, less grooming, and small purses. They would occasionally be allowed to compete in a select few PGA tournaments but were denied membership in the organization for one reason only—the color of their skin.

If Sifford and other great Black players before him, such as Teddy Rhodes and Bill Spiller, were invited to play in a PGA tournament, their participation usually came at a cost. They endured on-the-course heckling and taunts, even death threats. They were routinely turned away from courses in the South until they stopped going altogether. They were barred from clubhouses, forced to eat and change clothes in parking lots. In one ugly incident in 1952, Sifford teed off with three other Black men in a tournament in Arizona, only to discover when they got to the first green that human excrement had been dumped in the hole.

Celebrities such as boxer Joe Louis and baseball great Jackie Robinson repeatedly called out the PGA for its racist ways but to no avail. Spiller and Rhodes had filed a doomed lawsuit against the PGA, targeting its restrictive clause, in 1948. The organization promised to allow Black players into its tournaments if the plaintiffs withdrew their lawsuit. The lawsuit was dropped but the discrimination continued. The PGA simply reneged on the deal.

Sifford picked up the fight with someone on his side who had the power and the commitment to demand change. Stanley Mosk had been elected attorney general of California in 1958. A liberal Democrat who had spent the previous fifteen years as a Superior Court judge, Mosk had ruled racially restrictive covenants unenforceable in 1947, a year before the US Supreme Court reached the same conclusion. He hired a civil rights lawyer and activist, Franklin Williams, who did much of the work while heading up the newly formed Division of Constitutional Rights in the Attorney General's office. Williams had worked alongside Thurgood Marshall for the NAACP in Washington and had been running the organization's West Coast office for a decade. He was the ideal complement to Mosk, content to do the behind-the-scenes work, while Mosk was equally content to speak forcefully and publicly, using his bully pulpit. Williams and Mosk proved to be the ideal allies to champion Sifford's cause, and they did so with energy and enthusiasm. Mosk browbeat the PGA incessantly whenever the organization misspoke, which was frequently. Williams threatened to sue the organization after being asked by a PGA lawyer, "Why do colored people want to go where they're not welcome?" Their joint actions forced the PGA to move its signature championship event out of the state of California. They enlisted support from fellow attorneys general across the country. The PGA caved under all the pressure.

Sifford forever credited Mosk with making things change.

"The Caucasian clause tumbled not because the rule was so inherently racist and wrong. It tumbled because I happened to meet a bright, liberal Jewish man who had a real problem with discrimination," Sifford said. "Within two years, Stanley accomplished something that no hot putter or public image could ever do."

Tiger Woods has called Sifford "the Jackie Robinson of our sport." The two became close friends, despite an age difference of more than fifty years. Woods called Sifford "the grandpa I never had" and named his first-born son Charlie. Further accolades poured in for Sifford long after he stopped playing. In 2004, he was inducted into the World Golf Hall of Fame, the first Black to be so honored. "That little old golf I played was all right, wasn't it?" he said during an emotional acceptance speech. Two years later, the University of St. Andrews in Scotland conferred an honorary Doctor of Law degree on Sifford "in recognition of your professional and personal achievements as a golfer." He became Dr. Sifford. In 2009, the tournament once known as the Los Angeles Open announced that one participant each year "who represents the advancement of diversity in golf" would be in the field due to the Charlie Sifford Exemption. Among those to have received the exemption are Harold Varner III and Cameron Champ, both of whom played and won on the PGA Tour.

In 2011, a public, nine-hole golf course in Sifford's hometown of Charlotte, North Carolina, was renamed the Dr. Charles L. Sifford Golf Course. Ironically, it was a course Sifford was not allowed to play while growing up in the city. A photograph of Sifford and an accompanying story hang on the wall of the pro shop.

President Barack Obama presented Sifford with the Presidential Medal of Freedom in 2014. "On the tour, Charlie was sometimes banned from clubhouse restaurants," Obama said at the ceremony. "Folks threatened him, shouted racial slurs from the gallery, kicked his ball in the rough. Charlie didn't have teammates to lean on. But he had plenty of guts and grit and that trademark cigar. Charlie won on the tour, twice. But it was never about the wins. As Charlie says, 'I wasn't just trying to do this for me. I was trying to do it for the world.'"

As Obama draped the medal around the neck of Sifford, then confined to a wheelchair, the other recipients that day looked on and applauded the ninety-two-year-old golfer sharing the stage with them. They included Meryl Streep, Stephen Sondheim, Tom Brokaw, Ethel Kennedy, Marlo Thomas, and Stevie Wonder. Sifford was only the third golfer to be so honored, joining Arnold Palmer and Jack Nicklaus. "Not bad company, huh?" Sifford said.

The day after insurrectionists stormed the US Capitol in January 2021, seeking to prevent Joe Biden from being formally declared the forty-sixth president of the United States, Donald Trump presented Gary Player and Annika Sorenstam with the Presidential Medal of Freedom.

Stanley Mosk would go on to become a towering judicial figure in California, serving thirty-seven years as an associate justice on the California Supreme Court. No one has served longer. After his death in 2001, several members of the California Congressional delegation paid tribute to the long-serving jurist in the *Congressional Record*. Rep. Maxine Waters said Mosk "leaves behind a legacy of his strong belief in civil rights and free speech. He was often on the forefront of legal issues." Another congresswoman, Juanita Millender-McDonald, said Mosk "had a tremendous impact on our country. *Libertas per Justitiam*—Liberty through Justice, was a phrase that Justice Mosk had sewn into his judicial robes. It is a fitting inscription for a man who embodied the phrase so completely."

The Los Angeles County Superior Courthouse was named in his honor in 2002, as was an elementary school in greater Los Angeles. Also in 2002, the California Library and Courts Building in Sacramento was renamed the Stanley Mosk Library and Courts Building. A giant bronze likeness of Mosk, in judicial robes, was unveiled outside the building. More than a few attendees noted it was taller than the actual Judge Mosk, who was always sensitive about his height. Or lack of it. He would wear lifts on occasion.

"Of course, the statue is larger than he was," noted his son, Richard, then an appellate court judge. "It reminds me of what his favorite philosopher, Woody Allen, once said: 'the government is unresponsive to the needs of the little people. If you're under 5 foot 7, it is impossible to get your congressman on the telephone.'"

But what Stanley Mosk lacked in height he more than made up for with a sharp legal mind, an adherence to law and fact, and a lifelong identification with the underdog.

"Stanley Mosk ruled for racial equality before the rest of the nation began moving forward," said Chief Justice Ronald M. George at the dedication ceremony. "He moved beyond the traditional law enforcement concerns of the Department of Justice and established a new section on Constitutional rights and consumer protection."

Ellen Corbett, then chair of the state assembly's Judiciary Committee, said, "the judicial landscape Judge Mosk painted is clear and unambiguous. Whether writing for the majority or teasing the majority from the back bench, Justice Mosk always did what he felt was fair and just, even when it could lead to painful criticism from those he most sought to protect."

None of the accolades or tributes accorded to either man could have been foreseen when Sifford and Mosk were fighting in the 1960s to end the rank racial discrimination that had been codified in the constitution of the PGA. Sifford had been fighting the PGA for years just to be able to compete with the white players. He had no greater hope or expectation. Mosk had no knowledge of the PGA, the sport of golf, or the fact that Blacks were being discriminated against by the organization's own bylaws. But the golfer had a cause that the attorney general was only too eager to champion. The two made for a powerful pair.

The Los Angeles Open, the second oldest tournament on the PGA schedule, was a rare haven for Sifford and the other Black golfers who came before him. Sponsored by the city's Junior Chamber of Commerce, the tournament had, since its inception in 1926, welcomed Black players. Spiller had played in the tournament in 1948 and shot a first-round 68 to match Ben Hogan. He had done that while working as a red cap at Union Station and playing golf when his schedule allowed. Ted Rhodes had played in the same tournament in 1948.

But even as Sifford continued to be refused invitations to participate in tournaments in the 1950s and 1960s, the Los Angeles Open was a constant. It did not require its participants to be members of the PGA, as many tournaments did. If you were good enough, you could play. In those days, it was one of two regular stops on the PGA Tour in the United States that didn't regularly discriminate or adhere to the PGA's discriminatory regulations. The other was George May's All-American Open at the Tam O'Shanter, the club he owned outside Chicago. May openly welcomed Blacks and criticized the golfers of the time (including Hogan, by name) for not being more supportive of Sifford and other Black players.

Due to its fortuitous scheduling as one of the first tournaments of the season, the Los Angeles Open generally drew most of golf's biggest names, despite a venue that was less than ideal. The tournament had had numerous homes over the first forty years, but had been at Rancho Park, a municipal, daily-fee course, from 1956 to 1972, with the exception of 1968, when it was held at Brookside, a course in Pasadena near the iconic Rose Bowl. Rancho Park had modest practice facilities, a tiny clubhouse, and was located across the street from a car wash and a fried chicken joint. The course fell far short of the manicured conditions of the private clubs in genteel neighborhoods that hosted most PGA events. Jack Nicklaus tried to avoid the Los Angeles Open if it was at Rancho Park. He preferred Riviera. Who didn't?

But the Los Angeles Open was known for breaking barriers, and not just the barriers that Charlie Sifford encountered week-in and week-out. The tournament welcomed Babe Didrikson as a participant in 1938, making her the first woman to play in a men's event on the PGA Tour. By then, she needed no introduction to the golfing world. She was one of the most famous athletes on the planet and, in a 1975 column in the *Los Angeles Times*, Jim Murray said Didrikson "was the greatest athlete this country has produced."

Charlie Sifford loved playing in Los Angeles in part because it was his adopted home since 1957. He quickly discovered the benefits of living in California if one wanted to play golf as much as possible. Before he moved to Los Angeles, he had rented an apartment over the winter months to work on his game and to meet Spiller, Rhodes, and others for games at Western Avenue, a public course not far from Los Angeles International Airport.

"I loved the LA Open," Sifford said. "It was a great feeling to play in my hometown and go home to my family every night. I was always looser and more relaxed in that tournament."

He surely felt something on that first day of play in 1969. Sifford called it "one of those magic rounds where everything comes together" and his assessment was spot-on. After shooting a ho-hum 35 on his first nine holes, Sifford shot a 28 on the back nine, twice chipping in, once for an eagle. He signed for a 63 and no one else in the field, which included Arnold Palmer, Lee Trevino (the defending US Open champion), and other big-name players, could get within three strokes of Sifford on what was a chilly day in Los Angeles. He was in position to win his second PGA tournament, having finally broken through in Hartford in 1967. But this was bigger. This was the Los Angeles Open. Virtually all of the big names in professional golf were in Los Angeles, where the purse was $100,000 with the winner getting $20,000.

Sifford had had success in this tournament with three straight top-twenty finishes, including a tie for eighth in 1966. After a second-round, even-par 71, he held a two-stroke lead. Another 71 kept him atop the leaderboard, this time by three strokes over South African Harold Henning and American Dave Hill heading into what would be a momentous final round.

"There's nothing like being ahead on the final day in your hometown," Sifford said.

The gallery was definitely pro-Charlie. But the fans saw Henning pull even with six holes to go, take a one-stroke lead with five holes to play, and then lose the lead when Sifford birdied the sixteenth hole. The two ended up in a tie at 276, 8 under par, and headed back to the fifteenth hole for a sudden-death playoff.

"How I made it through that tense day without a cigar, I'll never know," Sifford said.

After waiting for the huge gallery to make its way to the fifteenth tee, Sifford and Henning both hit good drives on the 382-yard, par-4 hole. Henning was away and reached for his 9-iron for his approach shot. The ball faded to the right and landed in an area that was marked ground-under-repair, just to the right of the green. This was, after all, Rancho Park.

Sifford also reached for his 9-iron, having come up short from the same distance the day before when he had tried to muscle a wedge onto the green. He sensed an advantage. Henning would be chipping his third shot, making it unlikely, though not impossible, that he would make a birdie 3. Sifford was feeling none of the nervousness that he had felt at Hartford. He felt confident. Even exhilarated. And he struck the 9-iron pure, landing his ball less than four feet from the hole.

Henning could have moved his ball from the ground-under-repair area, but the lie wasn't too bad, so he played it as it lay. His chip was a good one, but it came up a bit short. Sifford now knew he was one putt away from a second PGA Tour victory. He took a couple of practice strokes and then knocked the ball into the cup for the winning birdie.

The celebration was on. The gallery, which included former Dodgers' pitcher Don Newcombe, ran onto the course and surrounded the victor. Sifford, who had broken down and cried when he won at Hartford, basked in the adulation. This time, his family was there, and he smiled as he held the $20,000 winner's check with his wife, Rose, and two sons, Charles Jr. and two-and-a-half-year-old Craig, by his side. He was going to enjoy this one.

What he didn't know then, what he could not have known then, was that this would be his last victory on the tour he had fought so long and so hard to join. The victory proved to be his only top-ten finish of the season.

He would earn less than $15,000 in the thirty other official tournaments he entered. His next four events resulted in three missed cuts and a withdrawal from the Andy Williams tournament in San Diego.

There were forty-five winners on the PGA Tour that year. The youngest was twenty-four. All but three were under forty. At forty-six, Sifford was the oldest, and he would turn forty-seven in June. No one else came close. By the age of forty-six, Jack Nicklaus had won all of his eighteen major titles. Tiger Woods had won all of his fifteen majors and Ben Hogan all of his nine. They and all the other great players of their time never had to worry about where they played, how they would be accepted, or if their application for a specific tournament was returned. Woods has often said that if it hadn't been for Sifford's determination and diligence, he might never even have taken up the game.

That night, Sifford and his family joined other celebrants at Willie Davis's Center Field Lounge. Davis had been a Los Angeles Dodger mainstay in the 1960s, patrolling center field for a team that won three National League pennants and two World Series from 1963 to 1966. Other Black golfers were there as well, including Lee Elder, who would be the first Black to play in the Masters in 1975. Sifford also spent time with his friend Bill Spiller, who tried, unsuccessfully, to do what Sifford and Stanley Mosk had done.

And while Sifford's victory should have been front-page news on the nation's sport pages, it got overshadowed by another event across the country. On the same day Sifford won his second PGA event, Joe Namath and the New York Jets stunned the sporting world by upsetting the heavily favored Baltimore Colts in Super Bowl III in Miami. *That* was the shot heard round the sporting world on January 12, 1969.

Three weeks later, Sifford was honored by the City of Los Angeles. There was a small parade on 103rd Street, a section of the city that had been torched during the riots of 1965. The mayor, Sam Yorty, read a proclamation. It was Charlie Sifford Day and the honoree reveled in it. The road leading to Western Avenue, his favorite golf hangout in the city, was renamed Charlie Sifford Drive. The course, which had opened in 1927, was renamed in 1982 for Chester Washington, a celebrated Black journalist and publisher from the area. Western Avenue had been one of the first public golf courses in the Southland to allow Blacks to play.

Later that evening, Sifford was feted at a nightclub called The Black Fox. Asked to say a few words, Sifford said he was both overcome by the emotion of the evening and saddened by the feeling that his long, harrowing journey, one that had taken far too long, was coming to an end.

"It's just so wonderful," he said, "to think that a Black man can take a golf club and become so famous." He then paused, and added, "I just wish I could call back ten years."

Beginnings

$\mathcal{T}$here was no way Charlie Sifford could get back the years that racism had stolen from his career in professional golf. The man who won the 1969 Los Angeles Open against a strong integrated field had spent his prime golfing years honing his game on what Black players called "The Chitlin' Tour," a national competition sponsored by the United Golf Association. The UGA, originally called the United States Colored Golf Association, had been founded in 1925 for Blacks who were not welcome on the all-white Professional Golf Association, established nine years earlier.

There is no way to tell Sifford's story without centering the importance of the UGA to the development of Black talent in the game. Black golfers played for smaller purses on inferior courses than their white counterparts in the PGA but, not unlike baseball's Negro Leagues, the UGA provided stellar Black players with a place to shine. Sifford shone among the brightest, winning six UGA championships, including five in a row in the 1950s.

The crown jewel on the UGA schedule was its annual national championship, the National Negro Open. The first, on Labor Day weekend in 1926, was a two-day, seventy-two-hole open event for both professionals and amateurs at the Mapledale Country Club in Stow, Massachusetts, won by Harry Jackson. The club's owner, Robert H. Hawkins, was the first Black man to design and operate a country club in the United States. He carved the nine-hole course for Black golfers from an estate thirty miles west of Boston that he purchased after years working as general manager at the nearby Sandy Burr Country Club in Wayland, the first Black man to hold that post in any club in the United States.

The great Black golfers of the pre-civil rights era all played on the UGA tour every year from early spring to late summer. They traveled the circuit together, often pooling their money to buy gas and food and to pay the entrance fees of $25 or $50 to compete across the United States, almost always on public courses. Many were segregated.

Howard Wheeler from Atlanta won the Negro National Open six times, including the first three to be held after World War II. Robert "Pat" Ball, also from Atlanta, won the title four times before becoming the head professional at a municipal course outside Chicago. Bill Spiller, of Tulsa, won over one hundred UGA events, but never won the National Open. Teddy Rhodes, from Nashville, considered by Sifford to be the greatest Black player of them all, won the title four times.

That was all that was available for the Black golfers in the 1940s, 1950s, and early 1960s as the PGA Tour started to grow into the behemoth it is today. If any of them had any hope of eventually joining the PGA, the journey had to include all those weekends on the UGA tour.

"It launched my career," said Pete Brown of Port Gibson, Mississippi, who won the championship twice and was the first Black to win an official PGA Tour event at the 1964 Waco Turner Open. "Without the UGA, I never would have played professional golf."

The UGA was not simply a Black knockoff of the PGA tour. For one thing, unlike the PGA, the UGA did not discriminate. White golfers were welcome to play in its tournaments, and some did. Within its competitions, there were divisions for amateurs and, in 1930, a division for women formed, eight years before Babe Didrikson played in the Los Angeles Open. And for more than three decades, the UGA was the sole option for Black golfers to play in tournaments on a consistent basis since only three tournaments on the PGA schedule allowed Blacks to play—the Los Angeles Open, usually held in January; George May's All-American Tournament which was usually held over the Fourth of July weekend at his club, Tam O'Shanter, outside Chicago; and the Canadian Open.

Finding housing was a challenge when the UGA tour brought the Black golfers to courses in the South. Denied accommodation in segregated hotels, they bunked down with friends or supporters in private homes, just as Black tennis and baseball players were forced to do in the pre-civil rights era. Even the most famous Black entertainers of the time, such as Louis Armstrong, Count Basie, and Duke Ellington, were denied food and housing in hotels where they were playing to mostly white audiences in packed ballrooms.

It wasn't just Black sports and entertainment figures who were impacted. The first Black member of the presidential Secret Service detail, Abraham Bolden, was held off President John F. Kennedy's 1961 visit to Florida because he was not allowed to stay in the same hotels as the white Secret Service agents.

Haston Thornton attended many UGA events with his father, a bar owner and manager in Philadelphia known as Butch, who frequently shot in the 70s and competed against much bigger talents in the UGA. Butch Thornton and his golf buddies in Philadelphia played on public courses in and around the city, but also patronized a three-story social clubhouse they called the Fairview Golf Club.

"The first story was for eating. The second story was for gambling. The third story was for drinking," recalled the younger Thornton, known to everyone as Pancho. There also was a place on the third floor for members to hit golf balls.

"We would travel all summer to UGA events," Pancho Thornton said. "It was what I did on my summer vacation. We'd go all over—Chicago, St. Louis, Virginia, Florida, the Carolinas. It was always a fun time. Much of it was social. There were parties or banquets each night. But I'll tell you what, on the golf course it was anything but social. They were all collegial. But they all wanted to win. It was cutthroat out there. They didn't mess around. All the fun came after they played."

If the Black golfers were bitter about their exclusion from the PGA, Pancho Thornton didn't hear it. "All the time I was out there, I never heard anyone talk about how they wanted to play against Arnold Palmer or Sam Snead," he said.

Maybe they did not voice their resentment in front of Pancho, but Black golfers knew what they were missing by being denied the opportunity to compete regularly against their white counterparts. Dick Thomas was a schoolteacher from Annapolis, Maryland, and the only Black man to play in the 1958 US Open at Southern Hills Country Club in Tulsa. Before that tournament began, the USGA's executive director, Joe Dey, sent a letter to the general manager at Southern Hills, reminding him to treat any Black golfers in the tournament the same way as the white golfers would be treated: "I assume Southern Hills will accept any colored entrant who qualifies for the Open championship." That Dey would have to write such a note spoke of the times. While the USGA had no discriminatory clause, Dey nonetheless felt the need to remind the club members of that basic human right.

Thomas won his shot at the US Open at a qualifying round in Baltimore, but he did not make the cut in Tulsa after two rounds of play.

"The only way for a Negro golfer to go to the top in this game is to play with the pressure players throughout the tour," Thomas said then. The following year he won his first and only UGA National Open at Langston Golf Course in Washington, D.C.

He added, "I'm certain I could do a lot better playing against these guys on a regular basis."

It was not for lack of trying on the part of Black golfers. But they had no luck trying to integrate the PGA. The United States Golf Association, which was ostensibly color blind in running its tournaments, wasn't always a warm and hospitable host either. One of the more infamous examples of racism in the history of the USGA occurred when the organization held its 1928 Public Links Championship at Cobbs Creek in West Philadelphia, the course where Charlie Sifford honed his game as a young man.

The Publinx, as it was called, was an event designed for individuals who played at public courses, as the other big amateur, the US Amateur, was limited to individuals who belonged to USGA member private clubs, a restriction that remained until 1979. (In 1910, seventeen-year-old Francis Ouimet joined the Woodland Golf Club as a junior member to be eligible to participate in that year's US Amateur.) At the time, it was one of four events that the USGA ran, the US Open, the US Amateur, and the US Women's Amateur being the other three. It was discontinued in 2014.

In the 1928 Publinx, Pat Ball, who would go on to have a successful career in the UGA, and another Black golfer, Elmer Stout of Newark, qualified for the match play portion of the event after two rounds of stroke play. Ball was an interesting entrant, as he was the defending UGA National Negro Open champion, and those tournaments were considered to be professional and offered cash prizes. The USGA could have ruled him ineligible based on that fact alone. But it did not.

Instead, it sent two individuals to follow Ball and Stout as they played their two rounds of stroke play. These so-called witnesses reported back that both men had signed incorrect scorecards, a rules violation. The USGA in its infinite wisdom agreed, and both Ball's and Stout's names were removed from the list of the thirty-two players who would go on to match play. They were the only Black players in the tournament. The USGA kicked them to the curb.

Ball and Stout quickly filed an injunction to get readmitted into the tournament. Judge Raymond McNellie in the Court of Common Pleas ruled that the two players should be reinstated. He said the evidence presented at a hearing had not shown any rules violation and he directed the USGA "to remove the disqualifications." Amazingly, despite his ruling on the merits, McNellie also found that there had been no racial prejudice on the part of the USGA.

Even though Ball and Stout had won the right to be reinstated, the tournament had continued that morning without them. The players told Judge McNellie they preferred not to interfere with the tournament and would withdraw "in the spirit of good fellowship and sportsmanship."

The irony is that Cobbs Creek was a paradigm of what in the twenty-first century has become known as diversity, equity, and inclusion. But those who ran the course and maintained such a welcoming atmosphere were not in charge of the 1928 tournament. Although the court exonerated the USGA of racism, the fact remains that the only two Black players in the tournament were disqualified on baseless charges.

Ball was one of the best Black golfers in America in the first part of the twentieth century. The Atlanta native had picked up some of the finer points of the game by caddying for Bobby Jones at Jones's home course in Atlanta, East Lake Country Club. He moved to Chicago and quickly made a name for himself by winning the Cook County Amateur championship. He won the UGA National Open four times. His final UGA National Open victory had come in 1941 at Ponkapoag Golf Club outside Boston. His wife, Cleo, won the women's tournament that year and both were featured in a photograph that ran in the *Boston Daily Globe.*

Following that victory, a reporter for the *Chicago Defender* wrote, "The stories of Pat Ball and Negro golf are just about one in the same thing." Noting Ball's four UGA titles and two second-place finishes, the newspaper said that "none in his race can match his record." He turned forty-three in 1941 and spent the postwar years working as a golf instructor.

A year after his victory at Ponkapoag, Ball submitted an application to the USGA for the Hale America National Open in Chicago. The USGA had canceled its tournaments for the duration of World War II but announced that the Hale America would be played the same weekend in June as the originally scheduled US Open and that there would be two rounds of qualifying to get into the final field. Just like regular US Opens. The PGA was also one of the sponsors, but its job was to try and get its membership to participate in the tournament. Another sponsor, the Chicago District Golf Association, did the legwork and handled logistics.

But the USGA was in charge. If there was any doubt, the organization examined the clubs of one of the players, Sam Byrd, and found he had non-conforming grooves. Byrd had to scramble to find a set of clubs from a member of the host club, Ridgemoor Country Club.

Most of the big names at the time were exempted from qualifying, including Bobby Jones, who had retired from competitive golf in 1930. Jones still played three qualifying rounds at East Lake to try and shake off the rust from so many years of noncompetitive golf. The only real golf he had played had been at the Masters Tournament, which he had founded, and which had its first competition in 1934. He posted one of the lowest qualifying scores of anyone in the country.

Ball, Clyde Martin—who had been one of Joe Louis's golf instructors—and five other Black players sent in their $5 application fees and received confirmations from the USGA. The Hale America was trying to raise money for the war effort and encouraged as many people to apply as possible. At the end, a record 1,540 entered the tournament. Ball, Martin, and the five others, one of whom, Horace McDougal, was a member of the Northwestern University golf team, were assigned qualifying tee times at Olympia Fields Country Club, southwest of downtown Chicago. What followed was yet another blemish on golf and the USGA.

The *Chicago Defender* noted that two of the seven were able to play one round, but Ball and the others were told they would not be allowed to use the facilities at Olympia Fields and that their applications had been withdrawn. Never mind that this was a tournament encouraging entrants to raise money for the war effort. Never mind that there had been nothing in the application that prohibited Blacks. But here it was, front and center; Ball must have had Cobbs Creek flashbacks.

So did the USGA step in and order Olympia Fields to open its gates and course to the seven Black golfers? It did no such thing. In fact, the organization's president, George Blossom, who lived in the Chicago area, sided with the Olympia Fields policies and "respected the rights of a member club." What about the rights of Ball and the others? It's not like they were applying for membership to Olympia Fields (which would have been equally fruitless as the club did not admit its first Black member until 1992.) They simply wanted to play golf. They had done everything by the book and the USGA, as it had done to Ball and Stout in 1928, again kicked the seven to the curb.

A Black Chicago alderman sent a telegram to the USGA, calling its decision "undemocratic and unpatriotic." The alderman, Benjamin Grant, went on to say that the seven golfers "were denied the right to participate because of their color. The action definitely does not bolster the morale of the colored citizen and is not conducive to the democratic way of life for which all Americans are now fighting." The Black newspaper the *Chicago Defender* said the USGA "bowed to Jim Crowism" in a story with the headline, "Hale America Tourney Hitlerizes Seven Golfers."

The Hale America National Open went off as scheduled. Ben Hogan won the tournament, which featured a 62 by Hogan in the second round. Hogan and others later maintained that the victory should count as a real US Open, but the USGA has always insisted that the tournament was a one-time, wartime substitute for the US Open.

As long as the PGA's Caucasian-only clause stood, the UGA tour was the competitive option for Black golfers. Celebrities such as championship boxers Joe Louis and Sugar Ray Robinson, and big band leader and singer Billy Eckstine lent their support and dollars to the UGA tour. Louis employed Ted Rhodes and Clyde Martin; the two were both playing partners and traveling companions. This was all when Louis was the heavyweight champion of the world. Whenever he wasn't training for a fight, he was usually on the golf course. He became an excellent golfer, but he was known more for his wild spending and betting on the golf course. If he lost money, he didn't seem to mind, for it usually went to another Black golfer.

"Joe Louis was the most big-hearted man I have ever met in my life," Sifford said. "He was the most generous man I have ever seen, as well as one of the few Black men committed to making things better for his people. He was a towering symbol of strength and pride for the Black man. He was a true hero."

Louis sponsored a UGA tournament in Detroit and played in its amateur division, driving around tournaments in a golf cart with a caddie and his German shepherd. He spent so much time on the golf course that he found out his wife was divorcing him while playing a round at his home course in Detroit. Determined to reverse his fortunes in all of those friendly matches, he got serious when he got out of the Army in 1945. His regular coach, Martin, could no longer do the job. So, Louis hired Rhodes.

"After I'd worked with him for a while, I started doing better and winning some of my money back," Louis said.

Sugar Ray Robinson also sponsored a UGA tournament on Long Island and for four years in the 1940s had employed a Black golfer named Joe "Roach" Delancey as his teacher. Delancey played on the UGA Tour and won a number of events and, in 1956, reached the quarterfinals of the

USGA Publinx at Harding Park in San Francisco. But he remained an amateur and never reached the status of Sifford or Rhodes.

Eckstine was a regular at the UGA National Open and supported the Black golfers monetarily. Jackie Robinson would later use his celebrity to attack the racism on the PGA Tour in a syndicated newspaper column.

The UGA continued into the 1960s, even after Sifford succeeded in desegregating the PGA Tour; its most consistent winner was Lee Elder, who in one year won eighteen of the twenty-two tournaments on the schedule. Elder may have been the first Black golfer to play in the Masters, but Charlie Sifford went to his grave believing it should have been him instead. He had a point.

Charles Luther Sifford discovered the game that would define his life as a twelve-year-old growing up in Charlotte, North Carolina, in 1934. The third of six children of Eliza and Roscoe "Shug" Sifford, Charlie found his way onto the golf course the way many young golfers—white and Black—did, by caddying. Ben Hogan gave up hawking newspapers on the streets in Fort Worth, Texas, when he discovered he could make more money as a caddie at the Glen Garden Country Club. He sometimes slept in sand traps to snag a good customer the following morning. Byron Nelson was a caddie at the same club. Teddy Rhodes, a Black golfer who would become a mentor to Sifford, learned the game as a caddie at Belle Meade Country Club in Nashville, his hometown. Pete Brown did the same at a municipal course in Jackson, Mississippi.

In Sifford's case, his introduction to golf came at the all-white Carolina Country Club, now known as the Carolina Golf Club. It was not far from his house on South Tryon Street, a working-class neighborhood where whites and Blacks coexisted with few issues.

"The people who lived there were on the poor side of middle class, but they kept their houses and yards neat and they worked hard to make a living for themselves," Sifford said. "I guess I was fortunate. Because when I was growing up, there was no such thing as tension or segregation between blacks and whites."

Except for the whites-only restrooms and drinking fountains and the fact that the place young Charlie caddied was exclusively white. But, as Sifford put it, "most of the white people in the city couldn't afford to join that club, either."

The exclusive club was tucked discreetly behind tall trees down a long driveway that ended at a guard shack within view of a magnificent clubhouse and the Donald Ross–designed course. The Carolina Golf Club remains a Charlotte institution, sometimes used as a Monday qualifying site for the annual PGA tournament in the city.

Sifford's father worked in a local fertilizer plant, but, after a single day on the job, Charlie decided that lugging around heavy bales of manure was not for him. Instead, he earned sixty cents at Carolina for one eighteen-hole round carrying a single golf bag. "You had to be good to get that 60 cents," he said. "I was a good caddie because the game was so important to me." He would give his mother fifty cents and keep the extra dime, which he used to buy cigars. In the summer, he would often carry bags for thirty-six holes, doubling his daily income while learning the ins and outs of the game.

The caddies could play the course on Monday when it was closed to members. Sifford had permission to use a member's golf clubs on those days and it wasn't long before the teenager was shooting in the 70s. He quickly discovered he had a gift for the game.

It was at the Carolina Country Club that Sifford got to know Clayton Heafner, the club pro. He was known as the Candy Man for bringing candy to the caddies who were hanging around the club waiting to go out onto the course. Sifford frequently caddied for Heafner and, like other caddies who went on to become pro golfers, he got pointers from the soon-to-be PGA touring pro. They often played together on Mondays. "He was a big influence on my father in creating his interest in golf," said Charles Sifford Jr.

Heafner was a large man with a volcanic temper. He was said to wake up every morning feeling mean. And if he didn't, he was mean about that.

"Heafner was a tough guy, the kind of guy you wouldn't mind going on night patrol with, because you never thought he'd leave you," said Jack Burke Jr., the PGA's 1956 Player of the Year who won both the Masters and PGA championship that year. Burke and Heafner were teammates in a Ryder Cup match and Heafner tore into his playing partner during a round where not much was going well for Burke.

"You dumb little jackass," Heafner said. "Don't you ever try to play a *shot* in there? Don't you ever try to fade it in? Or hook it in? Quit shooting it straight!!"

One of the many stories of Heafner erupting during a round was when he held his putter in a water hazard and yelled, "Drown, you son of a bitch! Drown!" But he could hit the golf ball a country mile and soon took a liking to Sifford. Sifford caddied for Heafner, although he said Heafner's temper was an issue. Heafner routinely would fire him as a caddie during the first nine holes and then promptly rehire him for the second nine.

"He was large. He was huge," Sifford recalled. "He didn't take nothing, you know, no mess off of nobody."

When he and Sifford played in the mid- to late 1930s, Heafner had yet to make his mark in the professional game. But he made a big impression on Sifford as his cocky caddie began developing into an excellent golfer. "It was Heafner who taught me a valuable lesson about having the money to back up a bet," Sifford said, recalling the time he challenged his mentor to a match. When Sifford lost and admitted his inability to pay, Heafner picked him up, carried him over to a pond on the course, and deposited him in the water.

That was one unforgettable lesson. The other was even more valuable. He learned how to play the game of golf at an elite level by watching and mimicking Heafner. Asked what he retained from all his Monday matches with Heafner, Sifford said, simply, "All of it."

Heafner was eight years older than Sifford and became a force on the PGA Tour in the late 1940s and early 1950s when Ben Hogan, Sam Snead, Lloyd Mangrum, Cary Middlecoff, and Jimmy Demaret were on top of the game. Heafner won seven times on the PGA Tour and twice finished second at the US Open, to Middlecoff by one stroke in 1949 and to Hogan by two strokes in 1951. In the final round of the 1951 US Open, Hogan shot a 67 over the treacherous and punishing Oakland Hills layout. Heafner shot a 69 that same round. Those were the only two rounds in the 60s in the entire tournament. Heafner also played on two victorious Ryder Cup teams (1949, 1951) and won three of his four matches while halving the other.

Heafner's son, Vance, followed in his father's footsteps and won the Carolinas Open as an amateur in 1974 and turned pro. He teamed with Mike Holland to win the Walt Disney World National Team Championship in 1981.

Heafner's boss at Carolina, club owner Sutton Alexander, was another important Sifford ally in the late 1930s. Alexander had been a celebrated football player in the area, leading Charlotte's Central High School to the state championship as a senior. He attended Centre College in Kentucky to play football, but soon became interested—and quite good—at golf. As a senior at Centre, Alexander won the Kentucky Collegiate championship.

He returned to North Carolina to coach high school football at his alma mater and then went into private business. In 1934, he took over the

Carolina Country Club, which had opened for business five years earlier. He ran it for the next twenty-five years until he died in 1959.

Heafner died at the age of forty-six in 1960. He had left the professional grind behind in 1954 and became owner of an eighteen-hole public course in Charlotte, Eastwood Golf Club. Although he won seven PGA titles in his career and had those two second-place finishes at the US Open, Heafner told golf writer Darsie L. Darsie that his greatest day in golf had come in a tournament he lost by one shot. At the 1940 Los Angeles Open, persistent rain had turned the Los Angeles Country Club's North course into a quagmire. Heafner had played well in the miserable conditions and had what looked to be a comfortable five-shot lead after three rounds. He figured an even-par 71 in the horrible conditions would be plenty. He was wrong.

Lawson Little, one of the game's great amateur players in the 1930s, was now a professional and looking for a signature victory. He shot a spectacular 65 and passed Heafner, winning by one stroke.

"I will still look back on this as my greatest day in golf, a day where I played par golf under terrible conditions and was beaten by a man who couldn't make a mistake," he told Darsie. Little would go on that year to win the US Open at Canterbury Country Club outside Cleveland, beating Gene Sarazen in an eighteen-hole playoff.

After Sifford won the Los Angeles Open, he took a moment to reflect on the important roles Heafner and Alexander had played in his life. "I still owe both of them money," he said. "I'll never be able to pay them now because they're both dead." He owed them a lot more than money and he knew that.

But Heafner and Alexander were very much alive when the teenage Sifford started to consistently shoot in the 70s at Carolina, and both suspected the club's white membership might not appreciate getting shown up on the course by a Black golfer. They also understood that no Black golfer with dreams of being a professional was going to go anywhere in the South in the late 1930s and early 1940s. The two of them came up with a plan to get Sifford out of Charlotte and on to Philadelphia, where Sifford had relatives and he could play on integrated courses.

"I think he's the greatest person I ever met in my life," Sifford said of Alexander. "He told my mother and father, 'You should let Charles go to Philadelphia because I think he has the ability to play golf. And I don't want him to get hurt.'"

It was not an idle concern. A racial incident sealed the deal, sending Sifford off to Philadelphia. Sifford left his hometown after an altercation with the white owner of a neighborhood market. The owner was an abusive drunk, a racist, and a wife beater. His wife took shelter at the Sif-fords' home when things got ugly at home, which they often did. On one of those occasions, when Sifford went to the store, he was confronted by the owner about his wife's whereabouts. He threatened Sifford. He called him the N-word. Sifford warned him to stop. When the owner persisted, Sifford grabbed a bottle of Coca Cola and hit him between the eyes. Sif-ford recalled the man needed ten stitches to close the wound.

Suddenly, Sifford's departure from Charlotte became a "when" in-stead of an "if." He ran home and told his parents what had happened. They sent him to stay nearby with his aunt and uncle, Betsy and James. He was told to lie low in case the authorities were on the lookout for him. A Black teenager against a white store owner in 1939 North Carolina? What chance did he have in court?

He stayed in hiding with his relatives for a couple weeks, but he got antsy to get back on the golf course and, when he ventured out as a caddie one last time at Carolina Country Club, he was arrested on the twelfth hole. Sutton Alexander and Roscoe Sifford paid the fifty dollars bail and told Charlie to pack his bags. He was not going to wait around for a trial and verdict of an all-white jury. Sifford hopped a bus to Philadelphia where an uncle took him in.

He had dropped out of the eleventh grade, but that one-way bus ticket to Philadelphia would lead to a personal and professional trans-formation. In Philadelphia, Sifford found a job at the National Biscuit Company (Nabisco) and a place to play golf at Cobbs Creek Country Club. The municipal course in West Philadelphia soon would be his home away from home.

Opened in 1916, Cobbs Creek is one of the most important venues in the history of Black golf in the United States. It never discriminated against Blacks or against women, who were welcomed at Cobbs Creek even before they won the right to vote. "I was both surprised and de-lighted to see Blacks and whites playing side by side there," Sifford said. "I'd never seen anything like that in North Carolina."

It was, Sifford said, "just as Sutton Alexander had promised. A place I could play without having to worry about some groundskeeper coming by to run me off the course."

The course itself was a gem, designed by Hugh Wilson, who also designed the two championship courses at nearby Merion. (Cobbs Creek runs through part of Merion.) It has hosted UGA national opens, USGA events, and PGA tournaments. "Cobbs Creek was where everyone met," said Pancho Thornton, who played and caddied at the club. "It was the center for Black golf."

After the course fell into disrepair, a group formed the Cobbs Creek Foundation to rehabilitate the property, hiring golf architect Gil Hanse to redesign the eighteen-hole course. It was due to open in 2024 along with a thirty-thousand-square-foot facility that will house a learning lab in partnership with Tiger Woods's TGR Foundation. It will provide programs in science, technology, engineering, and mathematics for students in the area.

It was at Cobbs Creek that Charlie Sifford met Howard Wheeler, the de facto club champion, who played cross-handed and, at that time, had already been a two-time winner of the United Golfers Association national championship. Wheeler was one of the great Black golfers of his time and, like so many of them, is not well known because he never got the exposure that playing on the PGA Tour would have given him. But he knew the big names—Hogan, Snead—and they knew him. And one of the founders of the UGA called Wheeler "the black Arnold Palmer of his time."

Wheeler grew up in Atlanta and learned the game by caddying at Brookhaven Country Club and later moved over to East Lake as caddie master. He moved north, settling in Philadelphia and became a regular at Cobbs Creek. The cross-handed grip absolutely buffaloed Sifford, who had never seen anything like it.

"I was so busy telling myself that Wheeler couldn't possibly hit the ball right that I didn't pay attention to the shots he was making with that short, quick swing," Sifford said.

Wheeler could, and often did, hit golf balls from any surface, as he was a renowned trick shot artist. Sifford recalled Wheeler hitting a golf ball off the top of a Coca Cola bottle and never touching the bottle. "If he'd been alive 40 years later," Sifford said, "he could have made a fortune giving trick-shot exhibitions."

Instead, Wheeler took his considerable talents to the UGA. He was twenty-two when he won his first UGA National Negro Open in 1933 at Sunset Hills Country Club in Kankakee, Illinois. He was forty-seven when he won his last one in 1958 at South Park Golf Course in Pittsburgh. In between, he won four more, including three straight from 1946 to 1948. He rivaled the great Teddy Rhodes at that time for UGA dominance but, unlike Rhodes or Sifford, he professed no stated desire to play the PGA Tour. He was content to take money from the Cobbs Creek competitors.

When the US Open returned to Merion in 1950, Wheeler, then almost forty, qualified for the tournament by shooting rounds of 75 and 69 to make the cut by two shots. It marked the third consecutive year a Black golfer had qualified for the US Open; Teddy Rhodes had done so in 1948 and 1949. Wheeler was among 165 in the field and played the first two rounds with an amateur, Richard Whiting, and pro Charles Penna. But he did not play well. He shot rounds of 77 and 85 to miss the cut.

He qualified again in 1951 at Oakland Hills and was among the 162 starters at the fiendish golf course outside Detroit. That was the year that Clayton Heafner finished second to Ben Hogan. Wheeler's play improved, but his rounds of 75 and 78 put him one shot over the cut line.

In both US Open appearances, Wheeler got a taste of what life was like for Black golfers on the PGA Tour. At Merion, he had trouble finding partners for practice rounds; his Cobbs Creek buddies were not in the field. At Oakland Hills he had difficulty determining his tee time and was told by an official at the club to check the newspaper. That was it for Howard Wheeler, who returned to Cobbs Creek, where his rule as the unquestioned club alpha was soon to be challenged by a young, brash upstart from Charlotte.

Charlie Sifford immediately warmed to Philadelphia in general and Cobbs Creek in particular. It was his home course and he played there as often as his job allowed. He had discovered the course by accident. He noticed a Black man climbing onto a trolley car with a set of golf clubs and asked the man where he was headed. His destination was Cobbs Creek. Sifford tagged along and soon had made enough money at Nabisco to buy his first set of golf clubs.

He also became golfing buddies with Wheeler, who was eleven years his senior. At first, Wheeler met each and every challenge posed by the cocky North Carolinian. Eventually, the matches got closer, Sifford started to win a few, and they became partners, taking on all comers. Sifford recalled him and Wheeler beating PGA pro Ed "Porky" Oliver and another golfer in a match at Cobbs Creek and then traveling to Valley Forge to win a match against future PGA pro Mike Souchak and his brother.

That was how Black golfers survived in those days. Wheeler, as good as he was, never showed any interest in trying his luck on the PGA tour. He did just fine by winning bets on the golf course, playing in UGA events and supplementing those winnings with his work as a chauffeur for the singer Ethel Waters and her bandleader husband Eddie Mallory.

Wheeler was a year older than Hogan, Snead, and Byron Nelson, but he showed no interest in trying to compete against them.

"He was content to be the local favorite and take on anyone who wanted to challenge [him] on his home course," Sifford said of Wheeler.

For four years, Sifford worked at Nabisco, played golf at Cobbs Creek whenever he could, and also found time to catch a baseball game or attend a dance. In 1943, Eliza Sifford died in Charlotte. The last time Charlie Sifford had seen his mother was when he said good-bye to her before boarding that bus to Philadelphia. He also had met a young woman named Rose Crumbley at a local dance in Philadelphia and became instantly smitten. He was twenty-one years old.

The United States was fully engaged in World War II in two theaters by the time Sifford got his draft notice. In October of 1944, he began a two-year hitch in the Army. He remained stateside through July 17, 1945, and then began a seven-month stretch of foreign service. Sifford said he was sent to Okinawa as part of the Seventy-Ninth Signal Heavy Construction team. That would likely have required logistic and infrastructure work, as the battle of Okinawa had ended in June 1945.

A War Department Field Manual from June 1945 describes Sifford's work as "the building of open wire poles and lead-covered cable leads." The leads could be on the ground, in the air, or underwater. "The primary duty of the signal heavy construction battalion is to build all types of permanent or semi-permanent open wire or lead-covered cable construction," the manual reads. "The battalion may, however, be called upon to construct rubber-covered cable or field wire lines."

When the war ended with the Japanese surrender on September 2, 1945, Sifford said he was offered two choices—stay in Japan or join the Army Special Services, the entertainment branch of the military. That was a no-brainer as far as he was concerned. He chose the latter and became a member of a military golf team. One of his teammates was Mac Hunter, the son of Willie Hunter, the longtime pro at Riviera Country Club, who won the 1921 British Amateur.

The group played several matches in the Philippines, yet the one anecdote Sifford recalled more than any other from his time there was when Hunter challenged him to knock down a horse. It did not end well. Sifford had taken up boxing for a brief time in Charlotte, but he never had tried to punch a horse. The unfortunate animal was in front of a carriage, the driver waiting for a fare. Sifford, probably feeling the effects of what he termed "a few drinks," accepted Hunter's challenge. He punched the horse between the eyes and the animal did, in fact, go down. But that in turn led to collective outrage among the Filipinos who witnessed the event, and Sifford, Hunter, and the other golfers soon were in a free-for-all.

"They beat the living hell out of us," Sifford said. "We went back to the barracks all bloody and raggedy. It was the last time I punched a horse, or any other animal."

Sifford returned to the United States in March of 1946 and was honorably discharged on November 30, 1946. Available military records show that Sifford had watched his money while in the Army. A few months before his discharge, records show he received a cash payment of $100 and a check for $1,322.02. These are unusually high amounts, indicating he lived and spent frugally. He subsequently received two more payments, the final one of $110.65 written on the day of his discharge.

Then twenty-four, Sifford returned to Philadelphia with a plan. He went back to work at his old job at Nabisco, but stayed for only six months, which was just long enough to qualify for a paid vacation. He took his final check and began the life he had long dreamed about having —that of a professional golfer. He had heard all the UGA stories from Howard Wheeler and wanted to find out for himself what real, competitive golf was all about.

It was 1946 and, for Charlie Sifford, that would be a life-changing year.

On the opposite coast, meanwhile, another veteran had returned to his job as a Superior Court judge in Los Angeles in 1945. Stanley Mosk's military service had not involved foreign battlefields, though his name had been on a list to go to the Philippines when the war ended. The governor of California, Earl Warren, had not filled Mosk's seat on the court in the months that the judge had been in the Army. That job was ready for him to resume when he was discharged in the fall of 1945.

In 1947, while Charlie Sifford was just beginning to find a niche on the UGA circuit, Judge Stanley Mosk issued a decision from the Superior Court bench that reverberated across California and soon would be ratified by the US Supreme Court. It was a ruling, Mosk later said, that was one of the most important of his judicial career. It was totally in keeping with a man who spent his life fighting discrimination whether in a case about housing, as this case was, or in the matter of professional golf, as another pivotal case one day would be.

• *2* •

Stanley

*I*n 1947, Frank L. Drye, a decorated veteran of World War I and World War II, moved from Alabama to California. At the suggestion of an Army buddy, Drye settled his wife and five children into a five-bedroom, three-bathroom Mediterranean-style home in Hancock Park, an affluent neighborhood of Los Angeles.

It was the first house Drye had ever bought. He and his wife, Artoria, had saved for twenty-six years for just such a purchase. A leader of the Tuskegee Institute marching band, Drye had been a musician all his adult life. He had played the cornet in W. C. Handy's blues band and taught Ralph Ellison to play the trumpet. He played taps at the funeral of Tuskegee Institute founder Booker T. Washington.

A fifty-eight-year-old Black man, Drye had been awarded the Silver Star for "gallantry in action" in World War I, serving with the segregated Company E 365th Infantry near Pont-a-Mousson, France. His military records note that he had been "severely gassed" while leading his platoon on the day the Armistice was signed. More than eleven thousand casualties were recorded on November 11, 1918, in a war the Allies already had won. A United States Senate committee released a report in 1920 that called the carnage on Armistice Day "needless slaughter." Drye was one of the fortunate ones in that he was able to return home.

No sooner had the Drye family taken up residence in their new home than the pastor of the Presbyterian church, who lived across the street, sued the Dryes and two other Black families, charging that their presence in the neighborhood violated a racial covenant restricting home ownership to white people. "Nonwhite" was an expansive concept in those days, and it included Jews as well as Blacks. The pastor, Clarence Wright, sought a court order to enforce the covenant's racial restrictions. Seven other white families joined the lawsuit and distributed fliers around the neighborhood. Arthur Drye, one of the five children, recalled a flier in the family mailbox that "stated something like, 'These people are bringing down real estate prices in the neighborhood,'" he told the *Los Angeles Times* in 2007.

To the everlasting chagrin of the plaintiffs, the case landed on the docket of Superior Court Judge Stanley Mosk in October 1947. At age thirty-five, Mosk had already established himself as a liberal voice in California politics. In 1938, he had campaigned and then worked as executive secretary for Culbert Olson, the first Democrat elected governor of the state in forty-four years. As one of his last gubernatorial acts after his re-election defeat in 1942, Olson appointed his Jewish aide to the Superior Court bench.

Presented in *Wright v. Drye* with what he saw as a clear case of racial discrimination, Mosk wasted no time delivering what the *Los Angeles Sentinel*, a Black newspaper, called a "verbal lashing" to the plaintiffs. Mosk called the covenants "un-American" and ruled that they could not legally be enforced. The *Los Angeles Times* and other mainstream media outlets largely ignored the case.

"There is no allegation, and no suggestion, that any of these defendants would not be law-abiding neighbors and citizens of the community," Mosk said. "The only objection to them is their color and their race. This court feels there is no more reprehensible, un-American activity than to attempt to deprive persons of their own homes on a master race theory."

World War II had been over for only two years, Mosk reminded the plaintiffs, and the United States and its allies had defeated a nation that, in the name of racial superiority, had slaughtered six million Jews. He made specific reference to Drye's military service. "Our nation just fought against the Nazi race superiority doctrines. One of these defendants was in that war and this court would be callous to his Constitutional rights if it were now to permit him to be ousted from his own home by using 'race' as the measure of his worth as a citizen and neighbor." To enforce such racial covenants would violate the equal protection clause of the Fourteenth amendment, he ruled.

The Dryes remained in their home.

The following year, the United States Supreme Court, in a unanimous decision, held that judicial enforcement of racially restrictive housing covenants violated the Fourteenth Amendment. Shortly after the

Supreme Court ruling in *Shelley v. Kraemer*, Mosk wrote an article for the *Chicago Jewish Forum* magazine in which he said he doubted either ruling would banish housing segregation. But he did hope it would put the bigots on notice that the law stood on the side of integration. "The highest court in the land has put the torch to one of the major barriers, by stripping from housing segregation its only measure of sanctity, the cloth of legality," Mosk wrote.

Twenty years after the Supreme Court ruling, the Fair Housing Act outlawed racial covenants. But in 2021, an investigative unit from National Public Radio revealed that racial covenants are still on the books in municipalities across the United States. They may be unenforceable. They may be illegal. But no one has bothered to remove them from hundreds of deeded properties across the country.

As a judge, Stanley Mosk wrote more than fifteen hundred opinions over several decades. His grandson Matthew Mosk said his grandfather always pointed to the *Wright v. Drye* decision as among his proudest achievements. It spoke to the judge's twin passions of championing civil rights and fighting racial discrimination, passions formed at an early age in northern Illinois and nurtured through college, law school, and his positions of authority in the state of California, which included stints on two state courts and six years as the state's attorney general.

As a young man Stanley Mosk had wanted to be a newspaper reporter. He loved to write. He followed the news of the day. He collected baseball cards and followed sports with a passion. He was born in 1912 in San Antonio, Texas. His given name was Morey Stanley Mosk, but like William Ben Hogan and John Byron Nelson, he used his middle name as his first name throughout his life. At the age of three, Mosk's family, which soon would include his brother, Ed, moved to Rockford, Illinois, where Mosk spent his formative years. The city on the banks of the Rock River, close to the Wisconsin border, was one of the larger in the state. It was a ninety-minute drive to Chicago, close enough that the Mosks occasionally ventured into the Second City to see sporting events.

Stanley's fondest memories of high school were working for the school newspaper, *The Rockford Owl*, and writing articles for the local newspaper, *The Rockford Morning Star*, as part of a program called the Junior Press Club for young, would-be journalists. The newspaper set aside space each week for articles from several schools, and Mosk would sometimes write his articles in the *Morning Star* newsroom.

"This gave me a lot of enthusiasm for journalism. It taught me how to use a typewriter. I thought I would go into journalism," he said, a career ambition he quickly abandoned when he discovered that his hero at the *Morning Star*, the sports editor Frank Hicks, only made $35 a week.

Mosk's father, Paul, ran a men's clothing shop. The family supported the progressive politics of Robert La Follette, the Republican senator from neighboring Wisconsin and the Progressive Party's 1924 candidate for president of the United States, who championed regulation of the railroads and protection for workers and condemned political corruption and wartime restrictions on free speech, the latter cause being of particular interest to residents of Rockford. One hundred eighteen people were arrested there in 1920 during a protest led by the Industrial Workers of the World (IWW).

Mosk was the only Jewish student in a high school graduating class of four hundred, but he said he never felt the sting of discrimination there, describing Rockford as a liberal, religiously tolerant community. The Mosks were Reform Jews who did not go to temple or observe the Jewish holy days; Stanley did not have a bar mitzvah. He was elected class president and served on the debate team and as a captain in the Reserve Officer Training Corps.

Stanley Mosk's memories of Rockford as a city without religious prejudices softened one incident at his high school graduation. As senior-class president, Mosk led the graduates as they marched into the auditorium wearing their caps and gowns. The orchestra played "Onward Christian Soldiers." "Nowadays parents would have filed a lawsuit and would have tried to restrain the orchestra from playing a religious [song]," he said. "But my parents were broad-minded, and they just thought it was the funniest thing they'd ever heard." Mosk would recall his graduation march in 1991 while serving on the California Supreme Court when he joined the majority opinion that ruled that public high school graduations could not have religious invocations. In *Sands v. Morongo School District*, Mosk agreed with his fellow justices that prayers at graduation ceremonies violated the First Amendment of the US Constitution, but he argued, against the majority on the court, that it violated the Constitution of California as well.

Mosk enrolled at the University of Chicago following graduation, without a specific plan or career path, but he got his first taste of politics while at the university, campaigning for a reform city council candidate, Jim Cusack, from the city's fifth ward. Cusack's win against a candidate from the local political machine prompted Mosk to gravitate to political science as a field of study. He also joined a fraternity, Phi Sigma Delta, which boasted a number of alumni who had become lawyers. Lawyers frequented the fraternity for dinners and speaking engagements and Mosk liked what he heard.

He earned a bachelor's degree in philosophy, which allowed its students to also take classes in the law school. Mosk had completed his first year of law school by the end of his undergraduate studies and was set to continue his legal education at the University of Chicago when his father decided to move the family to California for better business opportunities. Stanley could not afford to remain in Chicago on his own, so he joined his family in Los Angeles, lived at home to save money, and finished his last two years of law school at the Southwestern School of Law. Dr. John J. Schumacher founded the school in 1911 as a private, nonprofit, and nonsectarian institution with a special mission to educate underserved students, particularly minorities and women.

Mosk passed the bar in 1935, the year he turned twenty-three. Armed with a law degree, the newly minted attorney went into private practice, sharing a law office in the Spring Arcade building on Spring Street with other attorneys to defray administrative costs during the lean years of the Great Depression. He took whatever cases came over the transom.

He met the woman who would become his wife through a friend, Ed Rau, who had invited Mosk to fill out a bridge foursome. Helen Edna Mitchell, who also went by her middle name, was one of the players and also Rau's date that night. She had moved to California with her parents from Winnipeg, Canada. Mitchell soon began dating the lively, witty, and attractive man who had just passed his bar exam. The couple was married at the bride's home in Beverly Hills, not far from the Wilshire Country Club.

Money was tight. Mosk remembered telling his wife, "I had a wonderful day today. I had a $25 case and two small ones." He supplemented his income doing legal work for his in-laws' cosmetic business, called Forty-Two Products, which marketed shampoo and after-shave lotion. Mosk also spent a good deal of his time on politics, becoming active in the Democratic Party after being moved by President Franklin D. Roosevelt's attempts to help those in need during the Great Depression. He had seen financial struggle firsthand in his own home, his father moving twice to try and make his business a success. "I suppose it came from the teachings of my parents, who themselves were always struggling to make a living. That certainly had an influence on me, I'm sure, and that's why I've always been an unashamed liberal," he said.

He got active at the local level and campaigned for an assembly candidate in the Fifty-Ninth District, the western part of Los Angeles. The candidate's name was Robert Heinlein, a retired naval officer who ended up losing that race to the Republican candidate, Charles Lyon. Heinlein turned his attention from politics to science fiction, instead, and his novel *Stranger in a Strange Land* became a classic of the genre.

Mosk supported the ill-fated 1934 gubernatorial campaign of the writer and muckraker Upton Sinclair while he worked on the state Senate campaign of Utah transplant Culbert Olson. Sinclair, who had lost a previous bid for governor and two campaigns for Congress on the Socialist Party ticket, was defeated yet again, this time as a Democrat. Sinclair "was a little farther to the left than I would desire," Mosk conceded. "He was pretty much . . . a socialist. But in support of his campaign in 1934, an organization called EPIC was organized, and I thought it was a very useful entrée to political activity."

EPIC was an acronym for End Poverty in California, Sinclair's bold plan to put the state's seven hundred thousand unemployed back to work by having the state take over factories and farms that were closing at alarming rates during the Great Depression. He also campaigned for a fifty-dollar monthly pension for the elderly and a state income tax to pay for it.

Sinclair lost that gubernatorial election, but during his campaign, more than eight hundred EPIC clubs formed across the state. The activists the EPIC movement nurtured would go on to influence California politics for decades to come.

For his part, Mosk was ready to have one of his candidates actually win. "I became interested in politics, Democratic politics in particular. I supported the candidate for the state Assembly for my district; he lost. I supported a candidate for the state Senate; he lost. I supported a candidate for district attorney; he lost," Mosk complained. "My record, if not effective, is at least consistent."

Mosk's candidate for district attorney, a progressive named George Rochester, finished fourth in a five-man race in August 1936. It marked the first political campaign in California in which Mosk participated. "The campaign was fun," he said. The result? Not so much.

Culbert Olson, who had been a state senator in Utah before moving to California, would break Mosk's losing streak. He won his race for state Senate. Four years later, Olson ran for governor, and Mosk threw himself into that campaign, becoming its Los Angeles County chairman. It wasn't an easy assignment. Olson had virtually no support from the influential conservative Los Angeles newspapers; Mosk referred to the political writers at the *Los Angeles Times* as "generally Republican hatchet men."

Olson ran a grassroots campaign. What he lacked in money and endorsements, he made up for with tireless volunteers knocking on doors, making telephone calls, and sending out mailers. After winning the Democratic primary, Olson soundly defeated incumbent Frank Merriman, who had angered liberals with his anti-union stance and alienated conservatives with his support of tax reform. Olson became the first Democrat to be elected governor since 1894.

Mosk admired Olson, a supporter of progressive causes during his legislative career in both Utah and California. Mosk acknowledged that "compromise" was not a word in the vocabulary of the man he called a "hard-headed Scandinavian." But Olson "was the most honest human being I've ever known. He had total integrity and, in a way, that was his downfall politically. If a legislator was with him 90 percent of the time, to Olson that man was no good because he opposed him 10 percent of the time."

Mosk stayed in Los Angeles after Olson took office in Sacramento—but not for long. He took a phone call from Phil Gibson, who had been one of his professors at Southwestern Law School and had just been named director of finance in the Olson administration. Gibson asked Mosk to join the administration as the governor's executive secretary.

"It took me about 15 minutes to wrap up my law practice" and move the family to Sacramento, Mosk said. He was twenty-six years old.

Mosk was paid $5,000 a year as one of the three administrative aides in Olson's office. There was the private secretary, who handled appointments and patronage issues. The assistant secretary served as press secretary. The executive secretary handled extradition, clemency, and other legislative or legal matters. One of Mosk's jobs was to visit inmates on death row at San Quentin and pass on his impressions to the governor. One of those prisoners was a woman, Juanita Spinelli, who was nicknamed "The Duchess." Mosk had a lifelong aversion to capital punishment, and he was very public about it, even as a judge. As Olson's clemency advisor, he recommended that Spinelli's death sentence for murder be commuted, even though the warden at San Quentin, Clinton Duffy, called Spinelli "the coldest, hardest character, male or female, I have ever known. The Duchess was a hag, evil as a witch, horrible to look at, impossible to like."

Mosk's recommendation did not pass muster with the governor. Spinelli received a thirty-day reprieve, but she became the first woman to die in the gas chamber at San Quentin on November 21, 1942. She was fifty-two and, as a final request, went to her death with family photos taped to her body.

Olson had a rough go of it right from the start. He collapsed from a heart ailment days after he assumed office. His wife of thirty-eight years died soon thereafter. The conservative state legislature stymied his proposals to regulate lobbyists, to provide universal health insurance, and to raise corporate taxes because of his "all-or-nothing" approach. He also took heat from the left flank of his own party on an issue over which he had no control. Democratic state committeeman John McEnery said Olson's agenda was hampered "by what we used to call in those days the leftwingers, and maybe sometimes we called them Communists although we weren't sure what they were." McEnery said that the group "all took the line that the national administration should have opened the second front to relieve the pressure on the Russians. Well, the United States wasn't ready to open the second front, but all the leftwingers kept agitating against Culbert Olson and the thing finally mounted until Culbert Olson just couldn't win."

The Republican Party, sensing victory, nominated Attorney General Earl Warren to try to unseat Olson in 1942. The two had warred over a murder case that Warren had prosecuted while serving as the district attorney for Alameda County. Three men had been charged and convicted based on the testimony of the actual killer. Warren insisted it was a murder for hire. Olson had thought Warren targeted the trio because of their ties to organized labor.

Mosk campaigned for his boss, but Warren won easily. He would be reelected in 1946 and 1950 before being confirmed as President Dwight D. Eisenhower's nominee for Chief Justice of the United States Supreme Court in 1953.

Olson, as governors have been known to do, dispensed some favors on his way out the door. One day, Olson gave Mosk the names of his selections to fill five court vacancies. Three appointments were to the Superior Court in Los Angeles. Two names were for the Los Angeles Municipal Court, one of which was Mosk's own. At only thirty years old, Mosk might have been thrilled by the prospect of any judicial appointment at all.

But that night Olson called Mosk at home. The aide expected to be chastised for his delay in delivering those signed commissions to the secretary of state's office. Instead, the governor said he wanted to withdraw Mosk's name for the municipal court. "My heart sank," Mosk said, until Olson told him he had decided to appoint Mosk to the Superior Court. "I've never forgotten that example of just pure, good fortune. And it changed my whole life."

As it happens, there was more than luck involved in Mosk's appointment to the Superior Court bench. On December 3, 1942, he had appealed to the governor directly—some might say, desperately—for just such a position. "Yesterday a capitol newspaper man said to me 'Stanley, the staff has taken a half-dozen trips East in the past four years and you always seem to be the one left behind to keep the office operating. I will bet $10 when the plums are passed out, that you will be left behind again.' If I am the first executive secretary in California history not to be appointed to the bench, I shall be looked upon with suspicion for many, many years by lawyers, the bench, by members of our own and opposing political parties," Mosk wrote to Olson.

"I do not contend that I am qualified to sit on the bench solely because I have been your executive secretary. I have the necessary temperament and other qualifications, including education, sufficient years of trial practice, experience at holding hearings and [I] write [for] legal and other publications. If you need any convincing on any of these points, merely ask any of the judges on the bench, from municipal court to [California Supreme Court] Chief Justice Phil Gibson."

Not everyone was as impressed by Mosk's credentials as he thought. He spent his first six months on the Superior Court bench not in Los Angeles but in Long Beach. The presiding judge in Los Angeles had not been thrilled to have a young, untested judge in his courthouse so he refused to assign him a courtroom or any cases.

However, the presiding judge in Long Beach, Alfred Paonessa, was happy to have him. One of Mosk's lasting memories of his time in Long Beach was joining Paonessa for lunch breaks in the judge's office high in the Jurgen's Trust building, overlooking the beach. He would walk in to see Paonessa with his binoculars, scanning the beach for pretty girls.

Elevated to the bench in early 1943, Mosk faced the voters for the first time in 1944 in what are known in California as retention elections; they occur every six years for Superior Court judges and every twelve years for justices on the Supreme Court. Because Mosk had just been appointed to the bench, he had to stand for election soon after he arrived. Two Municipal Court judges ran against the young jurist. Stanley Mosk wrote his brother, Ed, who was serving in the European Theater as a member of the Office of Strategic Services, "I drew the jackpot. It means I have a real battle on my hands, one of the toughest ever faced by an incumbent judge in the history of the court. . . . Feel certain of running 1st in the 3-cornered race. Only question being whether I can win at the primary and thus avoid a November run-of [*sic*]."

The judge hit up his friends for donations and tapped into the contacts he had made while working for Olson. Mosk won the first round of voting, but not by a majority, so he faced a runoff election against Municipal Court Judge LeRoy Dawson, who had taken to referring to his opponent as "the child judge." The third candidate, Judge Ida May Adams, threw her support behind Mosk as did most of the daily newspapers. He won by more than two hundred thousand votes. He would win retention elections for Superior Court again in 1950 and 1956.

Mosk commuted to Long Beach from his Beverly Hills-area home where he regularly hosted meetings of local Democratic Party clubs, one of whose members was Ronald Reagan, the actor and union activist with the Screen Actors Guild. Edna Mosk told her son that a lot of the club members felt that Reagan, who later would morph into a conservative Republican and be elected governor of California in 1966 and president of the United States in 1980, "was a little too far left for them."

Richard Mosk said their home also served as a wedding venue of sorts, with Stanley Mosk officiating at the marriages of celebrities such as Hedy LaMarr. "I always had to clean up the rice," Mosk's son recalled.

Mosk's courtroom also saw a number of Hollywood celebrities, most of whom were seeking divorces. The judge oversaw Joe DiMaggio's divorce from his first wife, actress Dorothy Arnold, in 1944 and Judy Garland's from her first husband, British-born composer and songwriter David Rose, also in 1944. In August 1944, Mosk wrote his brother that Lana Turner had appeared in his courtroom, seeking a divorce. "Turner was beautiful," Mosk wrote, "but the newspaper reporters were angry with her discourtesies." He did not elaborate. In the same note he said he had officiated at the marriage of actress Jean Parker, who one newspaper columnist called "the Liz Taylor of the 1930s." Parker, Mosk wrote, "is a lovely, little creature, quite bright. She married an Austrian refugee."

But by far the most publicity Mosk received was when Charlie Chaplin's paternity suit landed on his desk. In March 1944, Mosk wrote his brother that he "crowded the war off page one throughout the country by denying Charlie Chaplin's motion to dismiss the paternity suit against him and ordering the case to proceed to trial." Mosk told his brother that the ruling "was apparently a popular decision, for I have received fan mail from all parts of the country."

Chaplin, the actor and director, had had an affair with a young actress named Joan Berry while still married to his third wife Paulette Goddard, who had starred in *Modern Times*. (The actress is also known as Joan Barry. But the paternity suit is listed as *Berry v. Chaplin*.) Chaplin had hired Berry in 1941, signing her for $75 a week for a potential film to be called *Shadow and Substance*. The two soon became romantically involved. In October 1943, Berry gave birth to a daughter, Carol Ann, and when Chaplin denied being the father, she filed a paternity suit against him. Berry never appeared in a movie.

By the time the case got to court, the much-married Chaplin had wed his fourth wife Oona O'Neill, the daughter of playwright Eugene O'Neill, to whom he would stay married until his death in 1977 and with whom he fathered eight children. The oldest of those children, actress Geraldine Chaplin, is best known for her role as Tonya in David Lean's 1965 epic film *Doctor Zhivago*.

Mosk was asked to dismiss the case by Chaplin's attorney based on blood tests that, three doctors testified, indicated Chaplin was not the father. The judge refused to do so, citing state law, which said that while the results of paternity tests may be introduced as evidence, they are not to be seen as wholly exclusionary to other evidence. His decision sent the case to trial.

"To the adult parties to the action, this or any court owes only the obligation of impartiality and objectivity," Mosk said. "But to the infant, unable to maintain its own rights under the law, the court owes the additional duty of protection."

Mosk's ruling was upheld by the appeals court, and the state Supreme Court refused to take up the case. The jury ordered Chaplin to support Carol Ann until the age of 21. But the case also led to the reformation of paternity laws in California and across the country, a legislative fix that came too late for Charlie Chaplin. New Hampshire and Oregon also signed onto the wording of the Uniform Act on Blood Tests to Determine Paternity, which states: "If the court finds that the conclusions of all the experts as disclosed by the evidence based upon the tests are that the alleged father is not the father of the child, the question of paternity shall be resolved accordingly."

Mosk's letters to his brother touched on a variety of topics, from baseball (he was a diehard Chicago White Sox fan) to boxing to politics, both state and national. He noted that a dramatic comeback by USC against UCLA in a football game created more interest than the political campaign. In the spring of 1944, he noted that the major league baseball season had begun.

"The Cards and Yanks lead again, as usual. But your Cubs, woe is them! They fired (manager) Jimmy [*sic*] Wilson when they won their first game of the season, then lost 13 in a row! They are still wallowing in the cellar," he wrote.

"My White Sox, in fourth place, look good and with the best pitching in the league, are considered a real threat for the flag this year." Alas, Mosk's prediction for his beloved ChiSox proved to be premature. The White Sox finished 71–83, seventh in the eight-team American League. The Cubs were marginally better, finishing 75–79, fourth in the eight-team National League.

Mosk was much more comfortable writing about state and national politics. In June of 1944 he wrote that New York governor Thomas Dewey and Ohio governor John Bricker, the Republican ticket, "represent a combination bereft of ability, initiative or imagination. The platform of the GOP is a splendid 1924 document, except for its foreign policy plank, which reads like a chapter from a Harding speech in 1920." On Harry Truman, then seen as Roosevelt's likely running mate, Mosk wrote, "Yes, he's all right, an honest, able man. But colorless and possessive of no great vision."

When Roosevelt was reelected on November 7, 1944, Mosk wrote that it was "a great day for America, for the world—and for the Mosk family." The family reference was to his own victory in the retention election.

But the underlying feeling in many of Mosk's missives to his brother was one of guilt to the point of near exasperation. As a judge, Mosk was exempt from the draft. He nonetheless wanted to do *something* for the war effort. He had started serving in the Coast Guard reserve on a weekly basis, but that was not enough.

In July 1944, noting the improving situation for the Allies in Europe, Mosk wrote, "that brings me to the point of wondering if I'll not be delaying too long if I wait until November (the retention election) before getting into the show in some capacity. . . . That would mean that I would miss the boat, for I would never forgive myself if I failed to have some small role in this war." He asked his brother to make inquiries on his behalf, saying, "If a specific opportunity presents itself for something really worthwhile, I would go on a very short notice—leaving the (retention) campaign organized and to be run in my absence." "Please look into that for me, Ed, if you can possibly do so," he continued. "I don't want to delay too long. It may be later than I think."

It was also in 1944 that the Mosks' father died. Paul Mosk had been ill for some time with tuberculosis. Minna, his widow after thirty-four years of marriage, later opened a bookstore in downtown Los Angeles, something the brothers considered a huge accomplishment for someone with no retail or sales experience. "She handled that remarkably well for a person who had no business training," Stanley Mosk said. "It was a bookstore with cards and little gifts and a rental library for secretaries who lived in the area. She did this all by herself."

Two months after the 1944 election, Mosk waived his draft exemption and underwent the customary physical examination. His eyesight was listed as 20/800, which made him ineligible for the Navy. The Army, he told his brother, put him in the "Limited Service" class. That meant it was highly unlikely he would be called to active duty. "So, I fear I am right back where I began," he said.

Mosk appealed to the Office of War Information, which he said was only interested in hiring civilians. "And, of course, I am not interested in remaining a civilian."

He contacted attorney Arthur Goldberg both by telephone and mail. Goldberg, like Ed Mosk, was serving in the Office of Strategic Services. His role was head of the Labor Desk in the organization, which cultivated contacts and networks in the European underground to resist the Germans. But no help was forthcoming from Goldberg, who later would join President John F. Kennedy's cabinet as secretary of labor, and then become an associate justice on the US Supreme Court and the US ambassador to the United Nations during the administration of Lyndon Johnson.

"I have no illusion about service," he wrote to his brother early in 1945. "My bed is comfortable, the house is warm, privacy of the bathroom, meals of my own choice, hours that I set for myself, activities and thoughts of my own—these are precious things. I'm voluntarily changing them all for the ultimate in regimentation, discomfort, perhaps danger. But I am convinced that it is the best for me and, I hope, the country."

At his Army physical, according to his son Richard, the local Selective Service worker purposely left the room, giving Mosk time to memorize the eye chart and pass his physical examination. In early 1945, he was assigned to the Army's Transportation Corps. He was first sent to Fort Leonard Wood in Missouri for his basic training and then served out the war at Camp Plauche on the outskirts of New Orleans. During World War II, the camp was a staging area for troops passing through New Orleans to board ships for the Pacific Theater. It later was used as a training facility and a Prisoner of War camp for captured Italian and German servicemen.

It didn't pass as rigorous work. "I have to say, if you have to fight a war, New Orleans is not a bad place," Mosk said.

Mosk never made it overseas. His unit was scheduled to be sent to the Philippines when the war ended. He had been in the Army for only a handful of months. Phil Gibson, who had left the Olson administration for a seat on the California Supreme Court, first as an associate justice in 1939 and then as Chief Justice in 1940, called Mosk to ask if he was ready to resume his duties on the bench. There was a backload of cases in the Superior Courts; Mosk was needed back in California. Mosk was only too happy to return.

Governor Earl Warren, the man who had defeated Mosk's boss in 1942, had not filled the judicial vacancy in Los Angeles, although it was well within his power to do so. It was an act that Mosk never forgot. While Mosk and Warren had jousted frequently when Olson was in office, the two eventually became close friends and would sit together at the Rose Bowl every year.

As for the war he had tried so strenuously to join? "I don't know that the war had any significant influence on me," he said, beyond the horrific lessons the Holocaust had taught him and the world about dangerous theories of racial superiority.

It was not long after Judge Mosk returned to the bench in 1945 that the case of *Wright v. Drye* landed on his docket. In that ruling denouncing racial covenants designed to preserve all-white neighborhoods, Mosk made a stand for full civil rights for Black Americans and proved himself to be a man ahead of his time.

• 3 •

The Benefactors

$\mathscr{A}$s Stanley Mosk was striking down racial covenants in housing in California, Charlie Sifford was embarking on a professional career in a sport where Black golfers were uniformly assigned second-class status.

Professional golf was not the profitable pursuit at mid-century that it would become in the decades ahead when huge purses, lucrative endorsement deals, and enticing business opportunities would make multimillionaires of such talents as Tiger Woods, Arnold Palmer, Jack Nicklaus, Greg Norman, and Phil Mickelson.

In the 1940s, white golfers relied on family money, jobs as club pros at private country clubs, and personal financial backers to seed them at the beginning of their careers. Financial support was huge for those starting out. Marvin Leonard, a Fort Worth businessman, supported Ben Hogan financially in his early days. Byron Nelson received a much-needed loan of $500 to keep his golfing career alive.

But because Black golfers were prohibited from being members of the PGA, they were also not allowed to hold jobs as pros or assistant pros at most country clubs. That was the only avenue open to actually joining the PGA Tour back then. One had to work in a pro shop for five years, which is why when you look at leaderboards from that era you see the names of famous Texas-born golfers like Ben Hogan (Hershey, Pennsylvania), Jimmy Demaret (Darien, Connecticut) and Byron Nelson (Toledo, Ohio) listed according to which golf club they worked at, not their hometowns. Those pros didn't spend a lot of time at those clubs, but the affiliation was all that mattered. It benefited the club if the player achieved success on the PGA Tour. And the PGA itself didn't monitor how many days the pros spent in the pro shop or how many lessons they gave on the practice tee. The affiliation was sufficient.

There were, however, no exclusive country clubs or wealthy white golf enthusiasts lining up to help bankroll Charlie Sifford, Ted Rhodes, Howard Wheeler, Bill Spiller, and the other Black golfers on the Chitlin' Tour. For them, the fuel that propelled them was a passion for the game and faith that they one day might carve a place for themselves in professional golf.

That mix of passion and faith is what Sifford must have felt as he piled his clothes and golf clubs into Eddie Mallory's car for what he later would describe as "the most significant trip I would ever take in my life." Howard Wheeler joined them as they headed from Philadelphia to Pittsburgh for the 1946 UGA National Negro Open, being held at South Park Golf Course.

While Wheeler was an old pro at these tournaments, having already won two of them, Sifford was being introduced to competitive golf at a high level for the first time. All of the great Black players at the time descended upon South Park for what Sifford called "our Masters" tournament. The thirty-five-year-old Wheeler, the transplanted Atlantan who was a fixture at Cobbs Creek, was among the tournament favorites along with the thirty-two-year-old Rhodes. Wheeler won the third of his six UGA National Negro Open titles that week. Rhodes finished second, two shots astern.

And Sifford? His name is nowhere to be found in the saturation coverage provided by the *Pittsburgh Courier*, the city's legendary Black newspaper. He admitted to being overwhelmed by the whole event, awe-struck by both the talent of the other Black golfers and by the A-list celebrities who were on hand. It wasn't like anything he had ever experienced.

"For the first time in my life," Sifford said, "I was surrounded by guys who could really play. I had heard about some of them, but now they were up close, and one look at the way they hit the ball gave me a sinking feeling that I wasn't playing for no dollar bets at Cobbs Creek against businessmen."

While he did not score as well as he would have liked, Sifford's tournament play impressed his fellow golfers. Through Wheeler he met Rhodes and Spiller, who was playing as an amateur for the last time. They both encouraged him to go to Detroit for the tournament that bore the name of Joe Louis, the heavyweight champion of the world.

Louis was an internationally famous boxer, but he was also an aspiring Black golfer's best friend. In 1945, he had hired Rhodes to teach him the basics, providing the regular financial support that allowed Rhodes to play on the Black competitive tour. Louis, who bristled at the exclusion of Black golfers from PGA membership, had done the same for Clyde Martin, a golf pro at a Black course in Washington, D.C., earlier in the 1940s.

"The only person who could make a dent in the system was the one Black athlete whom everyone respected—Joe Louis," Sifford said. "It made him furious that his beloved game of golf was so racist. After Joe's fighting career was over, it became his passion to break Blacks into golf."

Sifford titled one of the chapters in his autobiography "Joe Louis Opens Doors." But those doors did not yield easily. Louis's son, Joe Barrow Jr., said his father was appalled at how stubborn racial discrimination remained in golf because "when he was heavyweight champion of the world, he fought all comers. He was more annoyed that Black golfers couldn't play against white golfers."

Louis, known as the Brown Bomber, reigned as heavyweight champion of the world for more than eleven years and fought twenty-five successful defenses. He attributed one of his few losses, a twelfth-round knockout to Max Schmeling in 1936, to his having paid more attention to his golf game than his boxing training. He had picked up golf the year before and hit the golf course whenever he could. In the rematch against Schmeling in 1938, Louis put more effort into his training and won with a knockout in the first round in a bout at Yankee Stadium before a crowd estimated at seventy thousand. The referee stopped the fight after Louis had knocked Schmeling down three times in the first two minutes, four seconds. This was during the Nazi's ascension to power in Germany and, like Jesse Owens's successes at the 1936 Olympics in Berlin, Louis had delivered a haymaker to the notion of white supremacy with his swift dispatching of Schmeling.

Louis enlisted in the Army in 1942. There was never a serious question of him actually serving in active combat. His popularity was more important, and it was used to convince the public to buy war bonds. He was more like a goodwill ambassador and eventually was sent overseas to the European Theater, but for the purpose of entertaining the troops.

He did defend his title once while in the Army, in March 1942 against Abe Simon, and donated his earnings to the Army Relief Fund. He was discharged in 1945, having attained the rank of staff sergeant.

Louis began competing in amateur golf tournaments while still at the height of his boxing career. And when Joe Louis played golf, people came out to watch. But the heavyweight champ had his standards, and he did not want to look like a duffer on the course. In the early 1940s, he hired

Martin to be his instructor. That relationship went on for two years until Louis enlisted in the Army. The year before, he had started the Joe Louis Open at his home course in Detroit, not only funding the $1,000 purse but also paying the travel expenses and entrance fees for those Black golfers who could not afford it. When the tournament resumed after World War II, Louis increased the purse to $2,000.

As his boxing career came to an end and Louis fought primarily in exhibitions, he turned more and more to golf, entering the amateur division championship of the UGA's National Negro Open whenever he could. He would win it in 1951. His legendary betting on the course enriched numerous Black golfers; Bill Spiller claimed he won $7,000 from Louis in a single match, enough for him to purchase his house in Los Angeles.

"He was one the most generous men I've ever seen, as well as one of the few Black men committed to making things better for his people," Sifford said of Louis.

When Louis hired Rhodes in 1945 to be his golf teacher and playing partner, many felt that Rhodes was already the greatest Black golfer of the period. Sifford thought so. He called Rhodes "the Black Nicklaus" and added, "Teddy was the undisputed master."

"God only knows what numbers Teddy would have put up if he had played on the white tour in those days, or what kind of influence he might have had on black kids to play golf. They would have had to write about him in every white newspaper in country," Sifford said.

Rhodes dressed as well as he played. Depending on which book you read about Rhodes, his nickname "Rags" either came from his youth, when he didn't possess the money to display the sartorial splendor he would later exhibit, or as a term of sarcasm because he was such a fashion plate on the UGA tour. He wore argyle socks, plus-fours, tams, and brightly colored cardigans and golf shoes to match each outfit. Dottie May Campbell, the daughter of the All-American tournament promoter George May, told *Golf Digest* in 1998 that Rhodes was every bit as charismatic as his wardrobe was elegant and fashionable.

"To me," she told the magazine, "he was a Black Clark Gable. He dressed like the cover of GQ. He'd walk into a room, everybody's head turned. He had star quality."

Rhodes had started caddying in Nashville at all-white courses when he was nine years old. His father died when he was still in elementary school. He soon went to work full-time at exclusive Belle Meade Country Club, a former plantation that once had been home to more than one hundred enslaved Black people, where his uncle was the caddie master. After high school, he joined Franklin D. Roosevelt's Civilian Conservation Corps during the Great Depression and served in the Navy during World War II, discharged early due to kidney stones.

Rhodes's big break came in 1945, when he entered a UGA tournament and did well enough to attract the attention of Joe Louis. He had a job working in a nightclub in Nashville, but golf was still his passion. He played with borrowed clubs and did well enough to attract the attention of Joe Louis, who also played in that tournament. The boxer was about to be discharged from the Army and was losing Martin as his golf instructor because of health issues.

Like everyone who came into contact with Rhodes, Louis was as impressed by the Black golfer's warm demeanor as his obvious talent for the game. A match was made. Rhodes went to work for Joe Louis as his valet, swing coach and traveling companion.

After his discharge from the service, Louis brought Rhodes to Los Angeles. To sharpen Rhodes's skills, Louis hired Ray Mangrum, a five-time winner on the PGA tour and the brother of 1946 US Open champion and Hall of Famer Lloyd Mangrum. Louis paid Ray Mangrum five dollars per session at Sunset Fields, a public course, to tutor Rhodes, who would soon become the best Black golfer in the game.

Rhodes's relationship with Louis changed his life. The salary Louis paid him allowed him to participate in UGA events, with his mentor also paying entry and transportation fees. Rhodes racked up his share of UGA events; one estimate has him winning as many as 150 tournaments. (The UGA's recordkeeping in those days was incomplete at best. There were only four recorded tournaments in the first year, 1926, and just eleven as late as 1949. There certainly were more than that, but it is impossible to know how many tournaments were held each year and to identify all the winners because of gaps in the records.)

Rhodes defeated Zeke Hartsfield in a playoff at a tournament in New Castle, Pennsylvania, the week before the 1946 UGA National Negro Open. It was one of three he had won prior to arriving in Pittsburgh. Earlier that summer, he had been in contention through three rounds of George May's All-American Open before a final-round 79 dropped him down the leaderboard.

But Rhodes's story is indicative of what that time was like for Black golfers. His non-confrontational manner served him well on the course, but often prevented him from voicing his opinions on the outright racism he fought. Several of the white pros of the 1940s and 1950s who had played with Rhodes attested to his talent. Bob Rosburg, the 1959 PGA champion who went on to become a television broadcaster, said of Rhodes, "he was a damn good player with a stylish swing. If he could have played every week on the tour, he'd have been in the top 20 at the end of the year."

But as much as Rosburg and others admired Rhodes's game, there is no evidence any of the white touring pros did much to get the Black players on the tour with them. And Rosburg was one of the more enlightened ones. He would join Charlie Sifford in the parking lot to eat as a show of solidarity because the Black golfer was banned from the clubhouse restaurant. But did Ben Hogan, Sam Snead, or Byron Nelson voice public concern over the plight of the Black golfer? They did not. Tommy Bolt and Jimmy Demaret, major champions from the 1950s, supplied Sifford with equipment and golf balls but were quiet otherwise. Of the great golfers of the 1960s, the one exception was Gary Player, who came from apartheid South Africa. But Player was a voice in the wilderness. Sure, they all liked Charlie Sifford and appreciated his game. But his struggle?

Still, just being around Rhodes, Spiller, and Wheeler in Pittsburgh that late-summer weekend was exhilarating for the twenty-four-year-old Sifford. That was the kind of heady company he was keeping when he drove out to Joe Louis's annual UGA tournament in Detroit, after his underwhelming performance in the National Negro Open. At the Rackham Golf Club, Louis and Rhodes introduced Sifford to one of the greatest entertainers of the era, the musician, singer, and bandleader Billy Eckstine, and Eckstine soon presented Sifford with an opportunity that would change the aspiring golfer's life.

According to Sifford, it was Rhodes who first approached Eckstine. "Look here, this guy is good," Rhodes told the musician and golf enthusiast. "He needs some help. Why don't you sponsor him, give him a job, and in return he'll teach you how to play?" Louis then showed up at Eckstine's room and explained how this young pro from Philadelphia had just crushed him in a match. That was enough to convince Eckstine to take the plunge.

Louis and Eckstine became the two most important benefactors in that era for Black golfers. Boxer Sugar Ray Robinson sponsored a UGA tournament on Long Island and briefly employed a Black golfer as his instructor, and Jackie Robinson used his fame to criticize the PGA for its racial discrimination. But neither directly subsidized players for as long as Louis and Eckstine did.

Eckstine offered to pay Sifford $150 a week to teach him the game. As Eckstine's son Ed explained, "Charlie was looking for a gig. Dad needed a valet and driver because he had just bought a new Cadillac to take him to his gigs. He would sleep in the back of the car and Charlie would drive. The deal was that they'd get up the next morning and find a golf course where Blacks could play. They would play 36 holes almost every day. And Billy Eckstine became a scratch golfer."

On the first night of their new relationship, Sifford told Eckstine to meet him at a driving range the following morning. As the two men left the club where Eckstine was performing, an inebriated man threatened the popular singer. Sifford intervened, brandishing a straight razor and indicating that it might be in the man's best interest to leave. The man left. Sifford kept a straight razor handy for the rest of their time together.

Eckstine was just getting into golf as a number of things were going on in his private life. The year 1947 would be the year he broke up his band and embarked on a solo career in Hollywood. The jazz scene at the time was rife with alcohol and easily available drugs, and Ed Eckstine said his father took up golf as a healthy alternative to the temptations of the road.

For Sifford, the job would mean being away from home more often than not, but it also would give him the freedom to play golf, make a decent wage, and start the long, slow process toward becoming a professional on the PGA Tour. He would be traveling the country with one of the most popular entertainers of the period. How could he say no to Billy Eckstine?

It was an extraordinary gesture from Eckstine, who was then just thirty-two years old. Sifford was part of a road show that could feature as many as seven different men traveling with Eckstine at a given time, with roles ranging from golf pro to press agent. The two men became close friends over the years and Sifford never forgot the huge impact Eckstine had on his life.

"It goes without saying that there would have been no Charlie Sifford, the pro golfer, and probably no Blacks in golf period without Billy Eckstine," Sifford said.

That one year traveling with Eckstine and his band was eye opening for Sifford, who would often catch a show at night. Eckstine is credited with creating the bebop sound, though he never warmed to the phrase. Throughout the years, his bandmates would include the likes of Charley Parker, Dizzy Gillespie, a young Miles Davis, and the jazz singer Sarah Vaughan, who would sing duets with Eckstine and also play some piano.

During its heyday, the band would spend forty weeks a year on the road, earning as much as $10,000 a week.

Many of the members had left Eckstine's band by the time that Sifford came aboard. But the golfer spent enough time in Eckstine's entourage to witness the power and the energy of the band's performances.

"Musically, it may have been the most important time in American history and Billy Eckstine kept the engine running with his hit songs and immense popularity," Sifford said. "He and his bands went out every night exploring new territory to play, and I sat on the side and loved every minute of it."

The singer-musician preferred warm-weather venues, the better to wake up the next morning and hit the nearest golf course. He befriended pro golfer Jimmy Demaret, which led to a long engagement at the Concord Resort Hotel in the Catskills, an area famously known as the Borscht Belt. It was a popular destination for New York City's Jewish population.

"I've heard it said that I was the first black headliner in the Catskills," Eckstine said. "I first appeared there in 1949. I don't want to sound naïve, but that was something I was never aware of. I don't remember breaking down walls—there were no walls to break down."

Comedian Nipsey Russell opened frequently for Eckstine at the Concord. He said Eckstine and singer Lena Horne differed from most Black variety entertainers at the time because they were the headliners. "And stars like Billy and Lena headlined everywhere," Russell said, "even though in some places they may have had to sleep on the beach."

One of the inns in the Catskills, the Tamarack Lodge, was run by Dave Levinson, whose parents had founded the establishment. He recalled a meeting in 1969 with the popular singing group The Four Tops, who were looking for a gig. The Tamarack and other places had started to book rock 'n' roll acts such as Blood, Sweat and Tears, Vanilla Fudge, and the Turtles.

"You don't remember us Dave," one of the Tops said to Levinson, "but we were the background music for Billy Eckstine when he sang at your hotel."

Billy Eckstine was born in Pittsburgh and attended high school in Washington, D.C. After a brief stint at the all-Black St. Paul Normal and Industrial School in Lawrenceville, Virginia, he enrolled in Howard University, a historically Black college in Washington, D.C. He was offered a music scholarship at the university, but instead he dropped out to pursue a singing career. He had discovered by then that he had a musical gift as well as the ability to do spot-on impersonations of Cab Calloway and others. He sang in various clubs in the Pittsburgh area. When he won an amateur music contest at the Howard Theater, he decided to sing full-time, joining drummer Tommy Myles's band, which toured the East and played in such famed venues as the Cotton Club in New York.

Eckstine was known primarily for his rich bass-baritone. He started his own band in the mid-1930s, Baron Billy and His Orchestra, but he struggled to find traction early on, bouncing around from city to city and gig to gig. After a year singing at the Club DeLisa in Chicago, earning $25 a week, Eckstine got his big break. Orchestra leader Earl Hines stopped by the DeLisa and was so impressed with Eckstine's performance that he told one of his orchestra's members, "I'm going to try and steal that boy! He will kill everybody." And Billy Eckstine found himself in 1939 as the lead singer for the Earl Hines Orchestra.

His renditions of "Stormy Monday Blues" and "Jelly, Jelly" catapulted him to fame. He tried to steer clear of blues numbers, feeling it would stereotype him. He also sang romantic ballads and soon became known as Mr. B. or, as Duke Ellington called him, the Sonorous B.

"Eckstine-style love songs opened new lines of communication for the man-woman merry-go-round and blues a la B were the essence of cool," Ellington wrote in his autobiography. "When he made a recording of 'Caravan,' I was happy and honored to watch one of our tunes help to take him into the stratosphere of universal acclaim."

Eckstine was bi-racial and dashingly handsome, radiating an appeal from the stage that attracted whites and Blacks, young and old, male and female. He would sell out famed New York clubs for week-long stints. His young female admirers were known as Billy Soxers. "Eckstine could drop his voice down basso, or send it skyward tenor, but it was that mellifluous, mesmerizing baritone that seduced a nation," wrote Richard Harrington in the *Washington Post*.

After several years leading a band, Eckstine decided to strike out on his own. His band had its final performance in Chicago at the Regal Theater in February 1947. The singer then moved to California, buying a house in Encino to avoid the housing discrimination against Blacks and Jews then so common in Los Angeles, but soon to be outlawed by Judge Stanley Mosk's ruling in *Wright v. Drye*. Eckstine's paternal grandparents were a mixed-race couple. His name was originally spelled Eckstein, but his agent convinced him to change the spelling to avoid appearing "too Jewish."

The Eckstine blended family included seven children. The oldest two were born to Eckstine's second wife before the two married in 1952.

Four children were born from 1953 to 1960. A seventh child, Billy Jr., or "Beezy," as he was known, was adopted by Eckstine during his first marriage. Family lore suggests Beezy was discovered wandering aimlessly around a brothel in a remote Wyoming town where Eckstine and his band had settled for the night. Eckstine took the boy back with him to California and Billy Jr. went on to serve three tours in Vietnam before joining the Pittsburgh Fire Department. He died in in 2013.

"The irony of him being Billy Jr. is that he had no musical acumen or interest in entertainment or show business," Ed Eckstine said.

Ed had a successful career in the music business as executive vice president of Quincy Jones Productions and later as president of Mercury Records. His brother Guy was a record company executive, and two others, Charlotte and Gina, were singers.

The Eckstine family were the only Blacks in their Encino neighborhood until a family named the Jacksons—yes, *those* Jacksons, Michael et al.—moved there in 1971.

While Eckstine's musical life changed when he became a solo artist, his itinerary did not. He would play clubs all over the country, testing out new songs, crooning out the standards to packed houses. He was returning to the staple that originally made him famous—his voice.

Ed Eckstine recalled a trip he made to Las Vegas with Quincy Jones and his wife, the actress Peggy Lipton, ten years before his father had died, to see Frank Sinatra at Caesar's Palace. After the show, the three went to visit Sinatra at his hotel suite.

"He took me aside and we talked for 15 minutes," Ed recalled. "He said, 'let me tell you something. I loved your dad. I loved the guy.' We got along great even though the media tried to paint us as adversaries. If the world had been different then, with no segregation, there would have been no need for me because we would already have had Billy Eckstine."

With Eckstine on the road, and Sifford right there with him, the families of both men learned to live with absent fathers. Billy Eckstine would check in on the phone every Sunday, with each of the children getting a few minutes to tell their father about their week. Sifford tried to call home every day.

Charlie Sifford had married Rose Crumbley after he accepted Billy Eckstine's offer to join him on the road. Rose and her mother remained in Philadelphia. Rose worked at the Woolworth department store and her mother at Horn & Hardart, which had the first food-service automats in the city. Charlie Sifford said his wife not only gave her blessing to him teaming up with Eckstine, but she was also excited her husband would be part of the musician's entourage. Their first son, Charles Jr., was born in 1948. His father would not be around very much for the next decade.

"It was definitely different, but I had a great mom and grandmother and some close friends so that kind of filled the void," the younger Sifford said. "It did bother me at times when the fathers of other kids came to baseball games and things like that, and they would always ask me where my dad was. I told them he was at work and couldn't make it.

"He called just about every day. And when he did come home, it was like a normal family. The little bit of time we did spend together we put as much as we could into it as possible. I just missed him being there for things fathers are normally there for."

When Ted Rhodes and Charlie Sifford weren't coaching their respective benefactors in golf, the pair were often traveling companions, sharing rides, rooms and money while trying to eke out a living on the UGA Tour that in 1947 offered a $2,000 purse with $700 going to the top finisher in its annual National Negro Open. The golfers, often joined by Wheeler and Hartsfield, would stay at the homes of friends. Sifford said the four generally split their wages. They drove across the country, two to a car.

Louis bought Rhodes a red Buick even though, at the time, Rhodes didn't know how to drive. Sifford did. He went up to Detroit and picked up the car, which Rhodes named "Alexander." "We were driving through Albuquerque on our way to California and Teddy was asleep," Sifford recalled of one trip. "My foot got kinda big and I had that speedometer hitting 80 and 90. Suddenly, Teddy woke up and said, 'Charlie Horse! Don't run Alexander so fast and hard!'"

While Rhodes was taking lessons from Ray Mangrum in Los Angeles, he met Bill Spiller. They had been born a fortnight apart in 1913 and had a shared passion for golf.

Spiller had been a basketball and track star at a segregated high school in Tulsa and went on to play sports at all-Black Wiley College in Marshall, Texas, from which he graduated in 1938. He wanted to go into teaching, but the best offer he could get was for $60 a month at a rural school in Texas. So he moved to Los Angeles to help out his mother, who had separated from Spiller's father when Spiller was a preschooler. It didn't take him long to get his red cap job and soon, as he put it, "I got stuck up in the golf game." He was twenty-nine.

But Spiller's athletic prowess in other sports served him well in picking up the game. Within four years he was winning amateur tournaments on the UGA circuit and, in 1947, he turned pro.

Rhodes had a head start on Spiller, but the two of them, along with Howard Wheeler, quickly rose to the head of the list of Black golfers in the mid- to late 1940s. In 1948, Spiller and Rhodes entered the Los Angeles Open. In the first round, eventual champion Ben Hogan shot a 68. So did Bill Spiller. Spiller faltered after that spectacular start and finished in a tie for twenty-ninth. Rhodes finished in a tie for twenty-second. Both golfers finished well within the top sixty, which should have automatically qualified them for the next PGA-sanctioned tournament, the Richmond Open outside Oakland. Except, of course, it did no such thing.

While white PGA members descended on the Monterrey Peninsula for Bing Crosby's annual Pro-Am tournament, which at the time was only fifty-four holes and thus not an official PGA event, Rhodes and Spiller bided their time. The following week, the two reported to the Richmond Golf Club for practice rounds but were informed by the PGA's tournament representative that they could not play. Madison Gunter, a Black amateur, was also turned away.

According to Spiller, the PGA representative, a man named George Schneiter, told them that the organization was merely following its own rules and regulations, without elaborating.

"Mr. Schneiter, I'm a college graduate," Spiller responded. "I understand English. So, if you want to say something to me, say it. I will understand." Spiller was then told that because he, Rhodes, and Gunter were not members of the PGA, they could not play in the tournament.

It was nothing personal, Schneiter assured them. Rules were rules. Schneiter was an accomplished player in his own right, a PGA tour player, and would compete in four Masters from 1946 to 1956, making the cut each time. But on this day in Richmond, California, he was a company man, an apparatchik, telling two golfers who had legitimately qualified for a PGA tournament that they had to pack their bags and leave because they were Black. Rules are rules.

The PGA's Caucasian-only clause had been in effect since 1934. It was all there, in black and white, Article III, Section I of the PGA's Constitution and By-Laws of the Professional Golfers Association of America. Under the heading "Members" it read, "Professional golfers of the Caucasian Race, over the age of eighteen (18) years, residing in North or South America and who have served at least five years in the profession (either in the employ of a golf club in the capacity as a professional or in the employ of a professional as his assistant) shall be eligible for membership."

How is it that professional golf, and no other major sport, decided to put something like that into its bylaws? It all goes back to a man named Dewey Brown who, in 1928, became the first Black member of the PGA. But because of his fair complexion, it took six years for the PGA members to discover that Brown was, well, Black.

Brown was born in North Carolina and was introduced to the game at a young age while caddying at the Madison (NJ) Golf Club. He soon developed into a skilled club maker and worked at high-end clubs like Shawnee-on-the-Delaware and Baltrusol Country Club. He made a set of clubs for President Warren G. Harding, Vice President Charles Dawes, and Chick Evans, who won the 1916 US Amateur and 1916 US Open, the first individual to do so in the same year. He developed a reputation as an excellent golf instructor as well.

"My idea of teaching golf is to teach the person," Brown said in an interview with *Golf Course Superintendent* magazine in July 1974. He went on to explain the fundamentals as he saw them, starting with the grip and proceeding all the way to putting. "If you have the confidence, you generally putt well."

Brown played in a number of local tournaments; at that time, there was no real established PGA tour. The PGA was almost exclusively composed of club pros, and Brown fit the membership criteria at the time due to his many years of working in pro shops.

Brown applied for PGA membership in 1928, was accepted, and was a dues-paying member of the organization for the next six years. It is not known why the PGA terminated his membership in 1934. But the very fact that the PGA rescinded Brown's membership and adopted the Caucasian-only clause in the same year cannot be a coincidence. Someone dropped a dime along the way because Brown checked all the boxes for PGA membership—except the one that would soon be adopted.

At the PGA's 1934 annual convention, the delegation from Michigan proposed limiting membership to Caucasians only. As to why that happened, one delegate to the convention was quoted as saying, "show us some good golf clubs Negroes have established and we can talk this over again." So, the PGA moved accordingly. And the Caucasian-only clause stood largely unnoticed and unreported upon until Bill Spiller and Ted Rhodes were denied entry into the 1948 Richmond Open because of the color of their skin.

After getting turned away, Spiller and Rhodes contacted Ira Blue, a well-known sportscaster at KGO Radio in San Francisco whose program was called *The Last Word in Sports*. He highlighted the issue of racial discrimination on his radio show and advised the golfers to hire a civil rights attorney in Redwood City named Jonathan Rowell.

Rowell agreed to represent the three golfers, filing a $315,000 lawsuit on their behalf against the golf club and the PGA on January 17 in the Superior Court for Contra Costa County, which is where Richmond was located. It was too bad for the golfers that the Richmond Golf Club was not in Los Angeles. The lawsuit might have landed on the docket of Superior Court Judge Stanley Mosk.

Three days after filing the suit, Rowell wrote to Thurgood Marshall, then chief counsel for the NAACP in Washington, asking for his assistance. The three-page letter described the golfers' situation; each of the three were seeking $5,000 for "actual damages by not being allowed to compete" and for what Rowell said was "humiliation, anguish and distress." Each player also sued the PGA for $100,000, arguing that the Caucasian-only clause made the PGA the equivalent of a closed shop, denying them the right to earn a living in violation of the Taft-Hartley Act.

"The cause of action against the golf club itself is that by signing the tournament contract with the Professional Golfers Association, an association which they knew discriminated against Negroes, the club thereby aided and incited the discrimination," Rowell wrote. "If this point can be made to stick, it may well have the result of causing many golf clubs to think twice before they ever put on another PGA tournament."

Rowell was asking for financial help from the NAACP; he estimated it would cost $250 to cover travel for expected depositions of PGA officials and players.

But the suit never got that far. In late September, a week before the trial was to begin, the case was dismissed at Rowell's request. What had happened? Behind the scenes, the PGA, through its attorney, had told Rowell that if he dropped the suit, the organization would allow Black players to participate in its tournaments. Spiller, Rhodes, and other Blacks could not be denied spots in tournaments, and the PGA escaped with what looked like a face-saving gesture.

Rowell took the organization at its word and the players withdrew the lawsuit. But they had been played. The PGA did not stop discriminating against Blacks. The tournaments that it sanctioned, which until then had been called "Opens," could now be called "Open Invitationals" and the sponsors could invite—or not invite—whomever they pleased. Most continued to shun Black players.

Spiller and Rhodes were satisfied in only one respect—more of the public was now aware that the PGA's operating bylaws limited its membership to Caucasians only. Both golfers turned thirty-five in 1948. They would have a few, precious years of professional golf left, but not nearly enough to benefit them when the Caucasian-only clause finally fell. The PGA would continue to be a closed shop for Black golfers for another thirteen years.

That summer of 1948, with the lawsuit pending, Rhodes became the first Black in thirty-five years to play in the US Open at Riviera. In 1913, John Shippen played in his sixth and final US Open. His first had been in 1896 at Shinnecock Hills. He was a caddy at Shinnecock and entered the tournament at the members' suggestion. He was half-Black and half-Shinnecock Indian and the US Open field, consisting mostly of European-born players, initially resisted playing in a tournament with Shippen and Oscar Bunn, a Shinnecock caddy and Native American. But the USGA stepped in and did the right thing, with organization president Theodore Havemeyer saying the tournament would proceed even if Shippen and Bunn were the only two contestants.

The rest of the field of thirty-five dropped their protest and played. James Foulis from Scotland won the tournament. Shippen finished tied for sixth. His best finish in a US Open was a tie for fifth in 1902. He went on to become a head golf professional at a number of Eastern golf clubs, including the Aronimink Golf Club in Newtown Square, Pennsylvania and the Shady Rest Golf Course in Scotch Plains, New Jersey, where he remained until he retired in 1960.

In 2021, Rocket Mortgage Company, which sponsors an annual PGA event in Detroit, along with Intersport, a media and marketing firm, and Woods and Watts Effect, a business consulting service, launched the John Shippen. It was a two-day tournament named in honor of America's first Black golf professional and its mission was to provide more opportunities for Black golfers, both amateur and professional. The John Shippen tournament was scheduled to immediately precede the Rocket Mortgage Classic in the Detroit area so that its champion could receive an exemption into the PGA tournament. There was also a women's division of the John Shippen, and its winner received an automatic exemption into an LPGA tournament.

The fact that it took thirty-five years for a Black golfer to make it to the US Open speaks as much to the sheer difficulty of getting there as anything else. The only option for Black golfers was to qualify for the tournament. Blacks weren't PGA members so there was no way for any of them to get exempt status for the USGA's signature event. Those spots went to players who had won the US Open or PGA Championship, had fared well in the previous US Open, had won the British Open, or were among the top money winners. No Black player had a chance to qualify under those criteria.

So, like thousands of others across the country, if they wanted to play in the US Open, Black golfers had to play in two rounds of qualifying. And that meant playing fifty-four holes over two weekends, weekends that a Black player might have spent elsewhere in a UGA event where he could make some money.

With time and money scarce, and the competition much stiffer than the UGA, a lot of Black players did not even bother to try and qualify for the US Open. That is one reason why Teddy Rhodes's presence at the US Open in 1948 was so notable. Rhodes attracted even more interest when the man called the 'Sepia Sharpshooter' by the *Los Angeles Times* shot a 67 in one of the practice rounds. There was no mention of his lawsuit in the story or the reason why it was so newsworthy that a Black golfer was participating in a US Open for the first time since before World War I.

Rhodes opened with a 70, three shots behind first-round leaders Ben Hogan (who would go on to win) and Lew Worsham, the defending champion. He struggled after that, however, and ended up finishing fifty-first. The *Times* noted that Rhodes's game "became more drab as his ensemble grew more vivid."

Rhodes qualified the following year for the US Open at Medinah outside Chicago, finishing second in the qualifying at Olympia Fields, the same course that had barred seven Black golfers from playing in the qualifying rounds for the Hale America tournament in 1942. Rhodes missed the cut by one shot after shooting 75–76 to finish ten strokes behind second-round leader Al Brosch. Cary Middlecoff won the first of his two US Opens that year, one stroke ahead of Sam Snead and Clayton Heafner.

Over the course of his career, Rhodes appeared in sixty-nine PGA tournaments. But his only option for regular, competitive golf was the UGA. And it was there that Rhodes became one of the tour's most successful players. Sifford recalled Rhodes blowing away the field at Sugar Ray Robinson's tournament on Long Island in 1949. Rhodes won the UGA National Negro Open three straight years from 1949 to 1951 until

Sifford finally was able to topple him. He won it again in 1957 at the age of forty-three.

Sifford marveled at Rhodes's ability while at the same time lamenting Rhodes's lack of professional opportunities. As good a player as Rhodes was, he didn't have the combative streak required to go up against the PGA at the time. If Bill Spiller was on one end of the spectrum, Rhodes was at the other. Charlie Sifford was somewhere in the middle, burning with rage inside but able to control his emotions on the outside.

"Teddy Rhodes was before his time and he knew better than to fight about it," Sifford said. "He played where they let him and when he played, he excelled. By the time things opened up a bit in early sixties, Teddy was too old and too sick to play."

The kidney stones that had led to his early discharge from the Navy still bothered him to the end. Lee Elder speculated that all the years traveling with Joe Louis also took a toll on Rhodes. He died on the fourth of July in 1969, four months shy of his fifty-sixth birthday.

But when Rhodes was still able to play, and play well, to Sifford he seemed like the ideal candidate to join the PGA. But if the talented, well-dressed and good-natured Teddy Rhodes was not good enough for the PGA, how was he, Sifford, ever going to get the opportunity?

• 4 •

Stanley, the Death Penalty, and the Democratic Revival in California

As the 1950s began, it was an improbable idea that a chance encounter between Charlie Sifford and Stanley Mosk would lead to the integration of the Professional Golfers Association. Neither man knew the other. Neither man even knew *of* the other.

Sifford was laser-focused then on his rapidly improving golf game. When he was not squiring singer Billy Eckstine around the country on concert tours, he was piling up victories on the UGA tour. He even played, with mixed results, in a few PGA tournaments open to Blacks. But Black golfers were no closer to their goal of membership in the PGA. That door was still closed.

For his part, Stanley Mosk spent the decade burnishing his progressive bona fides. Mosk may have been a judge, but he was also a proud liberal Democrat. He enjoyed widespread support in the Black community in the wake of his ruling that a racial covenant restricting property ownership to Caucasians was not enforceable. He supported a number of philanthropic causes important to the Los Angeles Jewish community, from B'nai B'rith to the Los Angeles Jewish Federation, the largest Jewish nonprofit organization in the city. For six years he was also board president of a children's service organization in Los Angeles.

A successful Democrat was a rarity in California politics then. In 1950, the Republican Party dominated all levels of state government. Earl Warren was reelected that year to a third consecutive term as governor. Both of the state's US senators were Republicans. Thirteen of its twenty-three members in the US House were Republicans, and both chambers of the state legislature were controlled by the GOP. Edmund G. "Pat"

Brown was the only Democrat elected in 1950 to one of the state's top offices. He had won the race for attorney general four years after losing a campaign for the same post in what was his first try at statewide office.

Mosk came to popular attention not because of his politics or his philanthropy, however. It was first the Charlie Chaplin paternity case in the 1940s. Then, a decade later, it was a gruesome murder case that landed him on the front pages. The 1955 trial of John Crooker "had all the overtones of intrigue, love, sex, hate, rejection, frustration and finally violence," Mosk later said, calling the homicide of a Bel Air socialite "one of the most dramatic trials I ever had as a trial judge."

The case also shone a bright light on one of Mosk's most passionate and complicated beliefs—his view of capital punishment. He hated it, but if the death penalty was mandated by law, as a judge he felt duty-bound to impose it. That didn't make it any easier or more just in his opinion.

"If we truly believe that only God renders such irrevocable decisions as life and death, then the judge who makes the pronouncement of the ultimate penalty is in fact playing God. He is ordering the elimination of a human being," Mosk wrote in an unpublished manuscript.

John Crooker had grown up in Maine with an abusive father, the only boy among seven children. He was a Navy veteran, twice divorced, handsome, and a serious student. He had just completed his first year of law school at UCLA at the age of thirty-one when he was arrested for the murder of Norma McCauley, his thirty-three-year-old former employer and lover.

Crooker had met McCauley in 1953 through the UCLA placement service. He was looking for a place to live and part-time work to help pay for his schooling. She was looking for someone to do odd jobs around the house and to watch her three children when the maid wasn't available. Crooker moved into the McCauley's elegant home on Somera Avenue in the city's posh Bel Air neighborhood and soon things took a predictable turn. The "houseboy," as the newspapers referred to Crooker, and the "attractive divorcee," as they characterized McCauley, fell for each other.

They would arrange their rendezvous far away from Bel Air, where McCauley's affluent social set would not see her. As Mosk put it later, "it would not do for a socialite to be observed out on the town with the help." The romance lasted for several months until McCauley called things off and Crooker moved out. Testimony at the trial later revealed that Crooker continued to try and see McCauley and was pressing her for money.

On the morning of July 5, the McCauley's maid asked five-year-old Kirk McCauley to check in on his mother, who had not appeared for breakfast. When the boy returned, he told the maid, "you better go in there. Mommy is in a mess." She was lying face down on a blood-soaked chaise lounge, still attired in the red dress she had worn the night before. A white stole festooned with rhinestones was knotted around her neck. She had been stabbed several times.

Police soon zeroed in on Crooker, arresting him later that same day. A search of the McCauley house uncovered a glass in a closet with what turned out to contain Crooker's urine. He had hidden in the closet much of the night, while McCauley and her date talked in the living room. When the date finally left in the early morning hours, Crooker emerged and confronted McCauley, asking her why she didn't want to see him anymore.

That is when Crooker grabbed a knife and stabbed her repeatedly. He choked her as well. All of this grisly information was contained in a confession, handwritten by Crooker on a yellow legal pad, after his hours-long interrogation by homicide detectives. He was charged with first-degree murder.

This was a decade before the US Supreme Court's landmark decision in *Miranda v. Arizona*, which mandates that police inform suspects that they have the right to remain silent and the right to consult with an attorney before and during questioning. Crooker subsequently claimed that his confession had been coerced, that he had been afraid of being beaten by police. He also said he had been denied legal help.

The key legal question before Judge Mosk was the admissibility of that confession. While he was aware of the liberties that unprincipled police officers could take with a suspect in an interrogation room, he did not find that Crooker's confession had been coerced and he admitted it into evidence. "I believed the confession was essentially voluntary, for the investigating officers did not obtain it by mere interrogation, with a stenographer writing down questions and answers," Mosk wrote well after the trial. "The police gave Crooker a pad and a pencil and told him to describe in his own words and in his own hand what had happened. Thus, there was a full and complete confession in handwriting by a defendant who was above average in intelligence and who fully appreciated the circumstances."

With the confession allowed into evidence, the jury convicted Crooker and then voted to send him to the gas chamber. For the first and only time as a trial judge, Stanley Mosk sentenced a man to die, calling it his "tragic duty."

The California Supreme Court upheld Mosk's ruling in a 6–1 decision. The US Supreme Court was more divided, ruling 5–4 that Crooker's defense was not compromised by a lack of initial legal representation because the defendant had already completed a year of law school.

By the time all of Crooker's appeals had been exhausted, Mosk had been elected attorney general, replacing Pat Brown, who had won the state's gubernatorial race in 1958. Crooker petitioned the governor to have his sentence commuted and Mosk played a role in that as well.

It was Brown's first clemency hearing as governor, and he wrestled with the decision. He had no doubt of Crooker's guilt but, like Mosk, he was not a fan of capital punishment. Crooker's attorney told Brown that Crooker had never been in trouble before meeting McCauley, had been honorably discharged from the Navy, and had been working his way through law school. He said Crooker came to the house without a weapon—police never found the knife—so there was no premeditation and that the US Supreme Court had only barely upheld the conviction.

Those arguments alone proved unpersuasive. Even testimony from Crooker's sister about his sterling character and sweet temperament before he met McCauley did not move the needle for Brown. But as the governor struggled to decide whether to commute Crooker's sentence of death to imprisonment for life without parole, Brown read a note from the judge who had presided at the trial. "This defendant's crime arose out of a relationship with the deceased under a set of circumstances that would not likely happen again," Mosk wrote. "He is an intelligent young man of some cultural attainment, and if personality defects could be cured or contained, he could in the distant future become rehabilitated and become a constructive member of society."

Here was the man who had just been elected to be California's top law enforcement official endorsing a clemency petition from a convicted murderer he himself had sentenced to die. As far as Brown was concerned, it was a game-changer.

"I listened carefully to all they had to say, but what really made up my mind was a note from Stanley Mosk in the report, stating that as the trial judge he would not object to a commutation of Crooker's sentence from death to life imprisonment." Brown took Mosk's advice and commuted the sentence.

The story did not end there. Crooker wrote a long, heartfelt letter of thanks to the governor and proved to be a model prisoner. In 1966, in one of his last acts before leaving office, Brown reduced Crooker's sentence to life with the possibility of parole. Six years later, Crooker was granted parole. Several years after that, Mosk, by then an associate justice of the California Supreme Court, received a wedding invitation in the mail. It was from Crooker. Mosk declined to attend the ceremony, but he sent a note offering his best wishes. He had had no idea that Crooker had been released from prison. The following Christmas he received the first of what would be annual Christmas cards from John Crooker and his wife, Valerie.

"I thought you would be pleased to know that Valerie and I have bought a house," the card read. "It is the first home I have ever owned. I have been promoted by my employer in the Bay area of California and am now earning a guarantee of $25,000 per year. Things are going really well for us. I wish you continued success in your career."

Mosk felt a sense of vindication. So did Brown, who said, simply, "I made the right decision." The decision did not cost Brown politically. He was reelected in 1962, defeating former vice president Richard M. Nixon. Brown's campaign for a third term in 1966 ended with a defeat to Ronald Reagan. Brown's son, Jerry, served as California's governor on two occasions, from 1975 to 1983 and from 2011 to 2019. Like his father, Jerry Brown also did a stint as the state's attorney general. Also like his father, Jerry Brown opposed capital punishment.

The Crooker case reaffirmed Mosk's belief in the jury system, even if its death-penalty decision personally repelled him. He was a trial judge after all, and he applied the law as required by the state of California. His rulings on the admissibility of Crooker's confession had been upheld twice on appeal. And his note to Brown expressing hope that Crooker might one day be rehabilitated once again drove home his belief that capital punishment was not the answer.

"It can be argued that the purpose of our criminal laws, rehabilitation of a criminal, was fulfilled in this case," Mosk wrote. "Obviously that would not have been possible if the lethal pellets had been dropped while this defendant was strapped to the chair in San Quentin's green gas chamber. And it would not have been possible were it not for the compassion of a governor. Pat Brown—the original Governor Brown—was that type of human being."

In his thirty-seven years on the California Supreme Court, Mosk was presented with scores of death penalty cases. Most of those cases were affirmed by the court and Mosk often voted with the majority. If he saw no miscarriage of justice, then he was bound by the law to affirm the decision. His views on capital punishment remained fixed, and he titled one of the chapters in his unpublished manuscript "Myth: Executions Are the Answer."

"In a way, I suppose, everything has been said about the death penalty that can be said," he wrote. "Yet we continue to discuss the penalty, the legal processes involved, the actual means of execution, the crimes for which death is to be imposed, and, at the cornerstone, the moral justification for society deliberately taking human lives. At the risk of appearing immodest, I claim to be peculiarly equipped to enter into this discussion because I have been on all sides of this issue—not, I hasten to explain, because of unconcern or ambivalence."

He said that as a young and fiery presenter on his high school debate team, he had argued for the abolition of the death penalty. As executive secretary to Governor Olson, one of his primary responsibilities was to interview death-row inmates and report back to the governor, who had the power to commute a sentence or let an inmate die. As a judge on the Superior Court, Mosk had been prepared to send John Crooker to his death. And as the attorney general, he testified three times before the California legislature urging repeal of capital punishment—to no avail.

In his final public role as the longest serving state Supreme Court justice in California history, Mosk said he took an oath of office to support the constitution and the laws of the state as they are, "and not as I prefer them to be." He concluded, "as you can see, my perceptions have varied with my responsibilities. When called upon to enforce the law, I have done so. When permitted the indulgence of personal opinion, I have expressed a clear preference for the elimination of capital punishment."

Prosecutors can still seek the death penalty in California, but no one has been put to death in the state since 2006. Arguing that the death penalty in the United States is disproportionately imposed on the poor and on people of color, Democratic governor Gavin Newsom in 2019 imposed a moratorium on executions and closed the death chamber at San Quentin, the nineteenth-century prison overlooking San Francisco Bay. In 2023, Newsom ordered all 671 death row inmates—all but 21 of whom were men—transferred to the general population of prisons in the state with high-security units.

"That's a helluva thing: The prospect of your ending up on death row has more to do with your wealth and race than it does your guilt or innocence," Newsom said. "Think about that. We talk about justice, we preach justice. But as a nation, we don't practice it on death row."

Stanley Mosk surely would have approved.

As much as he detested capital punishment, Mosk was equally appalled when authorities overstepped the law in collecting evidence, whether from illegal surveillance or harsh interrogations. The American Civil Liberties Union invited Mosk to be its main speaker when it celebrated its twenty-fifth anniversary in the state in 1948. Seven years later, a divided California Supreme Court ruled that evidence obtained by the Los Angeles Police Department from the warrantless bugging of a bookmaker's apartment could not be used at trial.

The 4–3 division castigated the LAPD for "police state" tactics and said it didn't take much to imagine a situation where the authorities would be "stamping out human rights" using such tactics. The decision drew widespread criticism, from law enforcement authorities to local attorneys to Pat Brown, then the state's attorney general. Brown said the court had erred and urged it to reconsider. Failing that, he asked the legislature to define more precisely what constituted a legal and reasonable search under state laws.

Stanley Mosk praised the ruling. Unreasonable searches had long been a problem, he asserted, and said that the importance of the Court's decision would remain "long after its detractors are forgotten." At a town hall in Los Angeles that year, he drove home the point with a fierceness and passion that did not sit well with the LAPD. "Only in a totalitarian state are the police beyond the reach of the law," Mosk said. "Perhaps law enforcement may be more deadly in that climate, but our Founding Fathers sacrificed efficiency for liberty. It was a wise choice. Essential though law and order may be, ominous though the inroads of crime may be, respect for our American legacy compels us to shelter the individual from an overzealous law enforcement agency."

He then delivered the zinger.

"Now, in all fairness, it must be said that in certain kinds of crime, the obtaining of evidence will be somewhat more difficult if law enforcement officers themselves obey the law—more officers may find it necessary to use their heads instead of their hobnailed boots."

LAPD chief William Parker, who had been lambasting the ruling ever since it had been handed down, did not appreciate the reference to "hobnailed boots." The German Army in World War I wore a hobnailed boot, with short nails protruding from the bottom, to protect the leather soles from wear and tear. The image of what Mosk called "overzealous law enforcement" stomping on individuals and individual rights was impossible to miss.

"He and I tangled constantly," Mosk said of Parker. "The town hall speech really infuriated him. He never let me forget that statement and opposed me at all times."

Two years later, the LAPD started to tail Mosk himself, although the then soon-to-be attorney general was unaware of the surveillance. It would become a major problem for Mosk in the next decade.

The California Democratic Party, an endangered species in 1950, made some gains statewide as the decade advanced. The California Democratic Council was formed with future US Senator Alan Cranston as its first president and soon claimed thousands of members to support Democratic candidates and causes.

One of its goals was simply to make sure that a Democratic candidate topped the Democratic ballot going forward. If that sounds obvious, it should. But California allowed cross-filing in elections and Republicans routinely filed for spots on Democratic ballots in addition to their own party's ballots. Earl Warren had won both primaries when he ran for re-election in 1946 and almost won the Democratic primary in 1942 (barely losing to Culbert Olson, whom he then trounced in the general election) and in 1950 (barely losing to James Roosevelt, the oldest of President Franklin Roosevelt's four sons, whom he also crushed in the general.)

As soon as strong Democratic candidates appeared on primary ballots in addition to the GOP cross-filers, good things happened for the beleaguered party. In 1954, Democrats picked up eleven seats in the assembly and Pat Brown was reelected as attorney general. Warren was now the Chief Justice of the US Supreme Court and his successor, Republican Goodwin Knight, won a full, four-year term as governor of California. Knight had been Warren's lieutenant governor and had taken over in 1953 when Warren left for Washington.

A Democratic tsunami in California occurred in 1958, when there were elections for the major state offices as well as a US Senate race. In-fighting among Republicans had led to a flip-flop of sorts. The governor, Knight, ran for the US Senate and the incumbent senator, William Knowland, ran for governor. Both lost. Pat Brown ran for governor and won. Democratic congressman Clair Engel replaced Knowland.

Stanley Mosk had never run for elective office, but "the idea of getting into the political arena in connection with a legal office appealed to me," he said. "I don't think I would have run for controller, or secretary of state or anything else. That would not have interested me. But a legal office did." Mosk had spent fourteen years on the Superior Court bench and knew the attorney general's office would present a new and intriguing challenge. He was well known and well respected in the legal community and in greater Los Angeles, which was where the majority of votes were.

Mosk quickly sought and won the endorsement of Cranston's California Democratic Council, emphasizing his many years on the bench. He also thought it to be advantageous that he wasn't trying to unseat an incumbent.

His primary opponent was a state senator from San Francisco, Bob McCarthy, whose family had long been donors to the Democratic Party. McCarthy was a father of nine and a World War II veteran of the European theater. He was every bit as well known and well liked in San Francisco as Mosk was in Los Angeles. McCarthy and his father were friendly with Pat Brown and Mosk was concerned that Brown would endorse his opponent out of loyalty. But Brown remained neutral in the race.

Mosk's biggest hurdle was getting his name and message out in northern California, where he was not well known. Future congressman John Burton recalled first meeting Mosk during that 1958 primary campaign.

"My brother Philip, and another member of Assembly, named John O'Connell, were the only people north of the Tehachapis supporting Stanley for attorney general," Burton recalled in 2002. "And they were supporting him against our own state senator and a neighbor of ours in San Francisco, Bob McCarthy.

"I could not understand how Philip could support someone from Los Angeles against one of our friends from O'Neil's drug store," Burton went on. "And he explained to me that there were things more important than playing the pinball machines at O'Neil's. He said, 'you have to meet Stanley Mosk.'"

Burton eventually went to work in Mosk's attorney general's office. Burton had thought his interview with one of Mosk's deputies had not gone well, mainly because of his attire. He wore an alpaca sweater, a pair of khaki pants and saddle shoes to the job interview. When Mosk's deputy mentioned Burton's wardrobe—he referred to Mosk as "general"—Mosk listened and said, according to Burton, "'Well, I am very close to the family and I hear he is a bright young man.' He must have heard that from Philip because he didn't know me. And then Mosk told his deputy, 'Even if he came in a bathing suit, we are going to hire him.'"

Mosk and McCarthy didn't know each other when their primary race began but would become close friends later on. It was, Mosk said, "the cleanest campaign I have ever seen." McCarthy did attack the CDC for endorsing Mosk, but both candidates refrained from ad hominem attacks and focused on the issues. "It's kind of gratifying to have political campaigns turn out that way," Mosk said. "We both ran hard campaigns and did our best, but neither of us said an unkind word about the other."

Both Mosk and McCarthy cross-filed in the race, and each picked up more than 149,000 votes from Republicans. The two primary Republican candidates, US representative Patrick Hillings and assemblyman and future secretary of defense Caspar Weinberger, cross-filed as well, and each received nearly 100,000 votes from Democratic voters.

Mosk raised $85,000 for the June primary and, it turned out, he needed every penny. The race was a nail-biter. The early returns pointed to a McCarthy victory. Votes in the San Francisco area, McCarthy's base, were counted by machine. Votes in the Los Angeles area were tallied by hand. The returns from the north came in quicker and showed McCarthy with a sizable early lead.

He remained ahead more than a day after the polls closed and his supporters claimed victory. Richard Mosk, then at Stanford University, recalled going to class the morning after the election and getting condolences from a professor about his father's anticipated defeat. Mosk's supporters told the candidate to wait until all the votes from Los Angeles had been counted. He was skeptical. "Bob McCarthy was ahead by a good number of votes," Mosk said. It was not until Thursday, two days after the election, that Mosk finally overtook McCarthy. The margin of victory was 135,000 votes out of more than 2 million cast. Later that day, McCarthy sent a congratulatory telegram to Mosk, conceding defeat, and wishing him well in the general election.

McCarthy and the Democratic Party lined up behind Mosk once the primary results were official. Pat Brown would later appoint McCarthy to be the state's director of the Department of Motor Vehicles. Three weeks after the primary, Mosk announced he would take an unpaid leave of absence from the bench until after the November election. He returned his paycheck every month while he was on the campaign trail.

His Republican opponent turned out to be Hillings who, like Mosk, had benefitted from the late tally of votes from the Los Angeles area, which is where he lived. Unlike his race with McCarthy, which had been run without rancor or name-calling, Mosk's race against Hillings would be rougher. He was going up against a candidate who was younger and a protégé of then vice president Richard Nixon.

Hillings was thirty-five when he took on the forty-six-year-old Mosk. A veteran of World War II, Hillings had served in the Pacific Theater for three years. He had been elected to Congress in 1950, winning the seat that Nixon had held before his election to the US Senate that same year. He is reputed to be the man who woke Nixon out of a nap to tell him that General Dwight D. Eisenhower wanted Nixon to be his running mate in 1952.

Hillings was combative and feisty, giving up a safe seat in Congress to run for attorney general. He called Mosk one of the architects of Culbert Olson's "socialistic administration which gave a setback to the state." He criticized Mosk for not taking a position on a loyalty oath for state employees, which had been adopted by the legislature in 1950 at the height of the country's anti-Communist hysteria whipped up by Wisconsin Republican Senator Joseph McCarthy and upheld by the state Supreme Court. In 1952, the loyalty oath was incorporated into the California state constitution. It required state workers to swear that they did not belong to or support any organization that wanted to overthrow the state or federal governments through force. Hillings avidly supported it, noting, "I consider the abolition of our loyalty oath . . . to be one of the most dangerous proposals ever made at a time when we are engaged in a life and death struggle against the Communist conspiracy at home and abroad."

Mosk stayed silent on the matter during the campaign, but years later, as an associate justice of the California Supreme Court, he voted with the court's majority in 1967 in ruling the loyalty oath unconstitutional.

Hillings also chastised Mosk for not resigning from the bench, even though Mosk was not being paid during his leave of absence. Hillings sent out campaign flyers highlighting the facts about each candidate, noting that he was a Catholic while Mosk was Jewish. No Jew had ever been elected to statewide office in California.

But Hillings was going nowhere—and at breakneck speed. A poll in early October gave Mosk a 2–1 lead over the congressman. A campaign visit by President Eisenhower two weeks before the election didn't help. A front-page editorial in the *Los Angeles Times* headlined 'Hilling's The Man' which ran the day before the election and called Mosk "a slick politician" didn't help either. The final preelection poll had Mosk ahead by twenty-two points.

And as the returns came in on November 4, they pointed to a historic Democratic landslide up and down the ballot. Pat Brown won his race for governor over William Knowland by more than a million votes. Clair Engle easily won the US Senate seat over Goodwin Knight. Democrats took control of both houses of the California legislature and also took seventeen of the thirty seats in the US House of Representatives. A right-to-work ballot question galvanized union support and was defeated.

Stanley Mosk outpolled them all. He defeated Hillings by well over a million votes, the largest victory margin of any election in the entire country. (He exceeded Brown's victory margin by a hundred thousand votes.) He carried every county in the state with the exception of Orange County, a longtime Republican stronghold, and captured more than 63 percent of the vote.

Patrick Hillings remained a friend and confidant of Richard Nixon for the rest of his life. He was one of Nixon's advisors in the 1968 presidential campaign. He ran for a seat in Congress in 1970 but lost in the primary. He remained active in Republican politics, however, and led Ronald Reagan's 1980 presidential campaign in Florida.

Stanley Mosk had never run for anything before. He had been his own boss as a young lawyer fresh out of law school. He was one of three secretaries working for the governor of California and he had spent the last fifteen years as a Superior Court judge. Now he would be overseeing a state agency of more than twelve hundred people, staffed almost exclusively by civil service employees who were exempt from being terminated by the new boss.

When he took office in January 1959, he had six open positions. But there was nothing to stop him from expanding the department and that is exactly what he set out to do.

"He shaped that office into a modern-day, multi-purpose, multi-issue public law firm," said Andrea Ordin, who joined the attorney general's office a year after Mosk left for the California Supreme Court. "He developed an outstanding group of lawyers, including African-Americans, Asians and women. Admittedly, they were in small numbers. But they joined long before many law firms hired a single woman or person of color."

Mosk created three new divisions in the attorney general's office—a Division of Constitutional Rights, a Consumer Fraud Division and an Anti-trust Division.

The state Constitutional Rights Division was the first of its kind in the country. Only two years before, the US Congress had created the Civil Rights Division of the US Justice Department as part of the Civil Rights Act of 1957. It would play a crucial federal role in the next decade in the struggle for civil rights by Black Americans.

Stanley Mosk wanted the attorney general's office of California to make a similar commitment. To run the Constitutional Rights Division, Mosk turned to Franklin Williams, a veteran NAACP lawyer and civil rights activist whose ancestry included Black freedmen, runaway slaves, Algonquin Indians, and Dutch and English immigrants. An honors graduate of Lincoln University and Fordham Law School, Williams had passed the New York State bar exam before he even graduated from law school in 1945.

Mosk knew Williams only by reputation, but what a reputation it was. He had served as assistant special counsel to Thurgood Marshall at the NAACP Legal Defense Fund, working some of the most egregious cases of racial injustice in an era when such cases were commonplace.

In 1946, Williams pressured the US Justice Department to investigate the case of Sergeant Isaac Woodard who was beaten by police in South Carolina just hours after his honorable discharge from the US Army. Struck repeatedly around the eyes with nightsticks, Woodard lost his eyesight and suffered memory loss. The all-white courtroom erupted in applause after the key officer charged with the beating was acquitted, but Williams had put racial violence on the national agenda.

In 1949, Williams represented four young Black men convicted of raping a white woman in Groveland, Florida. Williams and Marshall crafted the appeal, which Williams then successfully argued before the US Supreme Court. In April 2017, the Florida House of Representatives exonerated the men and apologized to their families.

In 1950, Williams argued before the US Supreme Court on behalf of the plaintiff in *McLaurin v. Oklahoma State Regents for Higher Education,* a case that laid the foundation for the landmark school desegregation ruling four years later in *Brown v. Board of Education of Topeka.* The University of Oklahoma had denied admission to its graduate school in education to a Black student, George McLaurin, because of the state's racial segregation law. The high court struck down that law as a violation of the Fourteenth Amendment.

Mosk and Williams had only met once, the previous year, at a Meet the Candidates forum sponsored by the Santa Monica NAACP when Mosk was running for attorney general. The organizer of the event had invited only the Democratic candidates, which infuriated Williams. He was determined that the NAACP be nonpartisan and let it be known to all in attendance.

Once Mosk was elected, Williams wrote to the new attorney general and urged him to establish a Civil Rights Division in the AG's office, just as Mosk had planned. He called Williams in for a chat. The attorney general told Williams he intended on establishing a Constitutional Rights

Division, which would cover civil rights. Mosk picked Williams's brain as to who should run the division, dismissing Williams's suggestion of two prominent civil rights attorneys, noting that they were both too busy and making more money than he could possibly offer them. Mosk then popped the question: "Well, how about you, Franklin, would you consider it?"

Williams had left Marshall and Washington after fourteen years in 1950 to become the West Coast regional director of the NAACP. It wasn't the position Williams had wanted; Washington was where the action was. But he hadn't always seen eye-to-eye with Marshall or with Roy Wilkins, the executive director of the NAACP. He was ready for a change. He had been out West for nearly a decade. "I had become completely disillusioned with my career opportunities in the NCAAP," he said. "I knew that Roy Wilkins would never let me rise in the organization and he would never bring me back East.

"So, I thought this was a wonderful opportunity," Williams said. "I've spent all of my professional life in the civil rights movement fighting for the rights of Blacks, primarily. Here was a chance to expand my interest into fighting for the rights of all minorities."

Williams accepted the position with Mosk and received a pay raise of nearly $3,000, to $12,500 a year. He was made the assistant attorney general and chief of the Division of Constitutional Rights. He remained there for two years before expanding a remarkable career of public service with the Peace Corps, the United Nations, and as President Lyndon Johnson's ambassador to Ghana.

His job with Mosk involved investigating allegations of civil rights infringements as well as intervening early to prevent those violations from occurring. He often acted as a mediator to ensure that legislation enacted to protect the rights of minorities and vulnerable people was implemented correctly.

Sometimes, he overstepped. Once, he simultaneously fired off letters to the musicians' union and to the press about its alleged discriminatory practices toward Black artists without informing Mosk. The president of that union was an influential Democratic labor leader. "Mosk called me in, and this was my first introduction to what happens when you are in a politically sensitive appointive job. All my professional life I had been with the NAACP, had been completely independent. . . . I was in effect my own boss. . . . I was free to determine strategy and how to implement it and I was running the show. Suddenly I was caught up short. Here I had done what I would have done over the prior years—I wrote a letter and let the press know about it. And suddenly I'm on the carpet with Stanley Mosk, who is very upset because he's a politico. This was a political goof, and I was rather shaken by that and made a little bit insecure, because I had never had that experience before."

Mosk's ire did not last long. He was too delighted to have Williams on his team to stay angry. John Burton, the Democratic politician who would go on to serve as chairman of the party and be elected to the state Assembly, the state Senate and the US House from California, came to work for Mosk as a young lawyer. "I was there when he had Franklin Williams in the Constitutional Rights department, first department ever on that. It was a wonderful place to work in those times. He was a wonderful, wonderful boss, but most importantly he was a wonderful person," Burton said of Mosk.

In their 2022 biography of Williams, authors Enid Gort and John M. Caher noted that Williams was seen as a bridge builder, not a grandstander, someone who worked behind the scenes to get things done. That was exactly the role he would play in Charlie Sifford's case against the PGA in 1960.

The Fight Continues

$\mathcal{E}$arl Warren had served most of his third term as governor of California when he was nominated by President Eisenhower to become the chief justice of the US Supreme Court. He left office in October 1953 and, in two years, the high court he oversaw issued some of the twentieth century's most important civil rights decisions.

In 1954, the court ruled unanimously in *Brown v. Board of Education of Topeka* that racial segregation in public schools was an unconstitutional violation of the Fourteenth Amendment. In November 1955, the court affirmed a lower court decision that outlawed segregation in public beaches and bathhouses in a case from Baltimore and reversed a lower court order that allowed the city of Atlanta to segregate its municipal golf courses.

But there was no such enlightenment coming from the offices of the PGA. Charlie Sifford won his first tournament as a professional in 1951 in Atlanta, a prestigious UGA event known as the Southern Open. He bested Howard Wheeler by three shots and collected a $500 check. He won the UGA National Negro Open championship in 1952 at South Park in Pittsburgh, the place where he had made his UGA debut six years earlier. He was thirty years old, playing the best golf of his life, but getting an opportunity to showcase his game regularly with the white golfers on the PGA Tour proved as exasperating as ever.

Once again, Joe Louis stepped in to lend his name and fame to the cause of the Black professional golfer. The sponsors of the San Diego Open, making its debut on the PGA calendar in January 1952, invited Louis to participate, keenly aware of the former heavyweight boxing champion's drawing power. But the PGA blocked Louis's participation because Louis was a Black man. It wasn't until the commercial sponsors, eager to cash in on his celebrity, noted that Louis could be exempted from the Caucasian-only clause because he was an amateur that Louis was cleared to compete.

There would be no such exemption for little-known golfer Eural Clark, a Black amateur; he was told he could not play. Bill Spiller qualified for the seventy-two-hole event but was also barred because, as a Black man, he was not a member of the PGA Tour, and the San Diego tournament was a PGA-sanctioned event. PGA President Horton Smith, who was in the field for the maiden tournament, cited the organization's bylaws to justify barring the two Blacks.

Louis was incensed. He called his friend, the radio commentator and newspaper columnist Walter Winchell, who offered support and aired the controversy. "Who the hell is Horton Smith? He must be another Hitler," Winchell told Louis, as Louis recounted the conversation in his autobiography.

Louis's fame and Winchell's megaphone had an impact. Smith convened a meeting before play began to try and iron out the situation. But Spiller, easily the most outspoken of all the Black golfers in that time frame, was not invited to attend. When Spiller crashed the meeting, after being tipped off by golfer Jimmy Demaret, he confronted Smith.

"I know and you know that we're going to play in the tournaments," Spiller told Smith. "We all know it's coming. So, if you like golf like you say you do, and I do, I think we should make an agreement so we can play without all this adverse publicity. And take the Caucasian-only clause out so we can have opportunities to get jobs as pros at clubs."

The PGA once again tried to have it both ways. Smith refused to bend on Spiller and Clark's exclusion from the tournament. Spiller was so upset by the decision that he staged a short sit-in on the first tee on the first morning of the tournament. Louis was allowed to play. Irony reached a new level when Louis and Smith, a two-time former Masters champion, were paired together for the first two rounds. Louis didn't make the cut. Smith did.

What came out of the weekend, however, was a small step forward for Black golfers. The PGA's seven-member tournament committee, of which Sifford's old mentor, Clayton Heafner, was a member, voted unanimously to eliminate one big obstacle to Black golfers playing in its tournaments. The Caucasian-only clause remained, but sponsors of individual tournaments could invite whomever they pleased. The PGA would no longer intervene to bar Black golfers as it had just done in San Diego and as it had done at Richmond four years earlier.

Smith was the president of the PGA for only two years, 1952 to 1954, having spent most of his life as a club pro. Despite his actions in 1952, Smith was showered with honors throughout his career and won most every important award the sport offers. He was inducted into the World Golf Hall of Fame in 1990. In 1960, he was given the Ben Hogan Award by the Golf Writers Association of America for overcoming a physical handicap. (Smith lost a lung to cancer.) In 1962, the year before he died of Hodgkin's disease, Smith received the Bob Jones Award, the highest honor accorded by the United States Golf Association. It is given in recognition of distinguished sportsmanship in golf. And in 1965, the PGA of America established the Horton Smith Award, which was given annually to a PGA professional who has made "outstanding and continuing contributions to PGA education."

What were these organizations thinking? Had they simply erased 1952 from their collective minds? The PGA of America finally saw the light, but not until the summer of 2020 and the massive demonstrations following the murder of George Floyd. It changed the name of the award to the more innocuous PGA Professional Development Award.

"In renaming the Horton Smith Award, the PGA of America is taking ownership of a failed chapter in our history that resulted in excluding many from achieving their dreams of earning the coveted PGA member badge and advancing the game of golf," PGA President Suzy Whaley said. "We need to do all we can to ensure the PGA of America is defined by inclusion. Part of our mission to grow the game is about welcoming all and bringing diversity to the sport."

Despite the compromise that Smith had brokered, Louis nonetheless called it "a breakthrough I was proud to be a part of." And the following week, Louis, Sifford, Spiller, Clark, Rhodes, and two other Black men submitted their entries to qualify for the Phoenix Open. They couldn't find a hotel that would accept Black guests, so they stayed at private homes of Louis's friends. They were not allowed to use the clubhouse facilities or the locker room at the golf club. And all the Black golfers were sent out for their qualifying round in the first two groups of the day.

"It was clearly a get-the-black-guys-out-of-the-way-so-we-can-get-on-with-the-tournament kind of deal," Sifford said. "But if that's all they were giving us, then that is what we would take."

It wasn't all that they were given. There was something else. Something so disgusting and appalling that it boggles the mind. What was so obtrusive or bothersome about seven Black golfers trying to qualify for a golf tournament on a Monday in Arizona?

Sifford was in the first group and was playing with Louis, Clark and Rhodes. When everyone had reached the first green, Sifford went over to remove the flagstick. "Something seemed funny," he said. "Someone had been there before us. The cup was full of human shit."

The golfers were understandably furious. Someone at the club had to have allowed the perpetrator onto the course. And it had to have been recently unless the person who put the flag in the cup in the morning somehow missed the unavoidable stench. "So, this was what we'd have to face on the white tour?" Sifford said to himself. "What a crude, disgusting thing to do to people."

The golfers refused to continue until the cup was replaced, holding up play for thirty minutes. Sifford was so disturbed by the incident that he shot a 75 and failed to qualify for the tournament. Louis did not qualify either, shooting an 81. Spiller, Clark, and Rhodes did qualify, but only Rhodes, who shot a first-round 71, stayed all four rounds, finishing well out of the money after additional rounds of 77, 75, and 79. Spiller and Clark withdrew after posting first-round scores of 79 and 81, respectively.

Spiller, determined as always, attempted to shower in the locker room after his round. Rhodes and the others tried to talk him out of it, but he was not to be dissuaded. So he entered the locker room by himself. Ten minutes later, someone from the club tracked down Louis and told him that Spiller had better get out of the building before something nasty happened to him. Louis was torn about what to do next. But the health of Spiller was the more immediate concern. He went into the locker room and came out with the disgruntled Spiller, who had managed to get a brief shower.

"After that introduction to the white professional golf tour, it's a wonder that we continued to try," Sifford said. "But try we did."

The Black golfers continued on to the next PGA stop in Tucson, where the popular Louis already had been granted an exemption. Sifford managed to qualify but did not make the cut. After Tucson, the tour headed to places Sifford saw no point in trying to go: Texas, Louisiana, Florida, the Carolinas. As long as the PGA washed its hands of the issue, sponsors and clubs could choose who they wanted to play in their tournaments. And no club or tournament in the deep South in the early 1950s was going to extend the welcome mat to a Black golfer.

A second integrated tournament in Canada emerged in the mid-1950s with the five-year run of the Labatt's Open. Sifford, Spiller, and

Rhodes all participated. Rhodes had the top finish of the three when he tied for fourth place in the inaugural Labatt's in 1953, earning $1,300. It was his best showing in an official PGA event. Sifford played in the tournament in 1956 and 1957 but finished no higher than thirtieth.

Sifford played in just two PGA events in 1953 and only five in 1954. He did win the UGA National Negro Open both years. But that was not what he had in mind when he set out on a professional golf career. "It kept me up at night sometimes . . . not knowing when my next chance to play competitive golf would come," he said. "How much of me had already been left behind that I would never get back? The years were going by fast. Why, why, WHY am I not allowed to play professional golf?"

In August 1955, Sifford and his favorite wingman, Teddy Rhodes, drove up to Toronto to try their luck in the $15,000 Canadian Open. Sifford had to go to Billy Eckstine to get the boss's approval. Eckstine not only okayed the request, but he also fronted the pair $200 for the drive north. "To have a man like Mr. B behind me was the most wonderful thing that ever happened to me," Sifford said. "He was the benefactor who made it possible for me to live my dream."

Both golfers easily qualified for the tournament, which had no issue with Black participants. Sifford then went out on the first day and, as he told reporters after the round, "I was really shufflin' and jazz-footin' down those nice green fairways." He led all players with a phenomenal 63. He didn't have a bogey on his card. He didn't have anything worse than a 4 on his card. He one-putted eleven greens. The 63 was a course record at the Weston Golf Club in suburban Toronto and equaled the lowest score in the history of the tournament, then in its forty-sixth year.

As the score was posted, a young, cocky PGA rookie who would go on to become one of the lions of the sport, and who had shot a 64, looked incredulously at the 63. "How did Charlie Sifford shoot a 63?" asked Arnold Palmer, who had yet to post his first win on the PGA Tour.

"Same way you shot a 64, except one better," Sifford replied. He was standing right behind Palmer. That is how the two met and they remained friends over the decades.

Rhodes opened with a 68, but neither he nor Sifford could regain the magic from that first day. Sifford closed with rounds of 74, 72, and 70, but still finished in the top twenty of a PGA tournament for the first time. He pocketed $205. Rhodes fared worse, finishing out of the money at 286. Palmer, meanwhile, followed his 64 with rounds of 67, 64, and 70 to post a comfortable four-shot victory over Jack Burke. The winner's check was $2,400 and marked the first of Palmer's 62 PGA career victories.

For Sifford, the Canadian Open of 1955 was a watershed moment for his confidence. He had four more top-twenty-five finishes the rest of the year, earning a shade more than $1,600. He added what by now seemed almost automatic—another UGA National Negro Open championship. It was his fourth straight. He would win again the following year, but his PGA attendance dwindled to just nine tournaments in 1956. After playing in the Los Angeles Open in January, he stayed away from Arizona and didn't play in a PGA event until the *Philadelphia Daily News* Open in June, where he tied for eighth place at his old haunting ground, Cobbs Creek.

That August, Sifford was driving to New York to meet up with Eckstine when he stopped to get gas. The service station attendant recognized him and asked him if he was in town for the Rhode Island Open. Sifford had no idea what the man was talking about but decided it might be worth his while to check it out.

He got permission from Eckstine to delay his arrival in New York and then reported to the Pawtucket Country Club for the two-day, fifty-four-hole tournament. It wasn't a PGA-sanctioned tournament by any stretch of the imagination. But it was a chance for Sifford to compete in a tournament for the first time in a month. He won it by five shots.

At this point, a decade had passed since Sifford had gone to work for Eckstine. But in 1957, Eckstine's golf game had improved to the point where he really didn't need any more of Sifford's tips. And Sifford was growing weary of all the time on the road and desperate to get his wife and son out of Philadelphia and move to Los Angeles.

Eckstine was still popular, but his fame had taken a hit in 1950 through no fault of his own. He was simply being Billy Eckstine, getting mobbed by Billy Soxers, when *Life* magazine photographer Martha Holmes snapped a picture that changed the singer's career.

Eckstine was in the middle of playing a sold-out stretch at the Paramount Theater in New York when *Life* assigned Holmes to follow him for a week. The actual photograph came after Eckstine had performed at a club called Bop City. As he came off the stage, a group of girls swarmed him, and one, laughing hysterically, rested her head into his right shoulder. Eckstine is laughing as well, the girls are ecstatic and Holmes, a celebrated photographer, took what in the twenty-first century looks to be a harmless, touching photograph.

But the girls were white. And Eckstine was not. And in 1950, that presented a problem to the photo editors at *Life*. The decision to run the photograph in the April 24, 1950, edition was made at the top by publisher Henry Luce. But the sanitized caption read, "Billy is swarmed by admirers. Most profess to have maternal feelings about him. He's just like a little boy, they say."

That was rubbish. This was no different than Elvis Presley or Frank Sinatra or Paul McCartney getting mobbed by their fans, who certainly had something other than "maternal feelings" in mind. Some of the letters to *Life* were vicious. How dare America's No. 1 picture magazine run such an offensive photograph? Some radio stations in the South refused to play Eckstine records. He had done nothing. But he was paying for whatever it was he did not do.

"It was really ugly," Eckstine's son, Ed, said. "Everything started to dry up after that."

Billy Eckstine had hoped his move to Los Angeles in 1947 and his contract with MGM would produce movie and television roles for him. The *Life* photograph and a subsequent shot of him socializing with a white actress in 1951 ended that possibility. When he was offered a movie role, it was as a butler. He told the film makers that he didn't carry his own luggage in real life so why would he agree to do so for actor Dan Dailey on the silver screen?

"He was in (the 1952 musical comedy) *Skirts Ahoy* with Esther Williams," Ed said, "but he couldn't be seen singing to her or looking at her because she was white."

Eckstine continued to perform for decades. He found new fans in Europe. But his career, which had been one meteoric rise, plateaued after the picture. He would appear on variety shows, but it was never the same as it had been. Holmes died in 2006 and, in an interview in advance of her *New York Times* obituary, she identified that photograph of Eckstine as her favorite "because it told just what the world should be like."

In 1957, the ten-year relationship between Sifford and Eckstine ended amicably. Eckstine had kept Sifford on his payroll until then, even though weeks would sometimes pass between the two seeing each other. Sifford was working on his golf game, trying to get into tournaments, and Eckstine's need for a driver/golfing companion had diminished.

For the first time in his professional life, Charlie Sifford was on his own, and he felt pressure he hadn't felt in years. He played in only eight events that year, earning a shade more than $1,200.

He had begun renting an apartment in Los Angeles during the winter and found the climate ideal. He found a golf course on Western Avenue where Teddy Rhodes and Bill Spiller played. He brought his wife out to look at houses they might one day be able to afford. It was just a matter of time, Sifford figured, where he could get enough money for a down payment.

But he wasn't going to get it with one top-ten finish in 1957, a tie for eighth place in the Eastern Open Invitational in July. He even saw his string of UGA National Negro Opens snapped at five when Teddy Rhodes won his fourth and final title in Washington, D.C. The way Sifford saw it, what good did it do to fight to get into tournaments if he wasn't playing well enough to succeed?

In November, with his chances dwindling to do something in 1957, Sifford entered the Long Beach Open. The tournament was not an "approved" PGA event because it was fifty-four holes. But many PGA touring pros competed in the event, including Billy Casper, Gene Littler, Paul Harney, Gay Brewer, Tony Lema, and Tommy Bolt. Because of the timing, many of the bigger name pros, who had competed in the San Diego Open the week before, didn't participate.

Concerned about his putting, Sifford switched to a putter given to him by Joe Louis. He had had problems the week before with his putting in San Diego, finishing tied for thirty-fourth and out of the money. That would soon change.

After opening with a 69, Sifford followed up with a 70. He was five shots behind the second-round leader, Dale Andreason, an established club professional in Southern California. He needed another round like his first round at the Canadian Open two years earlier—and he got it. He birdied four of the first five holes and then three in a row on the back side. After a bogey at seventeen, Sifford bounced back with a birdie on the eighteenth and signed for a 64.

It wasn't enough for an outright win. Sifford had been tied by Eric Monti, the longtime head professional at Hillcrest Country Club in Los Angeles. But Monti was more than just a club pro. He won nine professional tournaments, including three official PGA events. He tied for sixth in the 1961 US Open. After this tournament, he went on to win the Southern California PGA championship in a playoff over Bill Spiller. It was one of five times Monti won the event, which is the championship of the Southern California section of the PGA. Charlie Sifford's nephew, Curtis, won the tournament in 1980 and 1982.

At Long Beach, both Monti and Sifford had finished at 10 under par, 213 over the par-71 Lakewood Country Club. The men went to a sudden-death playoff, and to say Sifford was nerve-wracked would be an understatement. He said his stomach was churning as Monti made a birdie putt on the final hole, which forced the playoff. Sifford had been so close to winning a tournament with PGA players for the first time. Now he faced a playoff. Anything could happen. The nervousness disappeared.

"After all of the practice, and all of the heartache, and all of the doors slammed shut, I was suddenly in a position to win a big golf tournament," Sifford said. "And it was a wonderful feeling."

But he quickly found himself in a position to lose the playoff on the second extra hole. The first had passed uneventfully. On the second, Sifford missed a short putt and settled for a par. Monti was looking at a three-foot putt to win the tournament. But he missed. It was on to the next hole.

The situation reversed itself on the third extra hole. Monti missed the green and was looking at a short putt for par. Sifford had put his second shot on the green and was six feet from the hole. He just had to make it. After studying the putt from every conceivable angle, Sifford coolly knocked it into the dead center of the cup. He was now a winner on the PGA Tour, even if the PGA didn't term it an official event. It was more than that to Sifford. He was the first Black man to win a PGA event.

Sifford earned $1,200 for the victory and an extra $500 for shooting the lowest round of the tournament. It was more money than he had won participating in eight official PGA tournaments over the first ten months of 1957. "That paycheck would go a long way toward soothing some of the pain and frustration I'd been feeling all year," he said.

A banner headline in the *Long Beach Press-Telegram* on Monday, November 11, 1957, said, "Sifford First Negro Golf Champ." The first sentence of the story said Sifford had become "the first Negro in history to win a major golf tournament" and later compared Sifford to Jackie Robinson and tennis great Althea Gibson "as trailblazers of their race in the world of sports."

It had been a long time coming. Sifford had turned thirty-five in June, had appeared in PGA tournaments over the last decade, but his only real victories had come in UGA events. This was different. He was the only Black in the Long Beach field. Players who had won or would go on to win major championships like the Masters and the US Open were in the field. This was vindication. This was going to change everything, right?

"This is what I was waiting for," Sifford said. "Now I hope I'll really be able to go."

The next stop on the PGA Tour that year was in West Palm Beach, Florida. Needless to say, Sifford wasn't able to go. In the eyes of the PGA, nothing had changed. Winning a fifty-four-hole tournament and gaining national attention for it did nothing to improve Sifford's chances of joining many of the white players he had beaten in Long Beach on the PGA Tour.

"Even with public opinion on my side (never mind about right and wrong) the PGA wouldn't think twice about admitting me," Sifford said.

But there was one important change in Sifford's life. The money he made at Long Beach enabled him and Rose to put a down payment on a home in Los Angeles. On his scorecard, Sifford wrote "to my wife and Chas. Jr. This is the one that won the home." It remained a keepsake over the years. By the following year, the Siffords would be full-fledged Californians, having moved into a two-bedroom home in the city's Crenshaw district in south Los Angeles. Rose Sifford took a job working for the county and Charles Jr. enrolled in public school, eventually graduating from Dorsey High School.

With actual PGA membership out of the question, there was another possibility for Sifford that emerged in the 1950s. It was called Approved Tournament Player status. It was the next best thing to being a card-carrying PGA member because it had the PGA's stamp of approval. But the PGA also had to sign off on every ATP application, which proved to be problematic for Sifford.

Before the ATP was introduced, one could become a PGA touring player only after serving for five years as a club pro or assistant club pro. The PGA is and always has been comprised almost entirely of club pros from around the country. The number of touring pros was a tiny fraction of the PGA membership. But because membership in the PGA was limited to members of the Caucasian race, not only could Blacks not become PGA tour members, they also could not get jobs in pro shops and do their five years.

But after World War II and the emergence of college golf, the PGA realized its five-year service requirement was not practical when you had burgeoning stars like Arnold Palmer, Ken Venturi, and Gary Player ready to play tournament golf. It would have been suicidal to insist that Palmer spend five years in the pro shop at Laurel Valley Golf Club in Ligonier, Pennsylvania before he could join the tour. So the ATP was adopted.

All one needed was to be sponsored by your local PGA section and have two PGA members sign on to vouch for your ability to compete with the big boys. "Each applicant for playing privileges shall furnish evidence that he has sufficient ability to finish in the money in tournaments in which he competes, his lowest reported scores with the courses at which they are made, his average score, his reasons for wishing (to get ATP) and letters of reference which certify to his past achievements." The applicant must meet in person with the officials who run his PGA section and then the PGA would review the application.

The idea was that once a player was awarded ATP status, he would then be able to become a full-time PGA member by playing in twenty-five tournaments a year for the next five years. But Sifford, even while trying to get ATP status, knew how hard it would be for him to play in twenty-five tournaments because sponsors and hosts still held sway on invitations, and one-third of the PGA schedule was held in places that would be inhospitable or even hostile to a Black man.

But he kept at it. Sifford tried at least twice in the late 1950s to get ATP status. He had two California club pros support his bid for membership. But the PGA rejected his application. The organization proudly announced, however, that players with ATP classification had been extended invitations to the US Open and the PGA Championship. All of them were white.

Sifford played in only eight official events in 1958, none from January to June. In July, he was paired with eighteen-year-old amateur Jack Nicklaus in the first two rounds of the Rubber City Open at the Firestone Country Club in Akron, Ohio. It marked the first time that Nicklaus ever competed in a PGA event. He was one-shot better than Sifford over the first two rounds, but a third-round 76 dropped him down the leaderboard.

Nicklaus finished at 277, 7 under par, and left Akron convinced that he had what it took to compete on the PGA Tour. He took his talents to Ohio State, turned pro in 1961, and made his professional debut at the 1962 Los Angeles Open.

Sifford was two shots better than Nicklaus and one better than Arnold Palmer. But his lasting memory of that tournament was receiving a box of cigars from Jack Nicklaus's father. Charlie Nicklaus had followed his son and Sifford around the course the first two days and saw how much Sifford enjoyed a fine stogie.

It's unclear why Sifford played so sparingly in 1958, because he was much more active the following year. In 1959, he appeared in a personal-high sixteen official tournaments, "a full slate" according to the PGA Tour website. Since the tour had forty-six tournaments in 1959, sixteen appearances hardly made a "full slate." But the sixteen tournaments resulted in a career-best $2,926 in earnings, one top-ten finish (eighth place at the Portland Centennial Open in October) and five top-twenty-five finishes.

It also marked Sifford's first appearance in a US Open. Getting into the US Open field required three rounds of qualifying over two weekends, which Sifford wasn't all that keen to do. But Teddy Rhodes, who had qualified twice before, wanted to give it another try at age forty-five and urged Sifford to join him. "He wanted to give it one last shot," Sifford said.

The pair played two qualifying rounds at Medinah Country Club outside Chicago, which had hosted the 1949 US Open in which Rhodes competed. Both survived. The third qualifying round was at Skokie Country Club, and they emerged from that unscathed as well. It was on to Winged Foot Country Club in Mamaroneck, New York, one of the venerable East Coast layouts that had hosted a memorable US Open thirty years earlier in which Bobby Jones made a difficult putt on the final hole to tie Al Espinosa and then won the thirty-six-hole playoff by an astounding twenty-three strokes.

Sportswriter Dick Schaap penned a memorable piece about the 1959 US Open and it had nothing to do with Billy Casper, who won the tournament. It instead focused on Charlie Sifford, with the headline "The Golfer with the Big Handicap." The subhead noted that Sifford could only compete in select PGA events and needed to win a big tournament to get the attention he deserved. The US Open certainly qualified.

Sifford tied for thirty-first at Winged Foot with a score of 299, 19 over par at the difficult course. (Casper's winning score was 2 over par.) Sifford was never in contention to win the tournament. But what Schaap asked in his piece was whether a good final round by Sifford (and not the 76 he shot) might get him into the top sixteen finishers, which would mean an automatic invitation to the Masters, the ultimate bulwark of lily-white golf on the PGA tour.

Sifford had barely made the cut after opening with a 78 and then shooting a 72. Rhodes was not as fortunate. He had opened with a 77 (tying the amateur Jack Nicklaus) and followed with a 75, missing the cut by two shots. Sifford added a 73 in the third round and, Schaap wrote, would have made the top sixteen had he shot a 69 in the final round. But those kind of scores were rare at Winged Foot and, as Schaap wrote, "Sifford was eliminating the problem and was also eliminating himself" from Masters consideration.

Schaap had opened his piece with a conversation between two golf writers speculating about what would happen if Sifford had made the top sixteen. The writers are unnamed and one of them, said to be from Georgia, succinctly summarized the status of Black golfers in 1959. "If Sifford makes the top 16, they'll change the rules so only the top 15 qualify," the Georgia writer said of the Masters. "If he finishes 11th, it'll become the top 10. They ain't gonna have no Negroes playing at Augusta." Sifford predicted that he wouldn't be allowed to play at the Masters until some of the organizers of the Augusta tournament "fell dead." The first Black appeared in the Masters in 1975, four years after tournament founder Bobby Jones died.

There was some noteworthy racial progress to celebrate in golf in 1959. Twenty-three-year-old Bill Wright of Seattle became the first Black golfer to win an event sponsored by the United States Golf Association with a victory in the Amateur Public Links Championships outside Denver. He beat Frank Campbell, a former professional who had regained his amateur status, in the finals. After nearly not making the match-play portion of the event, Wright dominated throughout the tournament, never trailing in any of his six matches. He was believed to have been the first Black to compete in the tournament since its inception in 1922. Of course, that is because Pat Ball and Elmer Stout were disqualified from the 1928 Publinx before ever getting to the match-play portion of the event.

That victory earned Wright a spot in the 1959 US Amateur at the Broadmoor Club in Colorado Springs, Colorado. But Wright told *Golfweek* in a 2009 article that none of the other players from Washington in the tournament, all of whom were white, would travel or practice with him. He was prepared to practice as a single when a man asked him to join his threesome. The man was Chick Evans, who decades before had won the US Amateur and the US Open and was sixty-nine years old. The other two members of the group were much closer to Wright in age: future PGA Commissioner Deane Beman and a nineteen-year-old sensation from Ohio who would go on to win the tournament—Jack Nicklaus. After the round was completed, Evans made sure that Wright sat next to him at the head table along with the other former champions.

Wright played college golf at Western Washington College of Education, now known simply as Western Washington University, and also won the 1960 men's golf championship of the National Association of Intercollegiate Athletics in Bemidji, Minnesota. The NAIA is different from the NCAA in that it oversees athletics for roughly 250 small colleges and universities in the United States.

He turned professional but did not enjoy much success on the tour. He never played in the Masters or the PGA and missed the cut in his one US Open appearance at the Olympic Club in San Francisco in 1966.

"We just didn't seem to get the exemptions that would let us into tournaments," Wright said. He ended up going into private business but did play several events on what was then known as the PGA Senior Tour.

And while the USGA always maintained a Welcome to All policy, it would be another twenty-three years before a Black golfer won one of its tournaments when Alton Duhon won the US Senior Amateur in 1982.

Charlie Sifford played in eleven more official tournaments in 1959 after the US Open. His best finish of the year happened at the Portland tournament in October. In November, Sifford entered the $6,000 Gardena Valley Open, which was not a PGA event.

It was contested on a course Sifford knew quite well—Western Avenue in Los Angeles. The field included a few PGA regulars such as Jim Ferrier and Jerry Barber, both of whom became PGA champions. Ferrier won the title in 1947 and Barber would claim it fourteen years later. Sifford won the fifty-four-hole tournament by four strokes and collected $750. Sifford couldn't help but observe afterward that the player who finished sixth in the regular PGA tournament that weekend in Louisiana won more than he did. Still, it was his first victory since his win two years earlier at Long Beach.

Sifford played in one more fifty-four-hole, non-sanctioned PGA event before the year was out. He entered the fourth annual $5,000 Pomona Valley Open, which was being held at Los Serranos Country Club in Chino, a city in the Sacramento Valley in Northern California. The tournament would conclude just before Christmas.

The field was pretty strong given the time of year, with PGA regulars US Open champion Billy Casper, Billy Maxwell, Jerry Barber, Gene Littler, and Tommy Jacobs. Also in the field: Teddy Rhodes. And what happened on the first day of that tournament went largely unnoticed, though it shouldn't have. Three men shot 67 to share that first round lead. Sifford and Rhodes were two of them.

Had two Black golfers ever done that in anything other than a UGA event? Rhodes was forty-six, and his game was winding down. But here they were, the two traveling companions from the late 1940s and 1950s, the instructors to the rich and famous, sharing the lead of a tournament, the top Black men in the field. Barber was the third player with a 67.

Casper led after the second round, one shot ahead of Sifford and two ahead of Rhodes. After three rounds, Casper and Sifford were tied at 204. Rhodes, who at one point led the tournament with nine holes to play, finished third at 206 and collected $450. Casper and Sifford had to report back to Los Serranos on Monday, December 23, for an eighteen-hole playoff.

It took nineteen holes, but Casper prevailed. Sifford received $600 to Casper's $1,000 and the players split the gate receipts from the extra day. In the last two months of 1959, Sifford had earned around $2,500. That constituted a banner year for him.

And there certainly was no shame in losing to Casper, a future Hall of Famer who won another US Open in 1966 and the Masters in 1970. He was one of the game's greatest players in the late 1950s, 1960s, and early 1970s, winning fifty-one times on the PGA Tour, seventh all-time. The way Sifford closed 1959 should have given him all the confidence and boost he needed to pick up where he left off when the calendar turned. But with PGA membership still not an option, his schedule would continue to be determined by geography and the color of his skin for the next two years.

Sifford's successes in late 1959 at the Gardena and Pomona Valley tournaments had come just after his chance meeting with the attorney general of the state of California. During that encounter at the Hillcrest Country Club in Los Angeles, Charlie Sifford joined forces with a man who not only hated discrimination as much as he did, but had the power and the will to do something about it. Bill Spiller and Teddy Rhodes had had no such ally in 1948 when they mounted their lawsuit challenging the PGA's Caucasian-only clause.

In Stanley Mosk, Sifford found an advocate who would not compromise in the fight for racial equity in professional golf. It didn't matter that Mosk didn't care much for the sport or even that, prior to meeting Sifford, he had had no idea that the PGA had codified racism into its constitution.

When he did find out, things began to change in a hurry.

· 6 ·

The Obnoxious Restriction

$\int$tanley Mosk made a critical decision after getting sworn in as the attorney general of California in January 1959. He decided to keep his home in Beverly Hills and rent an apartment in the state capital of Sacramento. He would thus be able to frequent one of his favorite places for his tennis matches—the Hillcrest Country Club.

There are a handful of venues that can claim an unchallenged spot in golf history.

The Country Club in Brookline, Massachusetts, was the site of the 1913 US Open, won by a twenty-year-old amateur, Francis Ouimet, in a stunning playoff upset against two British giants of that period—Ted Ray and Harry Vardon. It popularized golf in the United States and is widely viewed as one of the turning points in the history of the sport.

Merion, outside Philadelphia, was the setting of several historic victories. In 1930, amateur Bobby Jones completed what was then known as the Grand Slam by winning the US Amateur at Merion after victories in the US Open, the British Open, and the British Amateur. (Merion had also been the site where Jones made his US Amateur debut in 1916 and where he won the first of his five US Amateur championships in 1924.) In 1950, Ben Hogan, still suffering the effects of a near-fatal car crash sixteen months earlier, defeated Lloyd Mangrum and George Fazio in a playoff to win the US Open, enduring the thirty-six-hole final day plus an eighteen-hole playoff in what has been dubbed the "Miracle at Merion."

The Cypress Point Club in California was the scene of a surprisingly competitive match-play event in 1956 featuring Ben Hogan and Byron Nelson—legends who had won fourteen major championships but who were both in their early forties—against a pair of upstart young amateurs, Ken Venturi and Harvie Ward.

Pinehurst in North Carolina. Baltusrol in New Jersey. Winged Foot in New York. Oakmont in Pennsylvania. Oakland Hills in Michigan. The Olympic Club in California. All are memorable venues, each having hosted the US Open.

You won't find Hillcrest Country Club on any such list. But the Los Angeles club in the Cheviot Hills neighborhood made golf history of another kind the September day in 1959 that Billy Eckstine introduced Charlie Sifford to Stanley Mosk. Eckstine and Sifford had come to Hillcrest for a round of golf, Mosk for a game of tennis. None was a member of the historically Jewish club, formed in 1920 when Jews were routinely blackballed from membership in most country clubs across the country. Perhaps with that history in mind, Hillcrest opened its doors to nonmembers, particularly famous ones, regardless of race or religion.

That history also makes Hillcrest Country Club a fitting setting for the beginning of the end of segregation in professional golf.

Groucho Marx, who famously quipped that he would never join a club that would have him as a member, did, in fact, join Hillcrest. "Hillcrest is the only country club in greater Los Angeles that will accept Talmudic scholars such as myself as members," he cracked. Groucho left his Hillcrest membership to his son in his will. His brothers were members as well. Harpo Marx was once officially chastised for not wearing a shirt while playing golf. The dress code specified what type of shirt was permitted. Club lore holds that Harpo showed up the next day with a code-approved shirt, but with no pants because there was nothing in the dress code saying what kinds of trousers were allowed.

The club pro, Eric Monti, had lost the 1957 Long Beach Open playoff to Charlie Sifford. He was once described as "the most long-suffering soul in Hollywood" because so many of the celebrities who sought lessons from him turned out to be horrible golfers. Groucho Marx was probably the worst. "He's so terrible it hurts to watch him play," Monti said.

On any given day at Hillcrest, you could find George Burns, smoking a cigar and playing bridge at what was known as the Comedian's Round Table. He might be joined by Jack Benny, George Jessel, Danny Kaye, the Marx Brothers, and Milton Berle. According to Monti, Berle was almost as bad as Groucho Marx on the golf course: "He's awful, simply awful. How a man can be as smart as Milton and as terrible at golf is a real mystery to me."

Frank Sinatra was a member, but Monti said Old Blue Eyes rarely showed up on the golf course and was a no-show when he booked Monti for a lesson. On the other hand, Dinah Shore and Burt Lancaster proved to be quick studies.

When Los Angeles Dodgers pitcher Sandy Koufax was roasted at the club, among the few printable remarks came when Jessel referred to Koufax as "without question, the most important Hebrew athlete since Samson." The comedian David Steinberg said Hillcrest "is a little like an inverted New York Athletic Club: there is no discrimination, but it sure helps if you're Jewish and a comedian."

Many of the movie studio bosses such as the Warner brothers, Louis B. Mayer, Samuel Goldwyn, and Adolph Zukor were also members. Milton Sperling, an Academy Award–nominated screenplay writer for *The Court-Martial of Billy Mitchell* in 1955, had an office across the street from the club. When Hillcrest was seeking new members after the Great Depression, a club member knocked on Sperling's door, asked if he was Jewish, and invited him to lunch. Sperling agreed to join when told the entrance fee was only $100 and he could pay in installments.

The club founders hired a Scottish architect named William Watson to build its golf course. He was the eldest of seven children and raised in a town not far from St. Andrews. His father, John, was an avid golfer and became a member of St. Andrews when his oldest child was nine years old. William Watson apprenticed under the legendary Scottish architect Old Tom Morris and designed his first golf course at the age of thirty-two—a nine-hole course in England. He arrived in the Los Angeles area at the end of the nineteenth century when there were fewer than twenty golf courses in Southern California.

Watson was sixty when he undertook the Hillcrest design and, a year later, golf writer D. Scott Chisholm of the *Los Angeles Express* wrote, "I have no hesitancy in saying that William Watson has here worked out his masterpiece—at least his masterpiece when applied to the California courses." The course had a redesign in 2019. From the terrace outside the opulent, chandeliered clubhouse, there is a panoramic view of the course with glimpses of the Los Angeles skyline. Inside are displays of the club's history, including an Al Hirschfeld cartoon of the comedians at the Round Table and a copy of a letter from John F. Kennedy thanking Monti for his support in the 1960 presidential campaign.

Watson also worked on such historic layouts as The Olympic Club in San Francisco, Olympia Fields outside Chicago, Interlachen outside Minneapolis, and the jewel of San Francisco's public courses, Harding

Park. The first three all hosted US Opens and Harding Park hosted the 2020 PGA Championship. He also is credited with designing Brentwood Country Club, which plays an involuntary but important part in the story of the integration of the PGA.

Watson designed more than one hundred courses in the United States and Great Britain, including the Minikahda Club in Minnesota, which hosted the 1916 US Open won by amateur Chick Evans. Watson was a firm believer in making his course designs blend into the natural terrain. He also hated trees. While designing Interlachen, he proposed felling 146 trees on the property, saying, "You can't have trees and golf, too. The best golf courses in Scotland haven't a tree or bush anywhere on them."

Hillcrest also holds a place in golf history as the first club in California to host a major tournament. In 1929, nine years after William Watson's handiwork had been completed, Hillcrest hosted the PGA Championship. The tournament then bore no resemblance to the one today and because it was limited to professionals, the great amateur players of the day, such as Evans and Bobby Jones, were ineligible to compete. Most of the professionals at the time were from Great Britain and had taken club jobs in the United States.

The PGA had been founded only thirteen years earlier, the brainchild of Rodman Wanamaker, a wealthy New York department store owner. Wanamaker funded the first PGA Championship tournament and decreed it would be a match-play format, like the US and British Amateurs. Thirty-two golfers qualified for the tournament, which was held in October at Siwanoy Country Club outside New York City. Jim Barnes, a transplanted Englishman, defeated Jock Hutchison, a transplanted Scot, in a match that went the full thirty-six holes. Both Barnes and Hutchison were United States club professionals at the time.

In 1929, Leo Diegel, one of the great but forgotten players in PGA history, reported to Hillcrest as the defending PGA champion, having defeated four-time defending champion Walter Hagen and two-time PGA champion Gene Sarazen along the way. He repeated that scenario in 1929, defeating Sarazen in the quarterfinals and Hagen in the semifinals before dispatching Johnny Farrell in the finals. Farrell, Hagen, and Sarazen are all in the World Golf Hall of Fame. Diegel won twenty-eight tournaments that the PGA counts as official victories. Only nineteen golfers have won more. He finally was recognized by the Hall in 2003.

Diegel is most remembered for an original and unorthodox putting style which came to be known as "Diegeling." Putting had always been

Diegel's weak link—he was a fabulous iron player—and he experimented with a number of styles. He settled on one in which both elbows were akimbo; one observer said it looked like a car with both doors open. The style came to define Diegel to the point where Hagen quipped, "how are they going to fit him into the box?" at Diegel's funeral.

Diegel played on the first four Ryder Cup teams, won four Canadian Opens, and his accomplishment in 1929 is prominently displayed at Hillcrest. The club never hosted another PGA Championship, but it did host the Los Angeles Open in 1932 and 1942 and was a qualifying site for the 2023 US Open at nearby Los Angeles Country Club.

By 1959, Hillcrest was better known for the Comedians Round Table and the famous faces in its dining room than for any tournaments it hosted. Billy Eckstine was one such familiar face, so, on that September day in 1959, Stanley Mosk greeted him warmly when the singer came over to introduce him to his friend, the professional golfer.

As Sifford recounted in his memoir, Mosk appeared confused to hear that Sifford was not a member of the PGA, especially given his rising prominence in the game. In 1959, Sifford played in sixteen PGA select tour events, a personal high, and he had won the Gardena Valley Open.

"Why can't you play on the PGA Tour?" Mosk asked.

"Because of this Caucasian clause in their constitution that says only whites can join," Sifford replied.

"You mean to tell me that they actually have that in their organizational bylaws?" asked the astonished, and suddenly energized, attorney general.

Sifford provided Mosk with a copy of the PGA's bylaws containing the Caucasian-only clause and followed up with what Mosk called "a plaintive letter" asking for the attorney general's assistance. Mosk and his deputy, Franklin Williams, got to work.

There is a competing story about how Mosk got involved in helping to end the Caucasian-only clause. In "Getting To the Dance Floor, an Oral History of the PGA Tour," edited by Al Barkow, Bill Spiller said it was at his suggestion that Mosk be told. Spiller caddied at Hillcrest and one of the golfers he looped for was attorney Harry Braverman. Spiller told Braverman about the discrimination and said it was Braverman who contacted Mosk and made the attorney general aware of the situation. In subsequent articles on Spiller, Barkow has championed that claim. But this author could find no other source to confirm Spiller's story. In fact, Sifford goes into detail about his meeting with Mosk and subsequent correspondence by mail. In numerous interviews, Mosk continually referred to Sifford as the golfer who drew his attention to the matter. In his personal papers, Franklin Williams referenced Sifford as the golfer who was trying to get the PGA to drop its discriminatory clause. And when asked directly about Spiller's story by author John H. Kennedy, Mosk said, "Harry Braverman was a close friend of mine, and he may well have contacted me at the request of Bill Spiller. However, my recollection is that I received a letter from Charlie Sifford after his entry into a tournament had been rejected. He merely asked me to help him."

Mosk had one overriding question for the PGA: what was the reasoning for denying Sifford a chance to become a member and play in their tournaments? The PGA cited the bylaw that had been adopted in 1934. Mosk said that was not good enough. He warned he would go to court to get a restraining order against the PGA from holding tournaments in California if it denied qualified Black golfers an opportunity to play. The PGA did not budge.

In retrospect, it is not only stunning that the PGA was still a whites-only enterprise in 1959, but that even when confronted by the chief law enforcement official from the state that hosted several PGA tournaments every year, the organization would not bend. The *Los Angeles Times* columnist Jim Murray called the tour "the recreational arm of the Ku Klux Klan." Major League Baseball had been integrated since 1947, although the Boston Red Sox did not sign their first Black player until 1959, three years after Jackie Robinson retired. The National Football League, the National Basketball Association, and the National Hockey League all had Black players before 1959. Tennis great Althea Gibson suffered myriad racial indignities on tour in that predominately white sport, but she dominated pro tennis in the late 1950s. Only the PGA clung resolutely to its antebellum mentality.

Mosk had good company in his outrage at the PGA's undisguised racism. In March of 1960, Jackie Robinson would castigate the organization in a series of blistering newspaper columns. "Golf is the one major sport in America today in which rank and open racial prejudice is allowed to reign supreme. Though often called the sport of gentlemen, all too often golf courses, clubs and tournaments apply the ungentlemanly and un-American yardstick of race and color in determining who may or may not compete," Robinson wrote in the *New York Post*. "Even the president of the United States, Dwight D. Eisenhower, holds membership in a golf club which limits membership to 'Caucasians only'—the Augusta National Golf Club, where the Masters Tournament is held each year. And another famous and highly honored American, Bing Crosby, who annually sponsors a golf tournament bearing his name at Pebble Beach, California, has consistently refused to invite Negro professionals to compete."

Crosby's explanation that the tournament was limited to members of the PGA Tour might have been technically true, but it was a cop out. Sifford's winter in the West included just four tournaments and none after the Phoenix Open in February. He didn't play another tour event until June.

The pressure helped; soon enough, a crack appeared. The PGA granted Sifford Approved Tournament Player status in March 1960.

That meant that at age thirty-seven—he would turn thirty-eight in June 1960—Charlie Sifford was a rookie on the PGA Tour. But he still wasn't a member of the PGA Tour. He would have to play in twenty-five events in each of the next five years, assuming, of course, that by then the PGA would have come to its senses and allowed Blacks to become members. But Sifford only played in eighteen official PGA events in his rookie year, none in March, April, or May. The only way he could qualify for any tournament he chose was to win a PGA-sanctioned, seventy-two-hole tournament, or finish the season among the top sixty money winners. That was going to be difficult with his limited playing schedule.

"Approved tournament player or not, I still couldn't play the whole southern and southwestern swing of the tour," he said.

Despite the limited appearances, Sifford had, by far, his best year on the PGA Tour in 1960. He had a second-place finish at the Orange Country Open in October, having been tied for the lead after fifty-four holes with Al Geiberger, George Bayer, and Billy Casper, who ended up edging Sifford by one shot. The $1,500 check for second place was more than he had received for winning at Long Beach in 1957. Sifford had three top-ten finishes that year and placed in the top twenty-five on eight occasions. His official earnings for the year were nearly $7,000.

Mosk had spent the year campaigning for Massachusetts Senator John F. Kennedy, the Democratic nominee for president, and applying pressure to make the PGA stop discriminating against Sifford and other Black golfers. New York Attorney General Louis Lefkowitz opened an investigation in September 1960 and made it clear he would not allow the PGA to stage its tournaments in his state as long as it continued to discriminate against Blacks. That investigation prompted the Metropolitan Golf Association, which represented New York, Connecticut, and New Jersey, to submit a proposal to the PGA to eliminate the Caucasian-only clause at its upcoming annual meeting in November 1960. Making the pitch for the Metropolitan group was its head, Claude Harmon, who had won the 1947 Masters. The Southern California PGA delegation did the same.

On November 14, at the PGA's annual meeting in Scottsdale, Arizona, the motion by the two delegations to eliminate the Caucasian-only clause was brought to a vote. The motion, which required a two-thirds vote for approval, was defeated, 64–17. Before the delegates departed, they awarded the 1962 PGA Championship to Brentwood Country Club in Los Angeles. Brentwood was an interesting choice. The club, sometimes known as "Hillcrest Lite" had opened around the same time as Hillcrest and had hoped to host the inaugural Los Angeles Open in 1926. That honor went to the Los Angeles Country Club instead. Like Hillcrest, it had opened for primarily Jewish members who could not join most of the private clubs in the area. It lacked Hillcrest's roster of A-list celebrities, but it did have, in the words of former head pro Patrick Casey, "the agents, the producers and the behind-the-scenes people who make Hollywood go."

Its head pro until 1935 was Olin Dutra, who won the 1934 US Open and the 1932 PGA Championship playing out of Brentwood. He also finished third in the 1935 Masters and played on two Ryder Cup teams. Brentwood also was the course on which Babe Didrikson picked up the game of golf, starting in 1932, while she was competing at the Summer Olympics in Los Angeles. One of her hosts at Brentwood was the writer Grantland Rice.

In retrospect, it's hard to fathom what the PGA was thinking when it awarded its 1962 championship to a course in California at the same time the state's attorney general was threatening the organization with legal action over its racially restrictive bylaws. Not only was the PGA defying Mosk and Williams and keeping its codified racism clause intact, but it was also going to hold its most important tournament, its signature event, in California, right under their noses.

"Numerous attempts were made to persuade the PGA to voluntarily remove these restrictions," Williams wrote in a summation of the 1960 activities of the Division of Constitutional Rights. "The Association refused to amend its restrictive constitutional provisions and accordingly we announced our intent to move against their activities within the state."

Mosk and Williams told the PGA they would take action to prohibit the organization from holding any of its golf tournaments in California. Mosk, infuriated by the vote in Phoenix, then followed up with a public broadside against the organization. "We consider the refusal of the national PGA to eliminate its racial restrictive policy to be tantamount to open opposition to California law and policies," he said. "We intend to take every step available to us, both in and out of the courts, to force the PGA to eliminate this obnoxious restriction or to cease all activity of any kind in our state." He went on, "This state will not permit its citizens to be barricaded from employment and the opportunity to earn a living because of the accident of color or national origin."

Mosk contacted the Los Angeles Junior Chamber of Commerce, which was sponsoring the PGA's tournament in Brentwood (there was no Los Angeles Open scheduled for 1962 because of the Brentwood event) and told the organization he would not allow a tournament to be held in California that barred participants due to race. The chamber, which had always allowed Blacks to play in the Los Angeles Open, opted out of its sponsorship. Mosk then called attorneys general across the country, including Walter Mondale in Minnesota, Edward McCormack in Massachusetts, and Lefkowitz in New York. They all assured Mosk they would take similar action if the PGA moved into their jurisdictions.

All of this came a month after Sifford had won another nonofficial tournament with a field of approved players such as Bob Rosburg and Ken Venturi. He had earned his biggest paycheck to date, $2,000, for his victory in the $8,000 Almaden Open in San Jose, defeating Bill Eggers in yet another playoff. This one lasted one hole. Sifford had trailed Eggers by three shots entering the final round. The UPI account of the victory said Sifford "showed that his race—which has already done so much in and for boxing, baseball and football—can now produce champions in another sport."

In December, Mosk sent Williams to Washington, D.C., to meet with the counsel for the PGA. Williams was optimistic. The lawyer, Thurman Arnold, was a Washington rainmaker and had been famous for busting trusts when he had worked in Franklin D. Roosevelt's Department of Justice. He had then gone on to serve on the United States Court of Appeals for the District of Columbia. In 1946, he went into private practice and co-founded, with future Supreme Court justice Abe Fortas, a powerful Washington law firm. It was in that role that he invited Williams to sit down for a chat in his oak-paneled office, opening a bottle of Jack Daniels.

Arnold's contention was that the PGA was simply a membership organization. And when it staged a tournament, it was merely complying with the rules of the host club.

"You know that's ridiculous," Williams said. "The PGA totally controls the whole golf arena. And if it were to say to a club where it was sponsoring a tournament that they had to admit all persons, regardless of race or color, the club would have to comply. Otherwise, it would be deprived of the prestige of that tournament."

Then, Arnold delivered the line of the meeting.

"Well, why do colored people want to go where they're not welcome, anyhow?"

This was what Williams had been hearing for years in fighting for civil rights with the NAACP. But he was shocked to hear it from someone like Arnold.

Then, Williams said, he realized what Arnold meant. "The Roosevelt liberals were economic liberals and the issues of the 1950s and 1960s were social issues, and they had no conception of those," he said. "And I remembered very vividly as I sat there how Roosevelt had had advisors on Negro affairs . . . but had never appointed Blacks or Negroes to those positions. I also recalled how the public housing projects, which grew out of the New Deal, were all segregated by government fiat, as were the various government mortgage lending programs. They were imposing patterns of racial segregation on newly created residential areas. Rather than resisting them or destroying them, they were creating them. So, the Roosevelt New Deal liberal image was truly an economic perception and not a social perception at all."

That could be said of Franklin D. Roosevelt, but not of the First Lady, Eleanor Roosevelt. She was a powerful advocate for civil rights in the White House. The most famous example may have been in April 1939, when the Daughters of the American Revolution, of which she was a member in good standing, refused to allow the great, forty-two-year-old contralto Marian Anderson to sing in its Constitution Hall. It was Eleanor Roosevelt who arranged for Anderson to sing instead on the steps of the Lincoln Memorial. She sang "My Country, 'Tis of Thee" before a crowd of 75,000 at dusk. Eleanor Roosevelt promptly resigned from the Daughters of the American Revolution.

There would be no consensus reached at the meeting between Williams and Arnold, no matter how much Jack Daniels was consumed. Williams left Washington and consulted with Mosk, and they agreed that there might be no resolution short of suing the PGA.

Things started to improve for Charlie Sifford in 1961. He appeared in twenty-three events and earned $9,333, good enough to be among the top fifty money winners. For the first time, he was invited to play in both Bing Crosby's tournament on the Monterrey Peninsula and the Palm Springs Classic (which would become the Bob Hope Desert Classic in 1965.) He tied for thirty-eighth at the Crosby and tied for nineteenth at

Palm Springs. In between, he made his debut at a new tournament, the Lucky Invitational, in San Francisco and finished tied for thirteenth.

But after finishing in a tie for fourth at Tucson in mid-February, Sifford again found himself with no place to play. The tour went to Louisiana, Florida, and Georgia. Sifford did not. But in April, a surprise invitation came from the sponsors of the Greater Greensboro Open. The tournament organizers had been pressured by the local NAACP to invite Sifford and, a week before the tournament began, Sifford got the call. He would become the first Black golfer to play in a PGA Tournament in the South.

While Greensboro was not Montgomery, Alabama, or Jackson, Mississippi, the city had had its share of racial strife. In 1956, six Black golfers were charged with trespassing for playing at the Gillespie Golf Course in the city. They were convicted, but the conviction was set aside by the North Carolina Supreme Court. The city of Greensboro had leased Gillespie to a private organization, which in turn refused to allow Blacks to play. A separate ruling in a case filed by one of the six golfers, George Simkins, prevented Gillespie from discriminating against Blacks.

In 1960, four Black men staged a sit-in at a segregated lunch counter at Woolworth's. All were college students at North Carolina A&T. The four sat down at the lunch counter on February 1 and were denied service. They refused to leave their seats. Police were called, but did not remove the four, who stayed until the store closed. The students had alerted the local media and the sit-in was captured on television.

Within four days, some three hundred students had joined in the sit-in at Woolworth's and the movement spread to other cities. In July of 1960, when many of the students were not on campus, Woolworth's desegregated its lunch counter.

It was largely through the efforts of Simkins, then the head of the local chapter of the NAACP, that Sifford received the invitation to play in Greensboro. Sifford was eager to play but also knew what might happen back in his native state. After consulting with his wife, Sifford accepted the invitation and headed east.

He quickly was reintroduced to Jim Crow. Restaurants wouldn't serve him. He had to use separate toilets. And with no hotels willing to lodge him, he bunked at the historically Black North Carolina A&T. He moved in with a Black family after the dormitory proved too noisy.

Sifford's entry was the top story heading into the tournament. A spokesman for Sedgefield Country Club, said he expected there to be "a little grumbling from the strict segregationists" at the club but that things should be civil.

Sifford was hopeful that his recent, stellar play should suffice. He had played well enough in the pre-tournament Pro-Am to earn $163. The field wasn't as strong as it could have been; the tournament came the week after the Masters, and many of the big names, including Arnold Palmer, Masters champion Gary Player, and others were not in the field. To Sifford's delight, the players that were there treated him just like any other fellow competitor.

Then, on a wet and windy day, Sifford shot a 68, 3 under par, and emerged as the first-round leader of the tournament. It was a remarkable debut. He did not make a bogey and led the field by three shots. But before he teed off in the second round, Sifford received a phone call at the home of the family with whom he was staying.

"You better not bring your Black ass out to no golf course tomorrow if you know what's good for you, nigger," the caller told Sifford.

"I tee off at 10:15," Sifford told the man. "You do whatever it is you're going to do. I'll be there."

Walking down the first fairway on the second day, Sifford had flashbacks from Phoenix nine years earlier, minus the excrement in the cup. A group of about a dozen men started to heckle him, taunt him, and yell during his backswing. More than two hours elapsed before officials ejected the unruly men.

"I don't know how I managed to keep my poise because I was scared out there," Sifford said.

He shot a 72, 1 over par, which considering everything that had transpired, had to be one of Charlie Sifford's most remarkable rounds of golf. When he signed his scorecard, he pounded the pencil into the table in frustration over what he had just endured. But he recovered and finished fourth in the tournament, nine shots behind the winner, Mike Souchak.

"I hadn't won the tournament, but I felt a larger victory," Sifford said. "I had come through my first Southern tournament with the worst kinds of social pressures and discriminations around me and I hadn't cracked. I hadn't quit. Under the circumstances, I had exceeded my highest hopes while at the same time facing my worst fears."

Sifford returned to Greensboro every year for the remainder of the 1960s, but he never equaled that performance from 1961. His best effort was a fifth-place finish in 1967. He returned in 1968 and 1969 but missed the cut in both years.

The fourth-place finish in 1961 earned Sifford $1,300. He put his golf clubs in his car and began the drive to Texas for the $40,000 Houston Open. It was being held at a municipal course and Sifford had qualified by virtue of his play in Greensboro. But upon arrival, he was told by the tournament sponsors that he would not be allowed to play. A PGA official at the site washed his hands of the matter, deferring to the sponsors. When news broke that Sifford had been denied entry to the tournament, a group of about twenty Black protesters showed up at the golf course with picket signs saying, 'Sifford Makes Holes in One' and 'Why Can't Sifford Play?' and 'Why Is Houston Better Than Greensboro?'

He got the same message a week later in San Antonio, where he wasn't even allowed onto club property, and drove home to California. He wouldn't play in another PGA tournament until Memorial Day weekend.

In May, the PGA responded to Mosk's threats of legal action by announcing it would move its 1962 championship out of California. It did not say where. Mosk's unrelenting pressure had forced the organization's hand.

Lou Strong, the president of the PGA, said simply that "under present conditions in California, the PGA did not feel it would be possible to conduct a successful tournament of the magnitude of the PGA championship in that state." He insisted "the cancellation of the championship of Los Angeles had absolutely nothing to do with Charlie Sifford."

That denial fooled no one. "The PGA moved the tournament entirely as a result of my threat to get a court injunction against holding the tournament pursuant to discriminatory rules," Mosk told author John H. Kennedy years later. "What other possible motive could the PGA have?"

In a separate interview, Mosk said, "I don't see any reason for them moving the tournament at that late a date after having made preparations for the tournament to be held in Los Angeles, if not for the fact that they were going to exclude Charlie Sifford and others who might be Black."

Sifford said simply: "They went to all of that trouble just so they wouldn't have to allow a Black man—me—to play in their event."

In June, the PGA announced that Aronimink Golf Club outside Philadelphia would replace Brentwood as the site of its 1962 championship tournament. Mosk was stunned. He had been in contact with attorneys general and thought they all supported his position. "Apparently, Pennsylvania slipped through the cracks," he said.

In response to the PGA announcement, the NAACP wrote a letter of protest to Aronimink's president, W. W. K. Miller, and denounced the private club for participating in an "ugly tournament. We are extremely unhappy that Aronimink has decided to make itself a party to the continuing un-American practices of the Professional Golfers Association."

Even more egregious was Strong's contention that Sifford could have qualified for the 1962 PGA Championship just like any other Approved Tournament Player. But Sifford had no possible way of meeting most of the qualifying criteria, which Strong knew.

Still, all the pressure on the PGA seemed to be having an effect. A May 1961 editorial in *Sports Illustrated* called for the end of the Caucasian-only clause. "The PGA is far behind the times if it thinks that racial segregation has a place in sports. Professional basketball, baseball and football have long permitted Negro athletes to play. And all those sports have thrived. It is time for the PGA to put its musty store in order, too."

Mosk kept up the heat in his own state. The Southern California section of the PGA had an annual championship scheduled for July. With the regular PGA championship having adopted stroke play in 1958, this match-play tournament, scheduled to be held at a municipal course in Long Beach, was said by its sponsors to be the nation's top match-play event for professionals.

It offered a purse of $9,000. But it also limited the field to PGA members. That did not sit well with Mosk, who told the organization it could not hold the tournament in California unless it allowed anyone to qualify.

The Southern California section had proposed that the PGA eliminate the Caucasian-only clause at its last convention. But here it was, hosting a tournament that discriminated against Blacks. Faced with Mosk's threat, the section rescheduled the tournament and opened it up to all who could qualify.

Mosk called the move "a fine recognition of the right of athletes to compete solely on the basis of ability. We hope that your national PGA will follow your leadership in the cause of equal opportunity for all."

The PGA had two other incidents with its signature championship. In 1990, it awarded the tournament to Shoal Creek Country Club in Alabama. When it was reported that Shoal Creek had no Black members—shocker!—the PGA announced that going forward, it would not hold tournaments at clubs that refused membership to Blacks or people of color. It still held the tournament at Shoal Creek. In 2021, the organization announced it was moving its 2022 championship to Southern Hills in Tulsa. The tournament had been awarded to Trump Bedminster, but after the insurrection at the Capitol on January 6, 2021, the PGA acted swiftly to move the tournament, not wanting to associate its brand with the disgraced president.

Once the 1961 PGA Tour left the South, Sifford was back. He tied for seventeenth in the Western Open and then played pretty much every week from the beginning of July to the end of October. His best finish in that stretch was a tie for twelfth at the Canadian Open in July. It was one of fourteen top-twenty-five finishes for him in 1961.

As the tournament season moved into November, Sifford returned home. All the events were in Louisiana, Alabama, and Florida. His play had been strong enough to earn him entry into any tournament in 1962— any tournament that would have him, that is.

But in November, attention turned to the PGA annual meeting at the Diplomat Hotel in Hollywood, Florida. The organization earlier in the year had said it would offer a proposal to eliminate the Caucasian-only clause at the November meeting. Sifford, Mosk, and others were skeptical. Hadn't the organization voted to keep the clause by a huge margin the year before?

But Sifford's courage and grace coupled with Mosk's relentless pressure finally forced the PGA to act. Six sections of the PGA, including the section that comprised Alabama and Georgia, formally introduced the resolution to eliminate what Mosk had rightly called "the obnoxious restriction." A PGA official told delegates before the vote on the proposal that should it be defeated again, "we will be faced with an injunction suit restraining the PGA from operating in the state of New York. I am further convinced that we will have the same situation in California and confronted with a wave of litigation."

The delegates listened. By unanimous vote, the Caucasian-only clause was eliminated, as was the requirement that golfers had to be from either North or South America. Those four objectionable words—"of the Caucasian race"—were gone.

Prior to taking on Sifford's case, neither Mosk nor Franklin Williams had had any idea that the PGA was limiting its membership to only Caucasians. It made sense in a roundabout way for Mosk, whose sport was tennis. Williams, however, had started to pick up golf when he was transferred to California. He would stop at driving ranges and public courses while on the road, but eventually found the sport too time-consuming and too frustrating.

On one of those drives up the coast, Williams pulled over, parking his car near a beach. He then opened the trunk, removed his golf clubs, golf shoes, and everything else associated with the sport and tossed everything into the Pacific Ocean. He would be a huge factor in the PGA removing its Caucasian-only clause, but as a lawyer, not as a golfer.

Mosk said the decision to remove the clause "was a proud moment for the office of the attorney general, and demonstrated what can be done to further racial equality and opportunity when the will, and good-willed people, are involved." He called the resolution of the issue "perhaps my greatest satisfaction in the sports arena" while serving as the state's attorney general.

"I believed then, as I believe now," he said, "that society and the law can ultimately defeat overt bigotry every time."

· 7 ·

Aronimink—July 1962

$\mathcal{A}$s Charlie Sifford, Stanley Mosk, and the PGA of America knew, there would be no room for a Black golfer at the organization's 1962 championship, regardless of where it was held. Mosk had succeeded in bringing national attention to the PGA's racist constitution which, despite the protestations of organization president Lou Strong, did, in fact, make it virtually impossible for Sifford to play in the tournament. Even getting rid of the Caucasian-only clause had not done much to increase Sifford's slim chances of making the field.

To Sifford, the week of the PGA Championship was just like the week of the Masters; he could plan to have the time off. (He would be forty-three years old when he finally did play in his first PGA Championship.) But in 1962, that was an unreachable goal. While Arnold Palmer defended his British Open championship at Troon in mid-July, Sifford joined most of the touring pros at the Buick Open, where he tied for thirty-ninth. Most of the players in that tournament then headed East to suburban Philadelphia for the PGA Championship.

The host club, Aronimink, is one of those stately East Coast courses, complete with the obligatory, over-the-top, Tudor-style clubhouse and luscious grounds. It was a Donald Ross design and, in addition to the 1962 PGA, it has hosted a couple of US Amateurs and the KPMG Women's PGA. It will host the PGA again in 2026 on the one-hundredth anniversary of the Ross redesign. But because it hosted the 1962 championship, after getting withering criticism from the NAACP and being fully aware of *why* it had been selected, Aronimink has to deal with its own role in the segregation of the tour. It could have said, "no thanks." It did not. But in 1961, there likely would have been a long line of clubs eager to host the 1962 PGA had Aronimink not done so.

There was no blowback against the PGA, or the club, when the tournament opened on July 19. There were no protests on the grounds. Looking back at newsreel coverage, one can find no mention of why the tournament was being held at Aronimink. As far as the PGA was concerned, it had a championship to run.

"I think at the time, we didn't understand what had happened and why it was being played there," Gary Player recalled. "It was only later that we realized."

The golf calendar wasn't as neatly set up to accommodate the major tournaments in those days because the British Open was still an exotic and time-consuming event that most PGA pros avoided. Sam Snead had won it in 1946 in the first, post–World War II British Open. He did not return again until 1962, where, at the age of fifty, he finished tied for sixth. Ben Hogan famously won in 1953 at Carnoustie, the only time he participated in the tournament. In 1962, a handful of PGA pros made the trip across the pond to participate, including defending champion Arnold Palmer, US Open champion Jack Nicklaus (for his British Open debut), Phil Rodgers, Bruce Devlin, and Gene Littler. Player, who had won the tournament in 1959, was there as well, though not for as long as he had hoped to be.

The 1962 British Open was the last one that required all participants to qualify for the main event. It didn't matter if you were Arnold Palmer or the head pro from Clandeboye in County Down. Everyone had to play thirty-six holes of stroke play to make it into the field. That is another reason many US-based pros avoided the British Open.

But the PGA players had no trouble qualifying (the field was still dominated by British club pros) for the seventy-two-hole, three-day event, which ran from Wednesday to Friday. (The schedule allowed the British club pros to be able to return to their pro shops for the weekend.) The scheduling was also important because Gary Player figures it helped him win at Aronimink the following week. The two tournaments had sometimes been held at the same time. This time they were a week apart.

Player needed a par on the eighteenth hole in the second round of the British Open to make the cut. He still would have been well off the lead, but he would have been able to stick around for the final two rounds on Friday. Instead, he hit his approach shot over the green and missed the cut by one shot. He left for Aronimink the next day.

"I had my tail between my legs when I got there over not having made the cut. But that ended up being a huge advantage for me, because I got to play a lot of practice rounds on the course and got to know the course, got to know the membership, who were very kind to me," he said. "I loved the golf course, and the club made me an honorary member, which was great because my daughter lives in the area."

Player already had won two of the four legs of the modern-day Grand Slam, adding the 1961 Masters title to his 1959 British Open victory. He had come close to winning the 1958 US Open, finishing second to Tommy Bolt. By 1962, the new Grand Slam was getting accepted by the players and the public alike, and it wouldn't be long before the British Open changed its schedule and format to adjust to American television and become a regular tour stop.

The PGA itself had been a stroke-play tournament only since 1958, but while esteemed as a must-have by the golfers, its champions since then—Dow Finsterwald, Bob Rosburg, Jay Hebert, and Jerry Barber—had been an underwhelming group. Gary Player would put an end to that, but it took him a couple rounds to get his game going.

The first-round leader had a Charlie Sifford connection. He was fifty-one-year-old John Barnum, who shot a 66, and the following winter would win his only PGA event, the Jamaica Open, by two shots. Sifford was the runner-up. Player opened with a 72, 2 over par, then posted rounds of 67 and 69 to take a two-shot lead into the final round.

Player frequently used his 4-wood off the tee, rather than his driver, to ensure accuracy. And in his final round 70, he hit thirteen greens in regulation and one-putted six times.

"I putted like Tarzan," he said. "I was turning the 4-wood into a driver with a strong draw. I hit it almost as far as my driver but I kept it in play. But in tournaments like that, the putter is always the master. It wins golf tournaments."

The final round turned out to be a dogfight between Player and Bob Goalby. The two became good friends later in life, but on this day they were fierce competitors. Goalby was six shots behind as he went to the seventh tee. He made up five of them over the final twelve holes, finishing one shot back. Goalby marveled at Player's putting over the final nine holes.

"Nobody should make all the putts the way he did," he said of Player.

The $13,000 winner's check was the largest in the history of the tournament. Barber had earned $11,000 the year before.

"I had three legs of the Grand Slam and, to me, that was a mighty big plus," Player said.

The PGA Championship went off without a hitch, with no mention of Charlie Sifford, Brentwood Country Club, or Stanley Mosk. Lou Strong said his organization's signature tournament could not have been held in California given the conditions. He was right. But Pennsylvania and Aronimink proved more than accommodating. Gary Player would complete the Grand Slam with his only US Open victory in 1965.

The PGA Tour picked up the following week with the Canadian Open. Charlie Sifford was there and almost won the tournament. But he still was years away from breaking through to the winner's circle. Getting his PGA card had been hard enough. Getting a victory would prove to be just as hard.

The Drye family photo 1947: Arthur Drye, far left, is pictured with the rest of the family. His father (third from the left) was the lead defendant in the case in which Judge Stanley Mosk ruled racial covenants unenforceable and called them un-American. *Annie Wells/Getty Images*

Billy Eckstine and the Billy Soxers, 1950: Billy Eckstine is swarmed by young admirers after a 1950 performance. The photo enraged much of America, which wasn't ready to see a bi-racial man so close to white women. *Martha Holmes/ Shutterstock*

The Phoenix Open, 1952: L to R—Eural Clark, Ted Rhodes, and Charlie Sifford at the 1952 Phoenix Open. The players found human feces in the cup on the first green of their qualifying round. The 71 signifies Rhodes's score. Sifford shot a 75. *Bettman/ Getty Images*

Charlie Sifford's instructions helped turn Billy Eckstine into an excellent golfer in the 1950s. *Courtesy of Ed Eckstine*

Clayton Heafner: Clayton Heafner was influential in launching Charlie Sifford's golf career. He is seen here talking to reporters after a round at the 1953 Colonial Invitational at Colonial Country Club. *Courtesy, Fort Worth Star-Telegram Collection/Special Collections, The University of Texas at Arlington Libraries*

Joe Louis lining up a putt, 1950s: The boxing champion Joe Louis was an excellent golfer and fought just as hard outside the ring to get Charlie Sifford and other Black golfers into the PGA. *Bettman/Getty Images*

The attorney general's office, 1959: Stanley Mosk and Franklin H. Williams, the two men who fought the PGA on behalf of Charlie Sifford and helped end codified discrimination in professional golf. *University of Southern California/Corbis Historical Collection/Getty Images*

Hillcrest Country Club comedians table, 1959: Harpo Marx using an umbrella to tee off from the middle of the comedians table at Hillcrest Country Club. George Burns, Jack Benny and Milton Berle look on. *The Al Hirschfeld Foundation. www.AlHirschfeldFound ation.org*

Fundraising dinner 1960: Attorney General Stanley Mosk was an early and enthusiastic supporter of John F. Kennedy's presidential campaign. They are seated next to each other at a fundraiser at the Beverly Hilton in 1960. *University of Southern California/Corbis Historical Collection/Getty Images*

Mosk withdrawal, 1964: Attorney General Stanley Mosk can't hide his disappointment in announcing his withdrawal from the 1964 California US Senate race. *Gordon Dean/Valley Times Collection/Los Angeles Public Library*

Local man makes good, 1969: Charlie Sifford raises his putter in triumph after sinking the winning putt in a playoff against Harold Henning in the 1969 Los Angeles Open. *Bettman/Getty Images*

Alan Bakke, 1976: Alan Bakke, whose application for admission to the University of California–Davis Medical School was upheld in a ruling by the California Supreme Court. Judge Stanley Mosk wrote for the 6–1 majority. *Bettman/Getty Images*

Tiger and Charlie, 2009: Tiger Woods called Charlie Sifford a pioneer and the grandfather that he never had. Here, the two chat at a 2009 PGA tournament. *Stuart Franklin/Getty Images*

PMOF 2014: One of Charlie Sifford's heroes, President Barack Obama, presents Sifford with the Presidential Medal of Freedom in 2014 with Meryl Streep and Marlo Thomas looking on from behind. *Mandel Ngan/Getty Images*

· 8 ·

Charlie in the 1960s

The More Things Change . . .

$\mathcal{T}$he PGA was now an open shop. It had finally rid itself of the odious clause that had prohibited Blacks from being members of its organization. Charlie Sifford would now be treated like every other touring pro, finally on the way to achieving his lifelong goal.

But the mere removal of four words from the PGA's bylaws did not result in an attitudinal sea change among its sponsors and tournament hosts. Or the PGA itself. Sifford would still find it just as exasperating and infuriating to try and get his name in the field of one-third of the PGA tournaments. He was no more welcome in Florida or Louisiana in 1962 than he had been in 1961. There were no Stanley Mosks in Tallahassee or Baton Rouge.

Thanks to the pressure from the California attorney general, Blacks could no longer be prevented from joining the PGA or working in pro shops across the country. But they could be prevented, and were prevented, from playing in certain PGA tournaments because of the color of their skin. Charlie Sifford had helped to eliminate the Caucasian clause. He had endured countless indignities, insults, and death threats. He had won a couple tournaments with PGA players in the field and handled himself honorably in situations where someone else might have snapped.

But in 1962, he was told, again, that his presence would not be welcome at the Houston Open, which was contested on a public course. In 1963, finally getting accepted into the field at the Pensacola Open, he was prevented from using the clubhouse and dining in the restaurant, so he had to change and eat in the parking lot. In 1964, he was hoping to enter the New Orleans Open for the first time. But a PGA official called him and told him to wait a year. "There's a hater in office," Sifford was told. "We can't guarantee your safety." The reference was to Governor Jimmie Davis, an ardent opponent of efforts to desegregate the state.

"The 1960s were already bringing great changes," Sifford said, "but it still looked an awful lot like the 1950s to me."

In 1962, Sifford maintained as full a schedule as the temper of the times permitted. He won more than $12,000, coming close to winning for the first time at the Canadian Open. After taking the lead midway through the tournament, Sifford claimed that the Masters, seeing a Black man in contention, had suddenly changed its policy and decided not to invite the winner of the Canadian Open to its tournament the following April. He was wrong. In 1962, it was the policy of the Masters to invite the winner of the Canadian Open—if the winner was a Canadian.

Sifford clearly did not know that. While several non-Canadian winners of the Canadian Open had been invited to play in the Masters, it was because they qualified under the tournament's eligibility rules at the time. It was not simply due to winning the Canadian Open.

Instead, Sifford went after the Masters' officials, saying they were trying to ensure that their tournament remained "lily white." While it's undeniable that the Masters could have done more to integrate their tournament, this was a case of Sifford being uninformed.

And it became a moot point anyway when journeyman Ted Kroll overtook Sifford over the final nine holes to win the tournament. "I'd do anything to win a golf tournament," Kroll told Sifford afterward. "But I am truly sorry it was you who I had to beat."

From 1955 to 2022, no Canadian won his country's national open. Pat Fletcher, a transplanted Englishman who settled in the Montreal area, won in 1954 and received an invitation to the 1955 Masters. He finished in a tie for thirty-seventh place. In 2023, Winnipeg-born Nick Taylor triumphed in dramatic fashion, sinking a seventy-two-foot eagle putt to win a playoff over Tommy Fleetwood. He was the first native-born Canadian to win the Canadian Open since 1914.

In 1963, Sifford earned a personal best $16,565, playing in twenty-five official tournaments. That was good enough to be among the top sixty money winners, again, so he didn't have to worry about Monday qualifiers in 1964. But he was still miles behind Arnold Palmer, who became the first player to win more than $100,000 in a season.

Sifford finished two shots behind Gary Player in San Diego in 1963 in the first tournament of the season and tied for third place. He tied for third again at the end of January at the Lucky Invitational, four shots behind the winner, Jack Burke. Then, he did something for the first time in his career. When the PGA Tour went to places where he knew he would not be welcome, Sifford decided to play some tournaments in the Caribbean and South America.

He spent five weeks playing in Venezuela, Panama, Jamaica, and Puerto Rico. On the fourth leg of his trip, the Puerto Rico Open, Sifford won, defeating George Knudson by six shots to collect $1,200. The wire service story on Sifford's victory said it was the first time he had won a seventy-two-hole tournament in a PGA-sponsored event, which was the case. But it was not an "official" PGA event. While Sifford was winning in Puerto Rico, the regular PGA pros were competing at the Greater New Orleans Open.

The following week, at the Jamaica Open, Sifford nearly won again, finishing in second place, two shots behind John Barnum, the first-round leader of the 1962 PGA, who was fifty-one years old when he won his first and only official PGA tournament, the Cajun Classic in 1962. Sifford left with $1,000.

"Playing in Jamaica was one of the weirdest things I've ever encountered, because the Black people there were almost as rude to me as the white people in the South," Sifford said. "I took my $1,000, got out of there and didn't go back."

Back in the USA, Sifford made his debut at Pensacola, where he had to eat and change clothes in the parking lot, and finally got through the front door of the Houston Classic, where he tied for seventh. But he skipped three tournaments in Texas and another in Memphis before playing almost weekly for the rest of the year. The exceptions were the majors. Sifford did not play in the US Open that year at The Country Club in Brookline, Massachusetts. He had tied for forty-third at the 1962 US Open. He also did not play in the PGA Championship, which was held in Dallas. He would not make his debut in that tournament until 1965.

Life on the road had become somewhat more bearable because of two Black players who had joined the tour, Rafe Botts and Pete Brown. Botts had been the second Black to join the tour in 1961 and had an underwhelming professional career. The same could not be said for the man who followed Botts and became the third Black on the tour—Pete Brown. (Both Botts and Brown joined as Approved Tournament Players, with Sifford signing as one of the two established professionals for each man. Botts did not play well enough for long enough to keep his PGA card.)

Pete Brown was born in 1935 in Mississippi, which is where he started to learn the game of golf by caddying at the segregated municipal course in his hometown. Like Charlie Sifford, Brown developed into an accomplished golfer in his teens but had few places where he could showcase his skills. In 1953, the UGA held a tournament in Houston called The Lone Star Open. Sifford, Teddy Rhodes, and Bill Spiller were all in the field. Sifford had just begun his run of five straight National Negro Open titles.

After four rounds, Pete Brown finished ahead of every golfer in the field with the exception of Sifford. He earned $250. He came back the next year to the same tournament and won it, one of four times he would win the Lone Star Open. After a couple of other strong performances in 1953, Brown returned to Mississippi. It is here that his story starts to differ from most other Black golfers of the time. Pete Brown got himself a sponsor.

Randolph Wallace, who owned a construction company, a hotel, and other smaller businesses, had also grown up in Mississippi. But he relocated to Detroit and soon heard of Brown's golfing exploits. Wallace made his fellow Mississippian an offer—come to Detroit, all expenses paid, and teach his family how to play golf. So Brown headed to Detroit, where Wallace put him up at his hotel and Brown gave lessons to the Wallaces.

Wallace did more than just sponsor Brown as a golfer. When Brown nearly died in his early twenties from what doctors think was infectious mononucleosis, Wallace paid the young man's hospital bills. And when Brown gradually got back his strength and golf game, Wallace was there to help him. Brown won a pair of UGA National Negro Opens in 1961 and 1962 and got his Approved Tournament Player card from the PGA in 1963. He didn't have to wait very long to make a name for himself.

Since 1953, the PGA had had an event each year called the Tournament of Champions. The field was limited to those who had won a tournament in the year prior, which ruled out a sizable number of touring pros. For most of the 1960s, it was held in Las Vegas, either at the Desert Inn Country Club or the Stardust Country Club.

The PGA sponsored the Tournament of Champions. It also sponsored an event that ran the same week for all those who had not won a tournament the previous year. In 1964, it was called the Waco Turner Open. It was not held in Waco, Texas. It was held in Burneyville, Oklahoma, at the course that a wealthy promoter built especially for the tournament—and for himself.

The promoter's name was Waco Turner, and he was a millionaire oilman and larger than life. He filled potato sacks with cash and would dispense bonuses to players for good shots during a round. He would drive Cadillacs around his golf course until they ran out of gas and leave them there. No members complained because there weren't any members other than Turner and his wife, Opie.

The Turners hosted an LPGA event at their club in the late 1950s. It was called the Opie Turner Open and attracted a strong field, including Mickey Wright and Betsy Rawls. Always looking for a sideshow, the Turners invited the reigning Miss America, Mary Ann Mobley, to appear at the 1959 tournament.

Waco Turner's first PGA event was in 1961. The players loved it. There would be cash bonuses for birdies, eagles, chip-ins and the low daily score. But Turner also had one demand of his eventual winner: he could not play in the Tournament of Champions the following year.

Turner had to make an exception for the 1964 winner of his tournament because the Waco Turner Open ceased to exist from then on. So whoever won the 1964 Waco Turner Open could play in the Tournament of Champions the following year. That someone was Pete Brown.

Charlie Sifford had been the first Black to be admitted to the PGA as a member. Pete Brown was the first Black to win a PGA-sanctioned, seventy-two-hole tournament. It may have been known as The Poor Boy Open because all the winners were in Las Vegas. But it was a PGA event just like the San Diego Open and the Insurance City Open and, in 1964, the field included such PGA regulars as Miller Barber, Tommy Aaron, Charles Coody, Dan Sikes, and an up-and-coming twenty-one-year-old named Raymond Floyd. Sifford played in it as well and finished sixth.

Brown made a difficult par on the seventy-second hole to beat Sikes by one shot. He earned $2,700 for his victory. Immediately after winning, Brown received a phone call from Fort Worth, Texas. The sponsors of the Colonial Invitation requested his presence in the field for next week's tournament. Brown would have become the first Black to play in that prestigious tournament, held at the Colonial Country Club, which was Ben Hogan's home course for many years. But he did not make it, citing a back injury.

Brown did show up the following year to play in the Tournament of Champions but withdrew after one round. He played seventeen years on the PGA Tour and won one additional event, the 1970 Andy Williams San Diego Open. Brown ended up moving to Los Angeles and playing golf with Sifford. And when Sifford's son, Charles Jr., was married in March 1973, the wedding reception was held at Pete Brown's home.

The year 1964 was also a memorable one for Sifford in that he finally became a full-fledged member of the PGA. He had finished in the top sixty on the money list since 1960 and was thus no longer deemed to be an Approved Tournament Player. He was a tour regular, just like Arnie and Jack and Gary, the so-called Big Three. But he still had to be very careful about where he played. He averaged around twenty-seven tournaments a year from 1964 to 1966. The PGA schedule had no fewer than forty in any of those years.

In those three years, Sifford managed twelve top-ten finishes, but only one top-five, a tie for second at the St. Paul Open in August 1964. He finished in a three-way tie, three shots behind the winner, Chuck Courtney, earning $4,333.

Earlier that year, Sifford had played in his fourth US Open and finished twenty-seventh at sweltering Congressional Country Club in Bethesda, Maryland. But after the first two rounds, it looked like he might well earn that invitation to Augusta. He was tied for fourth place, six shots off the lead held by Tommy Jacobs. But on Saturday, in brutal heat and humidity, he shot 77 in the morning and matched that in the afternoon. "I just wanted to get out of there without fainting dead on the golf course," Sifford said.

The man who won the tournament, Ken Venturi, had been so ill after the morning round on Saturday that doctors advised him to withdraw. Venturi was in a fog of delirium and suffering from heat stroke when he did win. *Sports Illustrated* named him its Sportsman of the Year that year. Sifford's twenty-seventh-place finish was his best in a US Open to date, and he pocketed $400. It was the last time the US Open held its third and fourth rounds on the same day, an accommodation to television, not to Mother Nature.

By the time 1967 rolled around, Sifford was still without an official PGA win and would turn forty-five in June. He was beginning to wonder if he would be known merely as a survivor and not as a winner. He saw good young players coming onto the tour like Ray Floyd, Lee Trevino, and George Archer—all future Majors champions—and they were still in their twenties.

"You don't bounce back quite as fast from a sore back or a strained muscle when you're 45, and those golf courses seem to get a little longer every year when you're out there walking," he said.

But he started to finish in the money—an eighth place in Tucson, a fifth place in Greensboro, a sixth place in Dallas—and had amassed more than $20,000 in earnings by the end of July. That was more than he had made in any full season on the tour. So he was hopeful as he headed to Hartford for the Greater Hartford Open.

He had left Akron, Ohio, after finishing in a tie for nineteenth at the American Golf Classic and made the drive to Connecticut. He had always had a fondness for what was known then as the GHO. He stayed with friends, and he got acquainted with a Hartford lawyer named Gerard Roisman, who would become his de facto agent and personal attorney. Sifford had played in the tournament every year but one since 1955, although his previous two appearances resulted in a missed cut and a tie for fifty-first.

The 1967 field was reasonably strong for a late-summer event. Gary Player was among those shooting for the $20,000 first prize along with Art Wall, who was the defending champion, as well as Al Geiberger, Frank Beard, and Lee Trevino, who had had a coming-out party of sorts at the US Open in June, finishing fifth.

Sifford was in fifth place after the first round and was six shots out of the lead at the midway point. A third-round 69 matched his opening-day score, but he was still five strokes off the lead held by Terry Dill. Saturday is often called Moving Day on the PGA Tour, and Sifford's move was not to tumble too far down the leaderboard. It was still a huge deficit to make up in one round, but he gave himself a puncher's chance going into the final round.

And then, the magic reappeared. It was as if he had been transported back twelve years to the Canadian Open when he had opened with his 63. He shot a blistering 64, including a 31 on the back nine, which included a chip-in for an eagle at the fourteenth hole. As he walked up the eighteenth fairway, Sifford described the scene as if "the whole crowd funneled into me." They were chanting his name. They were cheering him on. Somehow, Sifford seemed to recognize what they were cheering about—he was about to win his first, official PGA tournament at the age of forty-five.

He finished at 12 under par over the Wethersfield Country Club course—and then waited. Steve Opperman missed a key birdie putt. Doug Ford missed a key birdie putt. Now, no one could catch Charlie Sifford. When he learned that his 12-under score would stand up, an emotional Sifford broke down and cried. He was too overcome to say anything much more than "Thank you" to the crowd as he accepted the $20,000 winner's check.

"You all make me feel at home," he said, fighting back tears. "If you try hard enough, anything can happen."

Later, reflecting on his breakthrough, Sifford said, "I thanked God for my victory and for giving me the strength to hang in there all those years when winning a golf tournament seemed like the most unlikeliest thing that would ever happen to me."

The victory assured Sifford of a year's exemption on the 1968 tour, although he had already attained that by virtue of his solid play to that point. He would finish twenty-fifth on the money list that year, well within the top sixty. It also meant he could book a trip to Las Vegas for the annual Tournament of Champions the following April.

But if Sifford had finally gained national recognition for winning his first official PGA tournament, the victory did not lead to a sudden awakening among the suits in corporate America. That may have had something to do with Sifford's underwhelming play over the final four months of 1967 after his victory in Hartford. He missed two cuts. He tied for fifty-fifth in the Thunderbird Classic. He closed the year with an eighth-place finish at a tournament called The West End Classic, which was played in December on Grand Bahama Island. It was a satellite event offering a smallish purse, but, for a lot of golfers, it was the final chance to earn enough money to make the coveted top-sixty list. Sifford was already there.

The following year, 1968, Sifford's itinerary read like that of a regular touring pro. Of course, he had been one since 1960, but there had been all those stops on the tour where he had not been welcomed. Now, in 1968, Sifford played in Florida, Memphis, and Atlanta, and he tied for eleventh in a tournament called the Rebel Yell Open. That was a one-time satellite tournament held in Knoxville, Tennessee, the same weekend as the Masters.

Could anyone ever have imagined Charlie Sifford playing in a tournament called the Rebel Yell Open? (It was named for the sponsoring bourbon company.) But he did. He also closed out his season with a second-place finish at the Cajun Classic in Louisiana, four shots behind the winner, Ron Cerrudo.

His trip to Las Vegas for the Tournament of Champions resulted in a tie for fourteenth place. In all, Sifford played in thirty-two events in 1968, but with only one top-10 finish he did not get any bounce from his win at Hartford in terms of endorsements, sponsorships, or other perks from American companies.

Sifford sought out super-agent Mark McCormack, who ran International Management Group and whose clients included Nicklaus and Palmer. Sifford said he was told he didn't make enough money to make it worth IMG's time. He figured a cigar endorsement would surely be in the offing after a picture of his victory in Hartford showed him with his stogie still clenched firmly in his teeth. But nothing arose. Sam Snead, who didn't smoke, got an endorsement deal to hawk Tiparillos for a couple years.

"I thought during the entire year of 1968 that I was bound to be offered a high-level sponsorship or endorsement," he said. "Never happened. I personally sent out letters to a number of big companies, as did my lawyers, expressing interest in having me endorse their products. All I got back were letters that said 'thanks. But no thanks.'"

Sifford wasn't surprised that offers didn't come flying over his transom. But he thought his story merited *something*, and if a white golfer had gone through what he had endured, he would have been able to cash in. He was experiencing exactly what he had experienced in the 1950s, only this time, it wasn't the PGA who was shunning him, it was corporate America closing its doors to him. How many more chances would he get?

"As I saw my opportunities to play on the tour slipping away, I mourned more than ever those years that I'd lost. I had given away more than a dozen years to Jim Crow and I wanted them back," he said.

But if 1968 proved to be a bit of a disappointment, the following year would turn out differently. And it wasn't solely because he added his second tour win to his resume. A seismic shift was happening on the PGA Tour, and Charlie Sifford would be the first golfer to win a PGA tournament under a new, more player-friendly arrangement that had been ironed out between the tour and its competitors just before Rancho Park welcomed the participants to the 1969 Los Angeles Open.

The 1969 Los Angeles Open was the first tournament played since the end of the so-called Civil War between the PGA and its touring pros. Less than one month had passed since the PGA, whose main responsibility was to its thousands of club pros around the country, and the touring pros, who were the week-to-week tournament golfers, had reached a settlement.

The players had been trying for years to have greater control over the tour. The PGA controlled everything including the size of the purses, which were about to explode due to television-rights fees. The touring pros felt that that money should be theirs. The PGA agreed, sort of, but still funneled money back to its clubs and to support its mission to "grow the game."

When Kermit Zarley joined the PGA Tour in 1964, he needed two PGA club pros who could vouch for his game. That was not an issue, as he won the 1962 NCAA Individual championship while playing for the University of Houston. To get into tournaments in those days required Monday qualifying unless the player was exempt by either having won a tournament in the previous year, having received a sponsor's exemption, or having finished among the top sixty money winners the year before.

What bothered Zarley and others was that tournament sponsors often would give out exemptions to local-area professionals—PGA members, but not touring pros. That may have appealed to the locals who purchased tickets, but it was not helpful to the pros who followed the tour. They needed to play.

The players' contention that the PGA had too much power over the tournament schedule, purses, and other revenues reached a head in 1966 when Frank Sinatra proposed hosting a $200,000 tournament in Palm Springs, which would have made it one of the biggest purses on the tour. Approval required a vote from the player-dominated Tournament Committee (which said yes) and a vote from the four-member Executive Committee, which had three PGA officers. It had veto power and it had never exercised it. But it did then, explaining that the Palm Springs area already was well served by the annual Bob Hope Desert Classic. Needless to say, that decision only fortified the players' resolve.

By 1968, things had gotten testy. The players had formed the American Professional Golfers, seeking "full and complete authority" to oversee and run the tour, with its prize money of more than $5 million. Both sides engaged outside counsel, with the PGA of America hiring William Rogers, who would soon be Richard Nixon's secretary of state.

In September, Leo Fraser, the secretary of the PGA, issued what the *New York Times* called a "scathing personal attack" on Jack Nicklaus. Fraser said Nicklaus, who was one of the leaders of the players' movement, "continues to pass out false information designed to mislead the public and camouflage the true intent of this plan to wrest the tour from the PGA." Fraser said of the players' motives, "It is this kind of irresponsibility and deliberate attempt to deceive" that only confirmed his view that the PGA should continue to run the tour. "Professional golf, which has made it possible for Nicklaus to become a wealthy man at age twenty-eight, is best protected under the structure of a respected and long-established organization which has only the integrity of the tour as its aim."

Fraser's broadside came a few days after Arnold Palmer, who had still not publicly backed the players, met with PGA officials in Washington, D.C., to try and find common ground. He went as an individual, not as a representative of the players. While still ostensibly on the fence, Palmer suggested a separate, self-governed section for the touring pros under the umbrella of the PGA. While his days as a winner of major tournaments had passed, Palmer, still only thirty-nine, was viewed as one of the sport's most important voices. Fraser accused Nicklaus of trying to undermine Palmer's efforts, which prompted an extraordinary reply from Nicklaus in a first-person article in *Sports Illustrated.*

Nicklaus conceded that the release had spelled his name correctly and that Fraser had been on the mark as to Nicklaus's age. "The rest of his cutting statement, though, was a personal assault," he wrote.

Nicklaus said the diatribe had been prompted by some remarks he had made earlier that year at the PGA Championship in San Antonio. Only 56 of the 168 players in the field were touring pros, which Nicklaus called "absurd and unfortunate." Only one-third of the field, he noted, was made up of touring pros, "in other words, the best players in the world."

That was why, Nicklaus wrote, it was imperative that the PGA touring pros run their own tour, set their own schedules, choose their own venues, control their own purses, but still within the PGA framework.

"We have formed the APG," Nicklaus wrote. "This is not designed to destroy the PGA. Instead, we want a better vehicle for the operation of professional golf tournaments. The next action rests with the PGA."

Two months later, the two sides came to an "amicable agreement" in the words of the PGA. The APG would become the Tournament Players Division within the PGA but have all the control it sought over scheduling, purses, and other tournament-related matters. The PGA would control its own championship and the Ryder Cup. The players division hired one of the most respected men in the sport, Joseph Dey, to be its first commissioner. The APG had lined up tournaments for 1969, as had the PGA, and while there was mostly overlap, there was one weekend in January where two tournaments were played in the same state, albeit with vastly different fields and purses.

The marquee event that particular weekend was still the Los Angeles Open, even though the PGA staged an event in Northern California, the Alameda County Open, at the same time. Virtually all of the big names in professional golf who chose to play that weekend chose to play in Los Angeles, where the purse was $100,000 with the winner getting $20,000. The biggest names in the Alameda field were Bob Lunn, by then a two-time winner on the PGA Tour, and Deane Beman, a two-time US Amateur champion, who would go on to succeed Dey as the players' commissioner in 1974. The purse for that event was $50,000 with the winner getting $10,000. Dick Lotz won the one-time-only event by one stroke over Don Whitt. As noted, most of the big names were in Los Angeles that weekend.

In addition to its exemplary civil rights history, the Los Angeles Open, perhaps more than any non-major, has, through the decades, contributed much to the sport's storied history. It has gone through a few name changes, has been played at a number of different venues, but if you are looking for a tournament with a lot of "firsts," look no further.

In 1938, Babe Didrikson was in the Los Angeles Open field, making her the first woman to play in a men's event on the PGA Tour. She had been an Olympic gold medalist in the javelin and the eighty-meter hurdles at the 1932 Olympics in Los Angeles. She had won a silver medal in the high jump. It was during that Olympiad that she first played golf. She was hooked.

She had no illusions about challenging the men. She was twenty-six and new to the game. She failed to make the cut after two rounds, shooting 84 and 81. Scotsman Jimmy Thomson won the event. The one positive Didrikson took from the experience was a life-changing one—she met her future husband, the professional wrestler George Zaharias. She returned to the LA Open in 1945 and made the thirty-six-hole cut, but she failed to make the fifty-four-hole cut. (Some tournaments had two cuts to winnow the field to a manageable number for the final eighteen holes.) In 1945, she entered the Phoenix and Tucson Opens and made the cut in each one.

Babe, as she would always be called, went on to a storied career in golf and became the sport's first female unqualified star. She won the 1946 US Amateur and the following year became the first American woman to win the British Ladies Amateur. The year after that, she won the US Women's Open, then in just its third year, by a stunning eight strokes. She would win it two more times by similarly ridiculous margins, nine strokes in 1950 and twelve strokes in 1954, a year after cancer surgery while wearing an ostomy bag. She applied to compete in the 1948 US Open, but her application was rejected. It was a men-only event, the USGA told her.

She was one of the founding members of the LPGA and one of the original thirteen inductees into the World Golf Hall of Fame in 1974. Overall, she won more than eighty tournaments, amateur and professional, in a career that came to an untimely end when she died of colon cancer in 1956. She was forty-five.

Twelve years after Didrikson's Los Angeles Open debut, the tournament welcomed Ben Hogan back to the world of professional golf in one of the most remarkable comebacks in sports history. The thirty-seven-year-old Hogan returned to the tour nearly a year after almost getting killed when a Greyhound bus struck his Cadillac on a rural Texas road in February 1949. Hogan spent weeks in an El Paso hospital with several broken bones and countless surgeries, but he deemed himself ready to play in January 1950. Amazingly, he tied with Sam Snead after seventy-two holes and lost in a playoff, which was delayed for more than a week due to inclement weather and unplayable course conditions. Less than five months later, Hogan won the US Open for a second time in a three-way playoff at Merion.

The 1961 Los Angeles Open was won by Bob Goalby. But it was Arnold Palmer who made the biggest headline, missing his only cut of the year. There was a good reason for that. In the first round, the defending Masters and US Open champion came to his final hole, a par 5, needing only a par to finish with a 1-under-par 70. After a perfect drive, the adventurous Palmer then proceeded to hit his next *four* shots out of bounds. He did not discriminate; two went out of bounds on the right and two on the left. Now hitting his tenth shot, he managed to get down in three from that original, disastrous spot, 230 yards from the green. The 12 ballooned him to a 77 and a second-round 72 forced him to miss the cut by a shot. Asked by incredulous sports writers after the round how he could post a 12, the genial Palmer quipped, "Well, I just missed the putt for an 11." Two years later, the Junior Chamber of Commerce, sponsors of the tournament, installed a plaque on the eighteenth tee box to commemorate Palmer's "achievement."

The following year, in one of the most eagerly anticipated professional debuts, two-time US Amateur champion Jack Nicklaus joined the field at Rancho Park. He did not like the course. Nicklaus finished in a tie for fiftieth, twenty-one shots behind winner Phil Rodgers, and earned a whopping $33.33. Nicklaus played in the Los Angeles Open at Rancho Park only twice more in the 1960s, his best finish being a tie for twenty-fourth in the 1967 event.

Nicklaus felt the tournament deserved a classier venue than Rancho Park. He was right, of course. The tournament is now held in February at the prestigious and difficult Riviera Country Club in Pacific Palisades.

Thirty years after Nicklaus's professional debut at the LA Open, a sixteen-year-old sophomore from Western High School in Anaheim named Tiger Woods played in his first PGA Tour event at the Los Angeles Open, then sponsored by Nissan. He missed the cut at Riviera after shooting rounds of 72 and 75 and said, prophetically, "I learned I have a long way to go." Six years later, when the tournament was held at Valencia Country Club (Riviera hosted the US Senior Open that year) Woods was twenty-two and already a household name and major champion. At the end of seventy-two holes, Woods was tied with Billy Mayfair, the 1987 US Amateur champion and, at the time, a three-time winner on the PGA Tour.

Mayfair won the playoff on the first extra hole. He remains the only player to defeat Woods in a PGA Tour playoff; Woods has an 11–1 record in such events, including 3–0 in major championships. He has lost two playoffs in non-tour events. Woods won eighty-two PGA events through the end of 2022, when injuries from an automobile accident drastically cut down on his appearances. The Los Angeles Open is not one of those eighty-two. But Woods has some pretty strong company in that department. Nicklaus never won it either, even after it had moved from Rancho Park to Riviera in 1973. His best finish was second place, two shots behind winner Gil Morgan in 1978, as he played the last four holes in 3 over par.

The 1969 Los Angeles Open was noteworthy as well, for the unexpected but rewarding victory for Charlie Sifford. It represented a validation that the victory in Hartford two years earlier did not consign him to the unwanted list of one-hit wonders. And it was particularly satisfying and fulfilling that the victory came in a tournament with a long and rich history, a tournament that always welcomed all comers, and at a golf course across the street from where Sifford had first met Stanley Mosk, ten years earlier, to ask for the attorney general's help in joining an organization that was determined to keep him out.

In a way, the circle had been closed. What had started one day in September 1959 at Hillcrest Country Club had closed one day in January 1969 at Rancho Park. The day after the tournament ended, Mosk received an unsigned telegram. It said, simply, "Thank you for opening the doors for the Charlie Siffords of this world." Mosk always assumed it had come from Charlie Sifford.

· 9 ·

Stanley in the 1960s

$\mathcal{B}$y the time the 1960s rolled around, Stanley Mosk was just getting settled into his new digs at the attorney general's office. But he had already established himself as one of the bright lights of the Democratic Party in California.

The Democratic National Convention was in Los Angeles in 1960, setting up a potential conflict for the new attorney general with the new governor, Pat Brown. Brown controlled the California delegation and, though he knew he had no prospect of winning the presidential nomination, he hoped to use the delegates' votes as leverage to secure the second spot on the Democratic ticket.

"I was an ardent Kennedy supporter from quite early. He captivated me, I must say," Mosk recalled years later. "I think Pat Brown had some idea in the back of his mind that he might end up as a vice presidential candidate. But obviously he could not be if Kennedy, another Catholic, were the presidential nominee."

As Mosk noted, "in the sixties, the religious issue was of consequence." So much so that Kennedy dealt with the issue in his acceptance speech at the Democratic National Convention, saying, "I am fully aware of the fact that the Democratic Party, by nominating someone of my faith, has taken on what many regard as a new and hazardous risk." Two months later, Kennedy felt compelled to address the issue again, this time in a speech to the Greater Houston Ministerial Association. He sought to dispel fears that, if elected, he would be beholden to the Vatican rather than the Constitution. "Contrary to common newspaper usage, I am not the Catholic candidate for President," Kennedy told the Protestant ministers. "I am the Democratic Party's candidate for President who happens also to be a Catholic."

As one of Kennedy's earliest and most ardent supporters in California, Mosk was soon to be Pat Brown's choice to replace Paul Ziffren as the state's Democratic National Committeeman. Brown wanted Ziffren out. There was too much friction in the party and Brown believed Ziffren, who was backing Adlai Stevenson, wanted to stop the governor from winning as a favorite son. Brown enlisted the help of Democratic fundraiser Bart Lytton to help him find a replacement for Ziffren.

"Paul Ziffren is Southern California. Paul Ziffren is a liberal. Paul Ziffren is articulate, attractive politically. And we have to get a like figure," Lytton told the governor.

"Well, who in the hell will that be?" Brown responded.

Lytton said, "Very simple. Stanley Mosk. He's Jewish, Southern California, liberal. If we can talk Stanley Mosk into doing this, then we have the one man we can knock Ziffren off with because we'll turn back the ire of the ultra-liberals; they also love Mosk. It isn't going to be a race issue, we're not knocking him off because he's Jewish, you see; and it isn't going to be Southern California versus Northern California. He's our man."

Brown lent his plane to Stanley and Edna Mosk to fly from Sacramento to Los Angeles in late May 1960 and have dinner with Lytton at Chasen's. It took some arm-twisting on Lytton's part to convince Mosk to take the position.

"Stanley was the attorney general at the time and he said, 'now what the hell do I want to be national committeeman for? I can't think of one good reason for it,'" Lytton said.

Mosk wavered as Lytton continued with the pitch. He wasn't sure. He knew and liked Ziffren.

"Look, Paul and I are friends. Why would I take out after him, A, and B; what would I want to be national committeeman for anyway? I'm the attorney general now," Mosk told Lytton.

Lytton responded, "Stanley, insofar as your being friends is concerned, you're supporting Kennedy and Paul is supporting Stevenson. All right. So, therefore, you're doing it on the basis of a presidential election; it's not a personal thing. And Paul wouldn't hesitate, as you know from the past."

Mosk agreed. Lytton then told Mosk that the attorney general needed a national forum, which being the national committeeman would provide.

"I told him, you're very well known in California, but you're not well known at all outside of California. . . . You have to get this. National committeeman will give it to you."

Lytton told Mosk that while the attorney general might have some prestige in California, "you don't have it in New Hampshire, and you don't have it in South Carolina. When you want a national forum, you're the national committeeman and you say something and you're in the national press."

A still hesitant Mosk finally acceded to Lytton's talking points, with some help from Edna, who had been on board from the outset. It likely severed the relationship between Mosk and Ziffren, whom Lytton had said was "among the unknockables, the untouchables, and immovables, and it was felt that it couldn't be done at all, but it was done and it was done very, very simply."

Kennedy barely edged Stevenson among the California delegation voters but support for the senator enabled him to win the Democratic nomination on the first ballot at the convention. Pat Brown later guessed that all the Stevenson support had been Ziffren's revenge for being ousted as national committeeman.

As Mosk was in the middle of trying to convince the PGA to end its racist ways in 1961, another project crossed his desk. Initially, it was a request from Brown that the attorney general investigate the growing influence of the ultra-conservative John Birch Society in California. Mosk refused to do so. As offensive and reprehensible as the Birchers were to him, he felt their beliefs and speech were protected by the First Amendment.

Instead, however, along with one of his deputies, Mosk prepared a report for the governor on the activities of the society. The report produced probably the six most famous and repeated words in Mosk's long history of speeches, decisions, dissents, and general observations.

Before QAnon, before anti-vaxxers, before reality-challenged conspiracists claimed the 2020 presidential election was stolen from Donald J. Trump, there was the John Birch Society.

More than half a century before Trump's rantings about a "deep state" operating in the federal government in the service of woke Democrats and "the Blacks," there was John Birch Society founder Robert Welch's claim that President Dwight D. Eisenhower was a "dedicated, conscious agent of the Communist conspiracy" and that the civil rights movement for racial equality was "fomented also entirely by the Communists."

At its height, the John Birch Society claimed no more than one hundred thousand members, but its numbers belied its political influence in conservative circles. Responding to US Supreme Court decisions up-holding civil liberties and endorsing racial desegregation, the John Birch Society erected billboards across the country calling for the impeachment of Chief Justice Earl Warren. Reacting to former vice president Richard M. Nixon's denunciation of the group in his 1962 campaign for California governor, the John Birch Society organized its ten thousand members in the state's one thousand chapters against his doomed candidacy.

Attorney General Stanley Mosk had been keeping a close eye on the group that also attributed to Communists public health efforts in the United States to add fluoride to the nation's drinking water to prevent tooth decay. Acting on Brown's request for general information on the society, Mosk and his assistant Howard H. Jewel produced a report on the John Birch Society in 1961 that was as notable for its prescience as for an extraordinary bluntness not typically found in official government documents.

"The cadre of the John Birch Society seems to be formed primarily of wealthy businessmen, retired military officers, and little old ladies in tennis shoes," wrote Mosk, contributing an iconic phrase to the American lexicon. Those were the six words—"little old ladies in tennis shoes." They would be forever linked to Mosk.

Mosk's office would soon be deluged with tennis shoes sent by the public and by members of the John Birch Society.

"I understand that Birch Society cells are being instructed to send me tennis shoes," Mosk said. "Since they so vigorously oppose foreign aid, we shall forward all shoes received to charitable agencies helping our needy, anti-Communist friends overseas. I hope, however, the shoes will not be for the right foot only. We prefer well balanced people, both at home and abroad."

There was more to the report. Mosk and Jewel said the Birchers

are bound together by an obsessive fear of "Communism" which they define to include any ideas differing from their own, even though these ideas may differ even more markedly from the ideas of Marx, Engels, Lenin and Khrushchev. In response to this fear they are willing to give up a large measure of the freedoms guaranteed them by the United States Constitution in favor of accepting the dictates of their "Founder." They seek, by fair means or foul, to force the rest of us to follow their example. They are pathetic.

Their founder in 1958 was Robert Welch, who convened a gathering of eleven business leaders at a private home in Indianapolis to discuss how to combat the internal threat of Communism in the United States. They named their fringe organization after US Army captain John M. Birch, an intelligence officer killed by Chinese Communists in 1945, making him—in Welch's view—the first casualty of the Cold War.

The son of North Carolina farmers, Welch enrolled in and dropped out of the US Naval Academy and Harvard Law School, in turn, put off both by the rigid discipline of military training and the progressive politics of the law professors in Cambridge. One of those professors was future Supreme Court justice Felix Frankfurter.

He stayed in Massachusetts to launch a candy company and, when it failed, joined his brother's successful candy business, which produced such popular mid-twentieth-century sweets as Sugar Babies, Sugar Daddies, and Junior Mints. Welch launched a failed campaign in 1950 for lieutenant governor of Massachusetts as an acolyte of Republican senator Joseph McCarthy of Wisconsin, then at full, evidence-free roar about the alleged infiltration of Communists into the US State Department and other warrens of the federal government.

While the rhetoric of McCarthy, and the Birchers who followed him, was extreme, the fear of Communism in the United States was pervasive in the 1950s and early 1960s. It led Attorney General Robert F. Kennedy to claim in 1961 that "Communist espionage here in this country is more active than it has ever been" and prompted President John F. Kennedy in 1963 to authorize the FBI director, J. Edgar Hoover, to place under surveillance Martin Luther King Jr. because the FBI suspected him of associating with Communists.

As big a fan as Stanley Mosk was of the Kennedy brothers, he took a different view of the Communist threat. In his report to the governor, Mosk characterized anti-Communist fervor as "self-induced terror." Bob Dylan would echo Mosk's mocking sentiments a year later in his folk song "Talkin' John Birch Paranoid Blues": "I was looking everywhere for them gol-darned Reds/I got up in the mornin' 'n' looked under my bed, looked behind the kitchen, behind the door, looked in the glove compartment of my car. Couldn't find any."

If anything, Mosk wrote in his report to Brown, the John Birch Society was inadvertently helping the Soviet Union.

He quoted an article in the April 4, 1961, edition of the *Literary Gazette* of Moscow to underscore that point. "Several years ago, an American Senator by the name of McCarthy performed a great service to world Communism by throwing suspicion of Communist affiliation on some very important personalities of the capitalist world. He was so involved in this particular activity that, instead of harming, he actually strengthened the Communist party in the U.S.A. Now the Communist movement has gained unexpectedly a new supporter. His name is Robert Welch." Mosk wrote,

> the entire Birch phenomenon is redolent with strong overtones of para-noia, with the "Communists," replacing the more conventional paranoid "they." For the paranoid, life is a nightmare. Only he understands the nature of the Peril. The more he acts on his systematized delusions, the more he is cast out by his fellow man for his oddness. This only serves to feed his dark suspicions and moves him to ever more bizarre beliefs. As these beliefs become more bizarre, he is ever more the outcast. The circle goes round and round centripetally until the victim is swept into a vortex of fanaticism and despair. This, I believe, is the future which awaits the Birchers. With the passage of time, I predict that they will be splintered and that internecine warfare will become intense as they interpret normal differences of opinion among themselves as treason.

Mosk's report brought a heated rebuke from Republican congressman John H. Rousselot of Southern California. "How long will the people of California stomach Mr. Mosk's bitter and bigoted attacks against the John Birch Society, an organization the California Senate Fact-finding Commission on American Activities found to be thoroughly dedicated to fundamental American ideals?"

Mosk was unbowed. "The orators of the radical-right have tried to pre-empt the term 'patriotism.' . . . Is it patriotic to demand that the chief justice of the United States Supreme Court be impeached? Is it patriotic to sow dissension by insisting that some of the very highest leaders of the United States are disloyal? Is it patriotic to debase free and open debate by heckling, and shouting and hooting? Is it patriotic to deride democracy by calling it a perennial fraud? Does this help America or hurt America?" he asked in response to his critics during a TV appearance in Oakland on February 5, 1962.

Notwithstanding Mosk's contempt for the ideas and the irrational fears of the Birchers and such like-minded extremists as Dr. Fred Schwarz's Christian Anti-Communist Crusade, he was clear in his report that the protection of their Constitutional rights was paramount.

"The Birchers have an equal right with the Prohibitionists, the Vegetarians, the Republicans, the Democrats, or, for that matter, with any Americans, acting singly or in a group, to an expression of their views; and no official, no matter how highly placed, can say them nay. In America, preposterousness prevents the acceptance, but not the expression, of ideas," he wrote, as clear a distillation of the heart of the First Amendment as any ever written.

For all the vitriol directed at him from right-wing zealots, Mosk easily won reelection as attorney general in 1962. His opponent was Tom Coakley, a former superior court judge in Mariposa County. Mosk said his new title as Democratic National Committeeman helped him convince former president Harry Truman to attend a fundraiser for the attorney general. Richard Mosk picked up Truman at the airport and plopped the former president in the back seat of his Plymouth. Truman finished off their conversation by asking to stop and get a bourbon. It was also a celebration of Stanley Mosk's fiftieth birthday in September.

"I must say," Mosk recalled, "that Truman was in rare form. And we packed the Fairmont Hotel at $100 a head and made a good deal of my campaign chest right there."

Coakley had tried to tie Mosk to what the challenger thought were groups that were soft on Communism, a potentially potent message in 1962. That didn't work. He spent the final days of his flailing campaign accusing Mosk of falsely using law enforcement officials in ads endorsing the attorney general's reelection. Mosk had the support of most of the sheriffs and district attorneys in the state and won reelection by nearly six hundred thousand votes.

The big election in California in 1962 was between Pat Brown and Richard Nixon. Two years removed from losing the presidential election, Nixon returned to California to try and unseat Brown. He had as much luck as he had two years earlier against John Kennedy. Brown won by more than three hundred thousand votes and Nixon vowed he'd not let the press kick him around anymore.

Some Democrats had suggested to Mosk that he challenge Republican senator Thomas Kuchel in 1962. Mosk wisely declined. Kuchel was popular, he was not a right-wing extremist, and he easily won reelection. But Mosk did have his eye on the 1964 Senate race. In October of 1963, Mosk sent a copy of a poll to the White House, the results of which showed he would be a formidable US Senate candidate in 1964.

"I have read with interest the polls," wrote Kenneth O'Donnell, a special assistant to President Kennedy, "and appreciate very much you sending them along."

Five months later, still ahead in the polls, Stanley Mosk's US Senate campaign came to an abrupt end.

Clair Engle, the Democrat who defeated former governor Goodwin Knight in 1958 for a Senate seat, could not seek reelection in 1964 due to health issues. He had been diagnosed with a brain tumor and underwent two surgeries. He would die before his term expired.

In April 1964, Engle officially ended his reelection campaign. But by then, it had already been presumed he would not be able to run.

Two candidates emerged on the Democratic side—Stanley Mosk and Alan Cranston. And this is where it started to unravel for Mosk, who had maintained a healthy lead in polls and later said he believed he would have won the race had he stayed in. But in March of 1964, Mosk held a news conference to announce he was not going to run to replace Engle.

What had happened?

Pat Brown inevitably caught some of the blame, and deservedly so. But, in reality, Stanley Mosk's worst enemy at that particular time in his life was the person he saw every morning in the mirror. His removal from the race amounted to a self-inflicted wound. Mosk had spent time schmoozing with the Kennedys and apparently thought he could or should be one of them. He met a woman, a twenty-two-year-old in Las Vegas named Sabrina Jourdan and soon the two were an item.

Mosk spent a lot of time with her. He went places with her. He used official state stationery to vouch for her opening a nightclub by recommending her club on the Sunset Strip receive a liquor license. But this was the 1960s and politicians' private lives were generally seen as just that.

As pieced together by Jacqueline Braitman and Gerald Uelman in their biography of Judge Mosk, and further enhanced in an illuminating story in 1994 by the newspaper *LA Weekly*, a picture emerges of a beautiful young woman and a man thirty years her elder clearly smitten both by the woman and the counterculture lifestyle of the Sunset Strip.

According to the *LA Weekly* article, Jourdan had been arrested for prostitution in Las Vegas in 1960. Her husband had a criminal record. Her sister was a forger and a smuggler.

The club she opened with Mosk's official blessing, Mr. Kon Ton's, served a questionable clientele. It was not the kind of place where Stanley Mosk would take Minna Mosk for Mother's Day brunch. And this was not the kind of company an attorney general or a Supreme Court justice should keep. It was seedy Sunset Strip and everything that entailed. As the television show *77 Sunset Strip* noted, it was an area for highbrows, hipsters, starlets, and phony tipsters.

Mosk was either oblivious or simply didn't care. Or he might have understood that no one would stoop so low as to write about such transgressions as long as they did not impact his work. Jourdan introduced him to her friends and had him tend bar at her parties. The couple made no attempt to hide their relationship.

The relationship continued even after Mosk had been elevated to the Supreme Court. Jourdan twice was found to have Mosk's credit cards in her possession and when authorities called the judge, he vouched for Jourdan and asked them to mail the cards back to him.

Investigators became interested in the early 1960s when Mosk's car was seen parked outside Jourdan's house in the Hollywood Hills. The LAPD started surveillance; it lasted until 1967 and produced enough damning evidence that Mosk would be denied a federal appointment. But the relationship spilled over to the California political arena in July of 1963.

Mosk and Jourdan boarded a plane in Los Angeles bound for Mexico City, where Mosk was attending a legal convention. Jourdan was quickly upgraded to join Mosk in first class. Someone snapped pictures of Mosk and Jourdan in a hotel room in Mexico City. Eight months later, the photographs of Mosk and the woman surfaced just as Mosk was getting ready to declare for the US Senate race. Pat Brown had seen them.

Cranston, then the state controller but also the man who launched the California Democratic Council, had already announced he would seek Engle's seat. Pat Brown was in his corner. According to the *LA Weekly* story, Cranston may have had access to the photographs and passed them along to Brown, who worried that they would fall into the wrong hands if Mosk got the nomination. Cranston denied that he had the pictures in the *LA Weekly* story.

Many things are still unclear. Who shot the photographs of Mosk and his paramour in the Mexico City hotel? Who hired the photographer? In whose hands did the photographs land? Was Brown the culprit here or was he acting in the best interests of the party?

And most perplexing of all, what was Mosk thinking? *Was* he thinking?

Mosk had prepared to announce his candidacy from his office and had made arrangements to have the announcement taped and then distributed to the appropriate outlets. Then, the morning the tape engineers were due in his office to record the announcement, he called everything off.

Had Brown confronted his attorney general with the pictures and told him not to run? Had Brown promised Mosk a seat on the Supreme Court as soon as a vacancy appeared if he, Mosk, got out of the race and ceded the Democratic field to Cranston? Had Edna Mosk, a spectacular fundraiser for her husband, intervened and, aware of her husband's dalliance, convinced him that it would be in everyone's best interests if he did not run?

We do know that Brown called President Lyndon Johnson on April 4, a month after Mosk pulled out, and spilled some of the beans.

"I worked like hell to bring unity," Brown told the president. "One of these days I'll tell you what I did to get Mosk out of it."

Johnson replied, "Yeah. Yeah."

Brown said he preferred not to divulge the full story over the telephone, to which Johnson responded, "Yeah. But I know."

"It wasn't any threats or anything like that," Brown said.

"I know that," Johnson said.

Mosk met reporters at the Statler Hilton in Los Angeles the day after it was announced that he was not going to run. He acknowledged his big lead in the polls and suggested that he probably would have won. But he said the prospect of fundraising, of hitting up friends and others for cash, was something he hated and would not do.

"I am unwilling to impose on my personal friends to give and to raise that tremendous sum of money," Mosk said, saying he would need more than $625,000 just in the primary. "I am equally unwilling to accept the obligations implicit in sizeable contributions from those who are not motivated by friendship."

Mosk denied being heavily pressured by Brown to drop out. But he did admit that he twice had talked to Brown about the governor's feeling that a contentious and expensive primary best be avoided. And he said other Democratic leaders in the state had told him the same thing.

What's revealing is how the name of Sabrina Jourdan never comes up in the oral histories when the topic turns to the 1964 Senate race. Two of them were done in the mid-1990s, well after the *LA Weekly* story.

Richard Mosk's oral history interview was in 1998. In it, he called the whole thing "a sad story." He referenced the phone call from Brown to Lyndon Johnson and said, "He did it, I guess, by circulating rumors about my father and drying up his financial support by inducing contributors not to contribute. And ultimately, even though my father was leading in the polls by a wide margin, he decided to pull out of the race."

He did so on March 4. There were no news reports at the time about Mosk's relationship with the woman or the trip to Mexico City. That all came out later. But the pictures had been seen by enough Democrats in high places. The LAPD certainly knew the story.

And when the *LA Weekly* interviewed Daryl Gates, then the captain of the intelligence division of the LAPD, he told the newspaper, "I was there when Governor Brown found out. That's when the big changes occurred."

Richard Mosk tried unsuccessfully to stop the *LA Weekly* from publishing. On the day the newspaper hit the stands, he sent family members and friends to every nearby newsstand to confiscate the papers. (It was a free paper.) The story got out anyway, but that's as far as it got. Richard Mosk and Susan Mosk were successful in getting major newspapers not to pick up on a thirty-year-old story.

One thing that perplexed Richard Mosk was how his father never held a grudge against Pat Brown.

"Aren't you really angry at the way Pat Brown treated you?" Richard Mosk asked his father.

"And he said, 'well, how can you dislike Pat Brown?'"

Richard Mosk said, "Well, I could."

As his son recalled, "That was Stanley. He got along with people and he didn't hold grudges. And he just took it as it came."

Susan Mosk was more direct.

"Pat put the screws to Stanley," she said.

Even though Mosk was out of the race, he still played a big part in his role as attorney general. He was asked by Pierre Salinger, who was then the press secretary for Lyndon Johnson, if he, Mosk, thought it was legal for Salinger to run for office in California. Salinger, a native Californian, had been a voting resident of Virginia for the last several years. But he had lived in the Bay Area before joining the Kennedy presidential campaign and then the administration as the president's press secretary.

Mosk researched the issue and determined Salinger could run. He thought at the time that Salinger was contemplating a run for a congressional seat in San Francisco. Salinger barely beat the primary filing deadline and instead launched a primary challenge against Cranston. It was just what Pat Brown had sought to avoid when he asked Mosk to pull out of the race.

The *Los Angeles Times* reported that Mosk would place his campaign war chest at Salinger's disposal. The Kennedys backed Salinger; Pat Kennedy Lawford, wife of actor Peter Lawford, lent her support to Salinger. So did Jackie Kennedy. This was five months after the president had been assassinated in Dallas, and his name and reputation were still beyond criticism in Democratic Party circles.

Salinger proved to be exactly what Cranston was not—energetic, comfortable with the press, and capitalizing on his Kennedy affiliation. He won the primary comfortably, and when Engle died in August, Brown appointed Salinger to fill out the remainder of the term.

Salinger had an interesting opponent in the general election. The Republicans nominated Hollywood actor George Murphy. He was a song and dance man in many big-budget Hollywood musicals in the 1930s, 1940s, and 1950s. He was smooth, handsome, a political novice and harped on Salinger being a carpetbagger. Salinger couldn't even vote in California, Murphy noted.

Murphy's strategy worked. On election day, Lyndon Johnson defeated Barry Goldwater by more than one million votes in California. Murphy defeated Salinger by more than 215,000. The victory was said to convince another Hollywood celebrity, Ronald Reagan, to run for governor in 1966. He did, and he defeated Pat Brown, who was seeking a third term. Brown later said that one of the biggest mistakes he made was running for a third term instead of letting Stanley Mosk try to beat Reagan.

Two months before the 1964 election, Brown elevated Roger Traynor from associate justice of the California Supreme Court to chief justice to replace the retiring Phil Gibson. That left a spot on the bench and Brown nominated his attorney general to take Traynor's spot. This is exactly what had been rumored back in March, that Brown would elevate Mosk to the high court if Mosk got out of the Senate race.

"I think there were some indications from Pat Brown that if there was no primary contest . . . that someday in the near future there would be a vacancy on the Supreme Court and though no commitment was made, he'd give me every consideration at the time," Mosk said.

On September 1, 1964, Stanley Mosk joined the seven-member court. Although tempted on occasion, he never left the bench and the voters of California approved his retention four times, the final time in 1998, when Mosk was eighty-six years old.

Mosk hadn't been on the Supreme Court for two years when the prospect of moving to the United States Supreme Court became an option in his mind. One note of support came in July of 1965 from George Killion, the president of the American President Lines shipping company and a prominent figure in California Democratic politics. Killion had worked with Mosk in the Culbert Olson administration.

In a telegram to presidential assistant Bill Moyers, Killion said that if President Johnson wanted a "fitting successor" to Supreme Court Justice Arthur Goldberg, "I think you would want to direct his attention to Associate Justice Stanley Mosk of the California Supreme Court." Killion said Mosk "represents the same ideals and principles Arthur Goldberg has espoused."

Goldberg, who had joined the court in 1962 as an appointee of John F. Kennedy, had been persuaded by Lyndon Johnson to resign his seat to replace Adlai Stevenson as the United States' ambassador to the United Nations.

Mosk, Killion wrote, "is a Democrat and has an enviable legal and judicial reputation in the courts. I submit his name for consideration with highest recommendations as to his integrity, loyalty and capabilities. I would appreciate it if you would be so kind to convey these views to the president."

Moyers responded the next day.

"I'll be glad to pass on your recommendation to the President," he said.

Did he? It probably had no impact, for Johnson was determined to put a close friend, Abe Fortas, on the high court and he did just that. Fortas replaced Goldberg in October 1965 and served on the court until May 1969, when he was pressured by the Nixon administration to resign following an exposé in *Life* magazine. In 1968, Johnson had tried to elevate Fortas to be the chief justice following the retirement of Earl Warren, but the move backfired when it was revealed Fortas received $20,000 from a financier under investigation for insider trading. Fortas returned the money, but it did little to stem the calls for his removal.

In August of 1965, Secretary of State Dean Rusk proposed Mosk for one of the United States' seats on the Permanent Court of Arbitration. This would not have required Mosk to leave the bench in California. In a memorandum to the president, Rusk wrote, "the Permanent Court of Arbitration is not a judicial tribunal sitting as a body to hear cases but a list of names from which parties to a dispute may choose arbitrators."

There were two positions available. Rusk proposed Mosk to fill the vacancy created by the expiration of Harold Smith's six-year term. "He is an outstanding jurist and has interested himself in international affairs. Justice Mosk is a Democrat."

Because of the nature of the appointment, a routine FBI investigation was initiated to vet the new candidate. (The other candidate was proposed for a second term.) And this is where Mosk's recent past caught up with him.

The FBI office in San Diego, in a special inquiry on Mosk, referenced a speech by Mosk's 1962 opponent for attorney general, Thomas Coakley.

In the speech, in early September of 1962, Coakley said Mosk had participated in programs sponsored by organizations that were listed as subversive
by the House Un-American Activities Committee. Mosk vehemently
denied the charges the next day. But in the 1960s, even being linked
to such groups as the American Civil Liberties Union or the California
Democratic Council—both of which were accused of being "soft on Communism" in Coakley's phraseology—could tarnish anyone's reputation.

Less than two months after proposing Mosk's name to join the
Permanent Court of Arbitration, the word came back from the White
House. "The answer on this one is a negative," wrote W. Marvin Watson,
the White House Appointments Secretary who was, in essence, Lyndon
Johnson's chief of staff.

In 1966, Mosk's name surfaced as a candidate for the post of assistant
secretary of state for African affairs. G. Mennen "Soapy" Williams was
stepping down from the position to run for the US Senate in Michigan.
He had been the state's governor for twelve years before joining the State
Department in the Kennedy administration.

A note to President Johnson recommended two men for Williams's
position—J. Wayne Fredericks, who was Williams's deputy at the time,
and Stanley Mosk. Johnson picked neither. He went instead with a career
diplomat, Joseph Palmer II. Fredericks held the post until Palmer was
sworn in and then retired from the State Department. Mosk was also
friends with Williams and had gone on a seven-week tour of Africa in
1965 on behalf of the State Department. That is likely why his name appeared on the short list.

In 1967, Mosk underwent a second FBI investigation for what the
agency listed as a presidential appointment. It was likely as a possible
replacement for Earl Warren on the Supreme Court. Warren had recommended Mosk to Johnson as one of a few candidates to take his place.
And Mosk had already let it be known, according to Vice President Hu-
bert Humphrey, that he was interested in the Supreme Court seat of the
soon-to-be-retiring Justice Tom Clark.

In a memo from April 1967, Humphrey wrote Johnson, "In the event
that you have not had this brought to your attention, I wanted you to
know of the interest of California Supreme Court Justice Stanley Mosk
in the forthcoming appointment to the Supreme Court."

Humphrey then quoted verbatim from a supposedly confidential
memo that Mosk had sent to him.

President Johnson's last appointment was Abe Fortas, directly from private practice to the highest court in the land. His next appointment should come from one of the Supreme Courts of the states. And, as indicated in my report, California desperately needs this recognition. In addition, the Supreme Court, to be properly balanced, needs one with experience in and concern for the problems of crime and law enforcement. This I have had in six years as Attorney General of California before going to the state high court. My opinions on the state court do, I believe, indicate respect for our individual constitutional guarantees, but a belief that they can be adapted to a society in which crime is a genuine problem. My attitudes in that regard are somewhat comparable to those of retiring Justice Tom Clark, for whom I have the highest regard.

Humphrey closed by saying he was not pressuring Johnson to appoint Mosk, but that he wanted the president to know of the judge's interest.

Toward the end of his administration, Johnson was playing a game of musical judges for the high court. He tried to move Fortas to take over for Warren, at the same time proposing a less liberal judge, Homer Thornberry, to take Fortas's associate seat. But with an election so close and Fortas's money issues surfacing, neither nomination got any traction.

Clark retired from the court in June 1967. It's not known if Johnson even considered Mosk for the seat, but the president certainly knew of Mosk, as was made clear when he and Pat Brown had chatted back in 1964. Johnson instead made one of the more important moves of his presidency, nominating Thurgood Marshall, who became the first Black to sit on the nation's highest court.

• *10* •

The Masters

Charlie Sifford set some ambitious goals for his professional golf career. He wanted to win a PGA tournament. He won two of them. He wanted to compete in the US Open. He played in twelve of them, his best finish a tie for twenty-first in 1972. He wanted to compete in the PGA Championship. He did so six times, his best finish a tie for thirty-third in 1965. He wanted to be enshrined in the World Golf Hall of Fame. He was, in 2004. And he wanted to compete in the Masters.

"I got four out of five," he told the audience in his acceptance speech upon being inducted into the Hall of Fame. "And I think the Hall of Fame is much greater than the Masters."

The crowd, which included a number of Masters' champions, applauded.

Charlie Sifford never set foot on the hallowed grounds of Augusta National Golf Club. He thought for the longest time that the men who ran the fabled tournament in Georgia discriminated against him because he was Black. But he also got no help from the long list of previous Masters' champions, who could have voted him into the field by way of a special invitation, but never did.

He was still bitter about it in 1992 when he wrote his autobiography.

"To my mind, the Masters was the most redneck tournament in the country, run by people who openly discriminated against blacks. How they could continually deny blacks the opportunity to play in their golf tournament while gaining popularity as the most prestigious tournament in the country is simply unbelievable to me."

In many ways, Sifford's relationship with Augusta National and the Masters mirrored his relationship with the PGA. The one notable difference: the Masters did not have a Caucasian-only rule written into its bylaws.

Sifford was only able to break into the PGA because of the help and legal support of Stanley Mosk. He was not able to crack Augusta National and its rigid adherence to its qualifying criteria, which it was known to bend on occasion. Just not for Blacks.

On merit alone, Charlie Sifford should have been the first Black golfer to play in the Masters, just as he was the first Black golfer to get a PGA membership card and the first Black golfer inducted into the World Golf Hall of Fame. But the host club ran its own show—and still does. It has its own rules for the tournament, it has its own rules officials, its own scorers, and it negotiates rights deal with whomever it pleases. Its membership, which is by invitation only, its income from rights fees, annual dues, and pretty much everything else is secretive. Until 2019, it held only one annual competitive tournament on the course—the Masters itself. Beginning in 2019, it hosted the final round of the Augusta National Women's Amateur.

"You have to understand what the Masters was like," said Gary Player. "It's like a law unto itself. I vividly remember asking at one dinner why Charlie Sifford could not be given an invitation. Given the time (the 1960s) and how young I was (20s) I thought that was pretty courageous. Their response was that they'd be happy to have Charlie, but he would have to qualify like everyone else. You gotta understand you're talking to people who in those days never had a Black man play in the tournament and never had a woman as a member. These guys were pretty stodgy and set in their ways."

The "guys" to which Player referred were the two men who built the Masters from the ground up: Bobby Jones and Clifford Roberts. Together, they ran the tournament from its inception in 1934 until 1971, when Jones died. Roberts continued on in his role as chairman until 1976. Ravaged by cancer, he committed suicide with a self-inflicted gunshot on the banks of one of the ponds at the par-3 course at Augusta National.

Jones had retired from competitive golf in 1930 and teamed with Roberts, then a New York investment banker, to acquire the land. Jones brought in architect Alister MacKenzie to help with the design. The tournament began play in 1934, although it wasn't called "The Masters" until later in the decade. Jones thought that title was too presumptuous.

The tournament quickly gained status as a must-play event and the PGA slotted it into its schedule in early April. It soon became a Major in the vernacular of twentieth-century golf. For the longest time, it insisted that players be assigned caddies—all of whom were Black—by the club. And as the civil rights era exploded in the 1960s, it just as quickly became a symbol of the antebellum South when a successful Black golfer emerged on the PGA Tour and could not wrangle an invitation to participate.

"As the golf tour grew mildly integrated, the Masters stood out like a hooded night rider at a civil rights rally," according to a 1979 article in *Sport* magazine.

Both Roberts and Jones had complicated histories regarding race. An article in *Golf Digest* in 2017 observed that the two men "might not have been any more bigoted than the average American born in 1894 (Roberts) or 1902 (Jones). But neither was a champion of affirmative action." No, they were not.

Outwardly, the two were contrasts in style. Jones was the genial host, beloved by the golf establishment. Roberts was the man who got the trains to run on time. He was feared as much as anything else. He knew who ran the show—he did—but he also was smart enough to let outsiders think Jones was the man in charge.

"Some men think they're God," wrote Frank Deford, the celebrated *Sports Illustrated* journalist. "In golf, at least, Mr. Roberts was sure he was God, only he had to go around telling everyone that Bobby Jones was God. It must have worn on him. No wonder he spoke so hesitantly."

Roberts grew up poor in Iowa before striking it rich as an oil and gas speculator. In the late 1920s, he became a partner in Reynolds & Company and, a few years later, cofounded Augusta National with Jones. He ruled Augusta like his own private fiefdom. The word *micromanager* only begins to describe Roberts's style. At Augusta National, spectators were called patrons. There was no rough. It was the "first cut" or the "second cut." Any mention of money or purses was strictly verboten. He banished Jack Whittaker from CBS broadcasts for a number of years when Whittaker rightly referred to an onrushing crowd approaching the eighteenth green as "a mob."

As long as Roberts and Jones ran the Masters, Sifford felt, there was no way that he, Sifford, would ever tee it up at Augusta National. "Throughout the fifties and sixties, the Masters kept its racial lines clearly defined between caddies and players," Sifford said. He attributed that philosophy to Roberts, whom he called "the autocratic chairman" of the tournament.

In 1972, Roberts sat down for an oral history interview conducted at Columbia University for what the university called its Eisenhower administration project. Roberts and Eisenhower were close friends; the thirty-fourth president of the United States joined Augusta National, visited the course more than fifty times, and counted Roberts as a trusted advisor. A special cabin built for him at the course while he was president, which the Secret Service helped design, still stands and is known as the Eisenhower Cabin.

The oral history is more than six hundred pages, but it offers no insights into how Roberts ran the Masters or his thoughts on the course or the club. It did, however, contain several passages in which Roberts reflected on race relations in the South in the 1950s and 1960s. He was asked about Eisenhower's 1957 decision to federalize the Arkansas National Guard to enforce a court order desegregating Little Rock Central High School. He said the actions of the governor, Orval Faubus, gave Eisenhower no choice. Faubus had called in the National Guard to prevent nine Black students from enrolling, claiming their attendance would lead to violence.

"I don't think the people in this part of the country," Roberts said, referring to New York, "have any realization as to the tremendous, the overwhelming percentage of the Southern white people that condemned Ike for his action. It was just like resuming the Civil War. And it was so bad that there was no possible way of discussing the matter in a sane fashion with the Southern white people at that point, because those who were ordinarily quite broad-minded and reasonable just couldn't be reasoned with at all on the subject of integration. To them, it meant just one thing in the end—mixed marriages."

Asked if the club and its members felt that way, Roberts said, "I'm talking about the members of Augusta National who lived in Augusta, and members of Augusta National who lived in Atlanta and various other Southern states. And many friends of mine that had no connection to Augusta, [but] people I knew in a business way, in banking, in the securities business, and people, officers of corporations, Southerners, running southern corporations."

While Augusta kept its membership secret, the club from its outset aspired to be a national one, with members from across the country who could only get through the front door if invited to join. More often than not, that included the elite of the business world. While Jones preferred friends and sons of friends as potential members, Roberts preferred captains of industry.

"(These were) very rational people about most any other subject in the world," Roberts said. "But when it came to this thing, almost to a man, they just said, 'integration means one thing. It means mixed marriages.' And in view of what's happened since, I don't mind admitting to you that those people were a lot more right about it than I thought they were at the time."

In that same interview, Roberts objected to a statement from Republican vice presidential nominee Henry Cabot Lodge suggesting that if Richard Nixon was elected president in 1960, there should be a Black member of his cabinet. It would, he said, cost the Republican Party some votes "because the country isn't ready for a black man in the cabinet by any matter of means at this point." He was probably right. John F. Kennedy did not appoint a Black member to his cabinet. It wasn't until 1966 that Lyndon Johnson appointed the first Black to a cabinet position, naming Robert C. Weaver as secretary of Housing and Urban Development.

When Roberts mentioned Augusta National members living in Atlanta, that could well have been a reference to his longtime partner. Unlike Roberts, Bobby Jones was a child of privilege who grew up in Atlanta, playing golf at segregated golf clubs like East Lake. But he was revered in the sport, was given two ticker-tape parades in New York City, and insisted time and again that he would welcome Charlie Sifford to Augusta if Sifford simply qualified under the tournament's guidelines. That was the black and white as Jones saw it—written clearly and concisely for all to see.

After getting spanked by *Los Angeles Times* columnist Jim Murray in 1969 for not inviting Sifford, a column that included a remark from Sifford that Jones had sent him a threatening letter, Jones responded privately to Murray. As recounted in Ron Rapaport's biography, *The Immortal Bobby*, Jones included a copy of the letter he sent Sifford, which was not threatening in the least. But it was condescending.

"Since I do not believe that you uttered any belligerent threats, I want to ask you if it will not be better in the future if you point out that you have seen no mention of color or race in the Masters' tournament qualifications," Jones wrote to Sifford. "And that you have every reason to believe that you will be invited whenever you fulfill one of these qualifications. Personally, I see no advantage either to you or the club to encourage newspaper reports of this nature."

This was the Lou Strong press release from 1961 all over again. Strong, the PGA president, had reiterated that Sifford was not being excluded from the 1962 championship because of his race, but because he hadn't qualified under the organization's guidelines. (Never mind that Sifford couldn't have met the guidelines because he couldn't gain entry to several PGA tournaments because of his race.) Here was Jones saying the exact same thing.

And what were those criteria to be allowed to make the drive down Magnolia Lane? In the late 1960s, when Murray was bashing Augusta National, there were fourteen ways a player could guarantee himself a spot in the Masters field. It should be noted that the Masters changed its admission policies over the years, but strictly enforced them when they were in effect.

The first entry point was for Masters champions. They received lifetime invitations. As Sifford had never been invited, it would be difficult for him to win the tournament. He could have gotten in by winning the US Open or finishing in the top sixteen of the previous year's US Open. As we saw in 1959 and again in 1964, Sifford almost did that. The US and British Amateur champions were automatically included. Sifford was neither of those and couldn't be. The British Open champion was included. Sifford never played in the tournament due to obvious reasons (cost, travel, time). A PGA Championship victory would have done it, except that Sifford didn't even compete in one of those until 1965. Had he finished in the top eight of the previous year's PGA Championship, he would have qualified. Members of the Ryder Cup team were included, too. As author Steve Eubanks noted, "in 1969, that was an opportunity as available for a deserving black man as being asked to accompany Neil Armstrong on a moon walk."

There were spots held for members of the Walker Cup and World Amateur teams "which, for blacks, made the moon walk look easy," Eubanks wrote. And Sifford was a professional. The Masters in the late 1960s offered spots to the *eight* quarterfinalists of the previous year's US Amateur. And Sifford could have gotten in by being among the tour's top sixteen money winners from the date of the last Masters to the beginning of the next one.

So, realistically, Sifford could have qualified for the Masters by winning the US Open or the PGA or being among the top finishers in those tournaments. There was one other way Sifford could have gotten in. One player could be selected by a vote of the Masters champions. In the 1960s, that included people like Jack Nicklaus, Gary Player, Arnold Palmer, Bob Goalby, Gay Brewer, and George Archer. Champions from the 1950s such as Ben Hogan, Sam Snead, Jimmy Demaret, and Jackie Burke could also vote.

In 2022, neither Player nor Nicklaus—the two most important champions of the 1960s who were still alive—remember the champions ever voting to invite a golfer to participate.

"I don't ever recall voting for somebody to play," Nicklaus said in an interview. "I never recall that anyone's name was ever brought up to play."

Player, who said he advocated for Sifford to be invited, also does not recall any vote from the champions.

"That's quite interesting. I don't remember us voting someone in. I mentioned Charlie Sifford a number of times, but I don't remember us voting. It's quite sad to think they didn't have Black players in the tournament," Player said.

But there *was* voting. Author David Owen, who wrote a book about the club and the tournament and was under contract to Augusta National, was given access to some of the voting. He noted that before those fourteen qualification categories were spelled out, previous criteria allowed former US Open winners, who enjoyed lifetime invitations until 1963, to pick a participant who otherwise did not qualify. That would have included many of the same men who later voted as Masters' champions. They could have voted in Charlie Sifford. They did not.

In 1969, the year Sifford won the Los Angeles Open, he received one vote from the Masters' champions, that of 1959 winner Art Wall Jr. Both Sifford and Lee Elder were on the ballot to be invited to the Masters, but a plurality of the previous champions voted for Bob Murphy. Chi Chi Rodriguez was also on that ballot and received a vote from Goalby.

Asked about Wall's vote for Sifford in 1969, Nicklaus said, "News to me." In 1973, Black journalist Maggie Hathaway from Los Angeles broached similar questions to Nicklaus.

"Don't you think that the pros who have won the Masters should vote your one invitation to be sent to Charles Sifford? Or Pete Brown?"

Nicklaus replied, "I shot my way in, and I am sure that most of the pros feel the same way."

Hathaway shot back, "what about the pros who did accept your invitation in the past decade?"

Nicklaus explained that the majority rules in those votes.

The vote of the Masters' champions to invite a player ended when the tournament adopted new qualifications in 1972. Under the new rules, anyone who had won an official PGA tournament in the previous year would receive an invitation. It was not applied retroactively, so it had no impact on Charlie Sifford. The new rules went into effect the year after Bobby Jones died.

But for all the list of qualifications to get into the Masters, there was one major difference between it and the PGA's ongoing refusal to admit Sifford as one of its members. The Masters was an invitational tournament. Yes, one got invited by virtue of meeting its qualification criteria. But a lot of other players got invitations for any number of reasons. At any time in the 1960s, or even in the 1950s when Sifford was dominating the UGA, the Masters could have recognized his achievements and extended an invitation. It did not.

Some of the players it did invite in the 1960s included Tomoo Ishii, Chen Ching-Po, Leopoldo Ruiz, Cobie Legrange, and Raul Travieso. They had not met any of the qualification criteria. Winning four amateur titles in Argentina was enough to get Travieso into the tournament.

"The Augusta tournament has a complicated formula for selecting its field," Murray wrote in 1969. "If you come from Formosa, it's easy to get in. If you come from a cotton patch in Carolina, it's impossible."

Sifford counted Nicklaus, Palmer, and Player as friends, though the first two never publicly said a word on his behalf. Sifford said he doubted it would have mattered had they done so, but he addressed this issue in his book.

> The questions are, did any of these guys ever exert any influence to get you into tournaments, or take you under their wing, or make that road any easier for you? Did they ever come out publicly on behalf of blacks playing the game in general, and for you to get a fair share?
>
> My feeling is this: No. I don't think Jack Nicklaus or Arnold Palmer ever tried to change anything for me, and I wouldn't have wanted them to. I am not someone who goes begging for help or a shoulder to cry on. . . . It's not their job. Those guys are golfers—the best in the world—but they're not politicians or civil rights activists or newspaper columnists. It's not their job to stump for the black man to get into the game, any more than it's their job to pop off about the state of the economy or the proliferation of nuclear weapons.

Well, yes and no. Nicklaus certainly didn't hesitate to endorse Donald Trump in 2020, saying, "His love of America and its citizens, and putting his country first, has come through loud and clear." That was a month before the 2020 election. Player accepted the Presidential Medal of Freedom from Trump the day after the January 6 riots at the US Capitol. When white golfers descended on apartheid South Africa to play in a rich tournament in 1987, Arthur Ashe told Scott Ostler of the *Los Angeles Times*, "Golfers all have their heads in the sand, all of 'em. They are the most apolitical bunch of athletes I know. They're all 5-11, blond, went to Oklahoma; they're all right-wing Republicans. As a group, they don't give a damn."

And that collective mindset as much as anything may have led to Charlie Sifford getting snubbed by the Masters' champions. As Jack Nicklaus said, the majority rules. And Clifford Roberts and Bobby Jones did nothing but stand by those rules (*eight players from the US Amateur?*) to defend the indefensible.

In 1973, with Lee Elder having taken over as the best Black player in the game, there still had been no invitation from Augusta to him—or any other Black player. Even with the new criteria, Elder came up short. Eighteen members of the US House of Representatives sent a telegram to Roberts demanding that the Masters invite a Black player. You can imagine how that went over in august Augusta. Roberts said he was a little surprised "as well as being flattered that eighteen congressmen would be able to take time out from trying to solve the nation's problems to help us operate a golf tournament."

One of Roberts's successors, Hootie Johnson, made a similar remark when Augusta was getting blowback in the early 2000s for having no women members. (It had admitted its first Black in 1990, plucking an executive from Gannett, Ron Townsend.) When someone mentioned to Johnson that Tiger Woods was in favor of admitting women to Augusta, Johnson said that he wouldn't begin to tell Woods how to play golf so Woods shouldn't tell him how to run his golf club. End of story. A decade later, Augusta admitted its first women members, Darla Moore, a former business colleague of Johnson, and former secretary of state Condoleezza Rice.

Sifford always knew he would have Masters weekend free on his schedule and so, in 1974, his final year on tour, the Cleveland chapter of the National Negro Golf Association held a testimonial dinner in his honor. It was during the Saturday of Masters' weekend and the association sent out invitations to golfers, celebrities, and politicos around the country. The point was not hard to miss.

"Mr. Sifford should not be in Cleveland this week," said Clarence Rogers, a Cleveland attorney who helped organize the testimonial. "He should be in Augusta. We purposely picked this particular weekend to honor him because it happens to be the weekend of the Masters. We knew he would be available."

Rogers flooded the zone with invitations to PGA players whom he knew would be in Augusta that weekend and unable to attend. Many players responded. One, Bruce Devlin, mentioned he'd be unable to attend because of the Masters. Others simply framed their responses to congratulate Sifford as a worthy honoree.

Tom Weiskopf, who tied for second in the 1974 Masters, weighed in from Columbus, Ohio, that he was "extremely disappointed" that he couldn't attend the testimonial. Johnny Miller, the defending US Open champion, who tied for fifteenth, checked in with a hand-written note saying Sifford was "a very good man and has done much for the Negro golf situation." He underlined the word "good."

Chi Chi Rodriguez, who tied for twentieth, enclosed a check for $125 to pay for ten tickets to be given to ten Black caddies "so they can see what a great person you are honoring."

Rodriguez wrote, "Charlie was always kind to me from the first day I came on tour. The only sad thing about Charlie's career is that no one really will ever know how great he could have been had he had a chance to play on the PGA Tour when he was in his prime and at his best. Charlie is to golf what Jackie Robinson was to baseball."

The Robinson comparison always irked Sifford. It was based solely on the fact that fourteen years after Robinson integrated major league baseball, Sifford was the man who broke down the PGA's "obnoxious restriction." Sifford counted Robinson as a friend and heeded Robinson's advice to be strong and stay committed.

But Sifford also noted that Robinson didn't have to do it by himself. Robinson had a support staff in place in the Dodgers' front office. Robinson had support from many (though not all) of his teammates.

More important to Sifford, his emergence as the game's first Black regular PGA Tour player did not open the floodgates for more Blacks. Robinson's did, especially in the National League, where, in the 1950s, five Black players—Roy Campanella, Willie Mays, Don Newcombe, Hank Aaron, and Ernie Banks—would win Most Valuable Player awards. A Black player was the National League's MVP from 1953 to 1959. The American League's first Black MVP was the Yankees' Elston Howard—in 1963.

"If I was the Jackie Robinson of golf, I sure didn't do a very good job of it," Sifford said, referring to the lack of Black golfers who followed him. "I would be proud to be compared to Jackie in almost anything, but not in the lie that says I'm the same symbol of freedom and racial equality in my sport that he was in his."

There was no mad rush from the UGA to the PGA. Lee Elder had dominated the UGA tour in the 1960s and he was the proverbial next-in-line. Pete Brown won a tournament in 1970. After Elder integrated the Masters, players such as Calvin Peete, Jim Dent, and Jim Thorpe emerged, but no one really made a lasting impact on the tour until Tiger Woods. And while Woods's presence resulted in exploding purses and boffo television ratings, it did not result in a new generation of Black golfers. It wasn't until 2011 that former Stanford star Joseph Bramlett became the first Black player to join the tour since Woods in 1996. Four years later, Harold Varner III became the first Black to qualify for the tour going through the PGA's feeder tour. In 2018, Cameron Champ became the first Black player since Woods to win a PGA Tour event and the seventh overall, joining Brown, Sifford, Elder, Peete, Thorpe, and Woods. Varner became the eighth with a victory in 2022.

There were only a few Black players on the PGA Tour in the 2020s. The 2022 Masters achieved a milestone of sorts in that it had a record number of Black players in the field—three. The same trio, Woods, Champ, and Varner, played again in 2023. There were no Black players in the 2023 US Open.

Sifford diplomatically declined to do any Masters-bashing at the Cleveland testimonial. He was fifty-one years old, and he understood he would never be invited to play in the tournament.

"I am not a militant," he said. "I have proven myself to be a pro golfer. I don't want anyone to think I have anything against the Masters. I feel like I have qualified to play in the Masters. I have won two tournaments. If they invited me now, though, I don't know if it would do any good. I'm spotting these kids fifteen years. If I can't win the damn Masters, I don't want to play in it."

The sponsor of the testimonial would soon play another important role in Sifford's life, helping him secure a job at Sleepy Hollow Country Club in suburban Cleveland. That is where Sifford moved his family from Los Angeles in 1974. With his PGA career over and with the Seniors Tour still a few years away, he was in limbo and needed a job. The only one he could find was at Sleepy Hollow.

The April 1974 testimonial included letters of regret from President Richard Nixon, Vice President Gerald Ford, and California Governor Ronald Reagan. But, of all the letters that came in supporting Sifford, the one that probably summed up his career the best came from Bill Beck, who was the president of the Golf Writers Association of America. Beck referenced a 1954 women's tournament in which Babe Didrikson Zaharias's husband moved a stone edifice that was in his wife's way. It gave her a clear shot to the green.

"I remember thinking," Beck wrote, "how simple! Everybody else played around it. Somehow, I have linked this in my mind with you, Charlie. In 1954 and the years before and after, you removed a man-made obstruction a million times bigger that everybody else had been playing around. I refer, of course, to prejudice.

"It rarely falls within the power of any man to improve a game he loves. But it fell within yours and you were equal to the opportunity."

Bakke, Bird, a Senior Moment, and an Elusive Buick

Charlie Sifford couldn't get into the Masters. Allan Bakke couldn't get into medical school in California. Neither man qualified for admission under the guidelines of the respective institutions. Sifford had no legal recourse to get Augusta National to change its ways. Allan Bakke did—and, like Sifford had when he fought the PGA, he found a receptive voice in Stanley Mosk.

Mosk's civil rights legacy will be forever linked to *Regents of the University of California v. Bakke*, a case that began in California in 1974 and ended in Washington, D.C., in 1978 when the US Supreme Court declared affirmative action programs in college admissions constitutional as long as they did not rely on racial quotas.

The debate about affirmative action programs was bound to be contentious, compelling Americans to confront the legacy of slavery and the scourge of racism that had outlived that "peculiar institution." Defenders and opponents of policies designed to give special consideration in education and employment to disadvantaged groups do not neatly fall into categories of "liberal" or "conservative." People of both political persuasions might well agree on the need for action to remedy past discrimination. The devil in dealing with such divisive social issues is always in the details.

The legal challenge to the use of affirmative action in university admissions began after Allan Bakke, a thirty-five-year-old white man, was twice rejected for admission to the medical school at the University of California at Davis. He argued that he was denied a seat because sixteen places in the one-hundred-person class were reserved for minority students, some of whom had weaker academic records and test scores than he had. That quota system, he argued, violated the Equal Protection Clause of the Fourteenth Amendment and Title VI of the Civil Rights Act of 1964, which prohibited institutions that receive federal funds from discriminating on the basis of race. Bakke sought an end to the minority program and immediate admission to the medical school.

For its part, the university argued that its special admission program was necessary to remedy past discrimination against minorities, to ensure diversity in its student body, and to provide a more equal playing field for minority applicants going forward.

Bakke's case was heard by Yolo County Superior Court Judge F. Leslie Manker, who ruled that the minority program was impermissible because "no race or ethnic group should ever be granted special privileges or immunities not given to every other race." He was unconvinced, however, that Bakke's rejection by the medical school was attributable to the existence of that program—in his mid-thirties, Bakke was older than the usual candidate—and Manker declined to order his admission to Davis.

Bakke appealed, and the university sought and gained direct review before the California Supreme Court, then one of the most liberal in the country. Dozens of amicus briefs addressed the issue of racial equality, pitting proponents of color-blind admissions policies in the name of fairness against advocates for affirmative action as a means of redressing the history of discrimination that had long disadvantaged minority applicants.

In a 6–1 ruling, the California Supreme Court on September 16, 1976, declared that the minority admissions program at Davis was unconstitutional. Writing for the majority, Justice Mosk praised as commendable the goal of creating a more racially diverse class of medical students, but he rejected the means Davis had chosen to achieve it. Mosk suggested the state expand the number of medical schools, providing greater opportunity for minority applicants.

"To uphold the University would call for the sacrifice of principle for the sake of dubious expediency and would represent a retreat in the struggle to assure that each man and woman shall be judged on the basis of individual merit alone, a struggle which has only lately achieved success in removing legal barriers to racial equality," Mosk wrote.

Mosk noted that, in the not-so-distant past, quotas had been a pernicious tool used to limit the number of racial and religious minorities admitted to prestigious universities, not to expand their opportunity to matriculate.

The Ivy League was a notorious example of using quotas to restrict access to bastions of white Anglo-Saxon privilege. Panic set in at Harvard, for example, when the percentage of Jewish students had tripled to 21 percent of the freshman class in 1922 from about 7 percent in 1900. Harvard's President A. Lawrence Lowell proposed a quota on the number of Jews admitted. He argued that limiting Jewish students to 15 percent would stem the anti-Semitism that was rife on campus, but his transparent goal was the preservation of Harvard's traditional WASP culture.

California Supreme Court Justice Matthew Tobriner, in the lone dissent in the Bakke case, criticized his colleagues for punishing the university for a praiseworthy effort to address the malignant effects of racial bigotry and he mocked Mosk's suggestion that the state build more medical schools as an alternative to affirmative action. "It is a cruel hoax to deny minorities participation in the medical profession on the basis of such fanciful speculation," Tobriner wrote. "Two centuries of slavery and racial discrimination have left our nation an awful legacy, a largely separated society in which wealth, educational resources, employment opportunities—indeed all of society's benefits—remain largely the preserve of the white-Anglo majority."

Mosk took no issue with Tobriner's analysis of the economic and social costs of de facto segregation, but adopting racial preferences was, in his view, a short-sighted solution. "The principle that the Constitution sanctions discrimination against a race—any race—is a dangerous concept fraught with potential for misuse in situations which involve far less laudable objectives than are manifest in the present case," Mosk wrote.

Years later, reflecting on the Bakke case, Mosk said he would not change anything in the opinion he wrote, "but I do have a gnawing sympathy for those who were disadvantaged because of race or color or economics, so that they cannot compete on a basis of equality with others. I've always seen the long-range solution to be roughly this: that those who have a disadvantage of any kind, whether it's race or economics or physical, ought to be given some special treatment during their early days of education in the public schools, so that when the competition begins later on for college admission, for professional school admission, or employment, that they will be able to compete on a basis of equality. But I concede that it's going to take some special training for many of these people in the early days of public schools, and I don't think we're doing that today."

Many liberals were aghast at the ruling in general and at Mosk in particular. Demonstrators gathered beneath his office window to denounce him. Placard-carrying protesters rallied to demand a reversal of the decision. He was heckled on the street.

"They really shouldn't have been surprised because the position he took, in which he deeply believed, sprang from his view of equal protection and his personal experience of being Jewish," said Peter Belton, the longtime legal assistant to Mosk at the California Supreme Court. "Jewish people in America and other countries had long suffered from quotas. It was an article of faith in Jewish social philosophy that these kinds of quotas were unfair and unwise, so it wasn't a big stretch for him."

B'nai B'rith would file an amicus brief in support of Bakke when the case went to the US Supreme Court.

The animosity toward Mosk peaked at the law school graduation ceremonies at the University of California at Davis, where he was the invited commencement speaker. When he rose to address the crowd, a few dozen of the 139 graduates, and about 150 guests, walked out. "Judges cannot be intimidated," the unflustered jurist told the members of the audience who remained. "Lawsuits are won and lost in the courtrooms, not in the streets."

Two years later, in a 5–4 decision on June 28, 1978, the US Supreme Court agreed with Mosk on two of the three main points he had made in his California Supreme Court ruling: the use of racial quotas in university admissions was unconstitutional, and Allan Bakke should be admitted to the medical school at Davis. The high court parted ways with Mosk in ruling that the use of racial preferences in admissions was sometimes permissible as long as it was only one of many factors being used to select an incoming class.

In his opinion, Justice Lewis F. Powell echoed Mosk when he wrote that the rigid use of racial quotas as applied by the school in the Bakke case violated the Equal Protection Clause of the Fourteenth Amendment. The fact that Blacks had been discriminated against historically was irrelevant, he wrote, because the use of racial quotas, is always "odious to a free people whose institutions are founded upon the doctrine of equality."

In an interview for an oral history project twenty years after his decision in Bakke, Mosk reflected on the ire directed at him in 1976. "Of course, the Bakke opinion is not without controversy. There are those who believe that there should be racial quotas. There are those who think that race should be a factor in determining college admissions. I respect those who have that point of view, but I don't share it," he said.

"I firmly believe that people should be judged solely on merit, objective merit, rather than their race or their color. So, it seemed to me that it was improper to reject Bakke in favor of persons who had less objective qualifications merely because of their racial complexion."

Mosk never actually met Allan Bakke, but the most famous litigant of his Supreme Court career did send him a telegram congratulating him on his twenty-fifth anniversary on the court. Bakke sent the telegram from Rochester, Minnesota, where he was on the medical staff of the Mayo Clinic. "For four years, I was scared to death that Bakke would flunk out of medical school and make our opinion look bad," Mosk recalled years later, noting that, in fact, Bakke had graduated with honors.

The same year that the United States Supreme Court ruled on the Bakke case, Mosk penned a decision that, once again, reflected his utter distaste for any kind of racial discrimination. It dealt with the method in which lawyers could summarily dismiss prospective jurors due to race in what is known as a peremptory challenge. The California case was *People v. Wheeler.*

Two convicted murderers, James Wheeler and Robert Willis, appealed to the California Supreme Court. They had robbed a grocery store owner of $6,000 and fatally wounded the store owner, Amaury Cedeno. The assailant ran from the store and jumped into a waiting car, which immediately drove away. A witness wrote down the license plate but did not see the driver.

In the 5–2 decision, authored by Mosk (with Tobriner concurring), the jurist wasted no time in zeroing in on what he saw as the most critical part of the trial. It wasn't the question over the identification of the two men or which one may have been driving the getaway car. It was something far more harmful in Mosk's eyes.

"We begin with a claim of error arising at the very outset of the trial and infecting the entire remainder of the proceedings," Mosk wrote. "Defendants are both black; the man they are accused of murdering is white." Mosk then noted that a number of Blacks were called from the jury pool and questioned. "Yet the prosecutor proceeded to strike each and every black by means of peremptory challenges and the jury that finally convicted these defendants was all white."

At one point in jury selection, both the prosecution and defense had agreed on three Blacks to serve. Then the prosecutor did an about-face and used peremptory challenges on all three. Defense attorney Edward Gritz rose to say, "It is obvious to me that there will be no blacks on this jury" and moved for a mistrial. "It is obvious to me that these defendants cannot get a jury of their peers." The mistrial motion was denied. Jury selection continued.

The prosecution had relied on a 1965 United States Supreme Court decision, *Swain v. Alabama*, in which five justices saw nothing amiss in an all-white jury convicting a Black man of rape and murder after six prospective Black jurors had been dismissed by the use of peremptory challenges. Mosk wrote, "The people nevertheless contend that we are compelled to allow this pernicious practice to continue in our courts."

As he often preferred to do, Mosk cited the constitution of the State of California in handing down the decision, saying it superseded *Swain*. "We conclude that the use of peremptory challenges to remove prospective jurors on the sole ground of group bias violates the right to trial by a jury drawn from a representative cross-section of the community. . . . The rule of *Swain v. Alabama* is not to be followed in our courts and the cases applying it are disapproved to that extent." As he later put it, "we were brutally frank about that."

As had been the case in *Wright v. Drye*, Mosk was ahead of the curve on this issue. It was not until 1986, eight years after *People v. Wheeler*, that the United States Supreme Court ruled that a prosecutor's use of peremptory challenges cannot be used to exclude potential jurors based solely on race. The decision was 7–2 with the first Black on the court, Thurgood Marshall, and the first woman on the court, Sandra Day O'Connor, siding with the majority.

"So that's an example," Mosk said later, "of how a state law can take the lead in protecting individual rights."

Mosk had been on the California Supreme Court for thirteen years when, in 1977, Donald Wright, the chief justice, retired. The expectation in legal circles was that Governor Jerry Brown would elevate Mosk to lead the court. Despite the controversy about the Bakke case, Mosk's otherwise reliably liberal voice made him the seemingly obvious choice for the state's progressive Democratic governor.

Brown, however, had other plans. He selected for chief justice Rose Elizabeth Bird, a forty-year-old lawyer then serving as his Agriculture Secretary, the first woman in any California governor's cabinet. Bird would also be the first woman to serve on the state's highest court, let alone lead it. An unpopular choice among her soon-to-be-colleagues because of her lack of judicial experience, Bird nonetheless won the required endorsement of the Commission on Judicial Appointments by a 2–1 vote.

"There was of course considerable surprise at the appointment. Frankly a lot of people expected Justice Mosk to be elevated to that position," Peter Belton, Mosk's legal assistant, recalled years later. "Everyone knew that he had major experience in administering a large agency, because he was the attorney general for six years and that is a big agency, and the job of chief justice does require administrative skills.

"Judge Mosk seemed to have everything that would fit the bill, and so we were all expecting him to be named. When he was not, it was a double surprise: first that it wasn't Justice Mosk and second, that it was someone that no one frankly had ever heard of."

Rose Bird was the daughter of chicken ranchers in Arizona. Encouraged by her mother to pursue education, Bird received a scholarship to Long Island University, graduating magna cum laude. In 1965, she graduated from the Boalt Hall School of Law at the University of California, Berkeley with academic distinction. Bird was the first female clerk for the Nevada Supreme Court and the first woman hired as a lawyer in the Santa Clara County Public Defender's office. She had volunteered in Brown's gubernatorial campaign and was part of his transition team when he named her to be the first non-farmer to lead the California Department of Food and Agriculture, the state's largest government agency.

She won no friends in agri-business when she outlawed the short hoe, a tool that caused serious back injuries, and when she supported the Agriculture Labor Relations Act, guaranteeing farm workers the right to organize and negotiate labor contracts. Jerry Brown was like-minded.

Shy by temperament, Bird had trouble fitting into a courthouse atmosphere described as "an old boys' club" by Belton. Mosk found her "aloof" because she kept her office door closed and, along with his colleagues, he bristled at her requirement that the justices make an appointment with her secretary if they wanted to discuss a case or court matters. They objected, as well, to the presence of her assistant at those meetings, taking notes.

"The biggest mistake Pat Brown ever made was not making (his son) Jerry appoint Stanley as chief justice instead of Rose Bird," said Mosk's second wife, Susan. "Stanley felt that way. Jerry Brown used to stay at our house and he and Stanley were very, very close until Jerry appointed Rose Bird. That was the end of that."

Bird first faced the voters in a 1978 retention election. Supreme Court justices must stand for reconfirmation in the first statewide election if they have replaced a justice who has retired or died. There is no opposition. It's an up-or-down vote. You stay on the bench, or you pack your bags. Bird barely survived, getting only 52 percent of the vote.

Bird, Mosk said, was "a very bright, intelligent, competent woman, but that does not necessarily equip her to be administrative and legal head of the entire judiciary of California." Mosk recalled telling her as much: "One of the first days that she was on the court, I was talking with her, and I remember vividly what I said. I said, 'I certainly cannot blame you for being here, but I blame Jerry Brown for putting you here.' She never let me forget that statement."

Mosk had personal reasons for resenting his new boss. He had heard from a state senator, who was also a friend, that Brown had been telling lawmakers privately: "I could never appoint Justice Mosk because of the Bakke case." Brown denied it, but Richard Mosk, the judge's son, said his father never hid his disappointment at being passed over.

"My father was a little bitter about the appointment, I think. I don't know if 'bitter' is the right word, but he was quite angry at Jerry for this," Richard Mosk said. "He also felt that Jerry had used the concept of affirmative action for the bench, which might be good policy in theory, to appoint judges who were not qualified, and that he . . . damaged the bench in the name of affirmative action or diversity."

If Stanley Mosk thought that Brown had named unqualified judges to the bench to court favor with women and minorities, he never said so publicly. In fact, he said quite the opposite, even about Bird. He called Wiley Manuel, the first Black jurist on the California Supreme Court, who was appointed by Brown at the same time as Bird, an "outstanding" jurist and he said Bird "would have made a fine judge or justice on any court." Just not sitting in the chief's seat that he thought more properly should have been reserved for him.

According to Belton, "Philosophically, she (Bird) and Judge Mosk had a lot in common." They were both firm in their personal opposition to capital punishment, for instance, an issue that would prove to be Bird's undoing after she had spent nearly a decade as chief justice.

Unlike Mosk, who deferred to state law and upheld the death penalty in cases deemed to warrant it, Bird never signed off on a single death penalty case. At the time, 80 percent of Californians supported capital punishment. More than sixty death penalty cases came before the court during her tenure as chief justice; she voted to overturn all of them.

A coalition of pro-business and anti-tax groups, eager to dilute the liberal majority on the state Supreme Court, targeted Bird for recall during the 1986 retention elections with an eye toward Republican Governor George Deukmejian naming a more conservative replacement. The groups raised more than $5.5 million, much of it in direct mailings. For good measure, the Bird opponents also took aim at two of her colleagues, Justices Joseph Grodin and Cruz Reynoso.

A well-funded, highly emotional television ad campaign successfully characterized Bird as "soft on crime" and more sympathetic to murderers than to their victims when, in fact, her deep-pocketed detractors were more concerned with what they viewed as her hostility to agri-business and the overall liberal sway on the court. The voters removed all three judges, Bird by a decisive 2-to-1 margin. It was the first time in state history that a Supreme Court chief justice had been removed via the retention process.

New York Times columnist Tom Wicker called the vote to remove Bird "a naked power grab" and said Bird's opposition to the death penalty "is only a trumped-up excuse for the anti-Bird campaign. The actual purpose is clearly to put a conservative majority on the California Supreme Court."

Mosk had also been up for retention in 1986 but easily prevailed. Why had the Republicans not sought to purge the great liberal jurist in addition to the other three?

Mosk attributed his survival to "a little political acumen" on his part. "First of all, I didn't announce my intention [to run for a new term] until the very last moment. By then the campaign against the other three had been developed. There was a feeling that I would not run (he was seventy-four at the time), and therefore they weren't going to waste their time opposing me. Then, I publicly announced I would not accept any campaign contributions and that my total expenditure would be twenty-two cents for a stamp to mail my petition to Sacramento. That got a lot of favorable editorial attention."

It did indeed. Friends of Mosk mailed him twenty-two-cent stamps to encourage him to continue on the court. Years later, the chief justice of the court, Ronald George, tweaked Mosk over the stamp anecdote in a ceremony naming a state building after the late jurist.

"He waited so long that when he finally decided to run, he feared his paperwork would not make it to Sacramento in time. So the populist plan for a 22-cent stamp went by the wayside. Stanley's papers were delivered by overnight mail at a cost of $10.25."

Mosk was dismayed by the loss of his colleagues, even Bird, arguing that judges should only be removed for incompetence or incapacity. "To vote against a judge because you disagree with an opinion of him or her, I think, is not justified," he said. "Of course, when Rose Bird was taken down, it was because of her alleged attitude on the death penalty. But it's doubly unfortunate because Joe Grodin and Cruz Reynoso were defeated at the same time; both of them were splendid judges." Deukmejian nominated Malcolm Lucas, a former law partner of his, to be chief justice.

Mosk would never become chief justice of the California Supreme Court, though he would earn the title of its longest-serving associate justice. On reflection, he said, he was not sure he would have been a great fit as chief justice. "I don't think I would have liked it, because of the requirement that you be effective as an administrator. I had to do a certain amount of that when I was attorney general, and frankly, I don't think I'm really equipped to decide who can work with whom, and if they don't get along, how to adjust that. So, I was really happy that I no longer had to do that when I left the attorney general's office and became an associate justice."

Rose Bird never recovered from the public humiliation of the 1986 retention defeat. She was said to have gone into hiding, becoming a recluse. A decade after her ouster, she was photocopying documents as a volunteer for a poverty law center in East Palo Alto. She did that for months before the lawyers at the center got tipped off that this was Rose Bird, the first female Supreme Court justice in California history. She had given her name when she volunteered, but no one connected the dots.

By then she was no longer even practicing law. She couldn't attract clients because of the lasting image of her as a coddler of murderers. She tended to her ill mother in Palo Alto and, in 1996, surfaced briefly to write an opinion piece for the local newspaper.

"If you have never experienced life under a microscope, you need to understand that those who live a public life are no longer seen as real persons—human beings. Rather, they are objects to be examined, manipulated, ridiculed and sometimes even hated," she wrote.

Rose Bird died in 1999 from complications of breast cancer. She was sixty-three.

Charlie Sifford knew quite a bit about living life under a microscope. He spent the latter part of the 1970s fighting what he perceived to be discrimination all over again. Here he was, just coming off a PGA career that had started way too late. Now, a new tour was beckoning, one where Sifford could finally play against players the same age on a regular basis. He only wished it were so.

Sifford's last year on the PGA Tour, 1974, was predictably uneventful. He finished one-hundredth on the money list and his best finish was a tie for ninth in the Sahara Invitational. He had had one more tournament victory three years earlier at the $30,000 Sea Pines Open in November 1971.

Sea Pines was being staged as a satellite event with the regular tour competing in the $110,000 Heritage Golf Classic. Both events were held on Hilton Head Island in South Carolina, less than two miles apart. Sifford won the $6,000 first prize against a less-than-glamorous field. "If I can't beat the big boys, I'll beat the little guys," Sifford said.

In 1975, Sifford won the Senior PGA Championship, a tournament that had been established back in 1937, when Augusta National staged the event, won by Jock Hutchison. It became recognized as a major championship for players on the PGA's Senior Tour.

The tournament eventually relocated to Florida, although it is now contested on different courses. When Sifford won the $7,500 first-place check in 1975, it was held at Walt Disney World. He also was given a 1975 Lincoln Continental Mark IV.

As was the case in his previous wins in Long Beach and Los Angeles, Sifford needed extra holes to prevail over Fred Wampler, making a twenty-five-foot birdie putt on the first playoff hole. Wampler, a former NCAA champion from Purdue, missed a ten-footer that would have extended the playoff.

Sifford topped a field that included Hall of Famers Julius Boros, Tommy Bolt, and Sam Snead as well a couple familiar names from the past, Eric Monti and Ted Kroll.

What followed after that victory was, to Sifford, mind-boggling. The PGA had an arrangement with its British counterpart to have the winners of their respective senior championships meet in a one-day, thirty-six-hole, match-play event, every other year. There had been a number of them prior to 1975. The British champion that year was Kel Nagle, an Australian who had won the 1960 British Open and lost the 1965 US Open in a playoff to Gary Player. He was inducted into the World Golf Hall of Fame in 2007.

What irked Sifford was not the competition or the format, but the venue. The Bide-A-Wee golf club in Portsmouth, Virginia, had hosted the same event the previous two times. Nagle was the British representative on both occasions, defeating Julius Boros in 1971 and losing to Sam Snead in 1973. But as Sifford recounted later, he quickly became aware of something when the players broke for lunch in between the two rounds. He was the first Black man to ever play the course.

The mayor of Portsmouth, a member of the club, said, simply, "I don't know why they (the PGA) brought Charlie down to play here."

Sifford was so upset that he considered not going out to play the final eighteen holes in the afternoon. Why, of all the possible places to play the match, did the PGA choose this one? He may not have been aware that it had been staged at Bide-A-Wee on two prior occasions or that the host pro at Bide-A-Wee and match coordinator was Chandler Harper, a former tour player who won the PGA Championship in 1950. Sifford went out for the second eighteen holes, but Nagle won the match by overtaking his opponent over the final seven holes.

As for Sifford, he left immediately and drove back to Cleveland.

By 1978, had Charlie Sifford accomplished enough to be considered a legend? Maybe not in the sense of a Snead, Hogan, Nelson, Nicklaus, or Palmer. But knowing his story, knowing that he won twice on the PGA Tour, had two other PGA-Lite victories and had also won in 1971 at Sea Pines and in 1975 at the PGA Seniors, that gave him some fairway cred, did it not?

He thought so. Then he found out, again, that he was back to knocking on doors he thought had been opened years before.

In 1978, in what turned out to be the precursor of the Senior Tour, a tournament was held in Austin, Texas, called The Legends of Golf. The format was twelve, two-man teams, playing a best-ball format over three days at Onion Creek Country Club.

The field for the 1978 event was legendary. Sam Snead, then sixty-six, was among the twenty-four as were seventy-six-year-old Gene Sarazen, sixty-eight-year-old Jimmy Demaret, and sixty-two-year-old Tommy Bolt. Also in the field was seventy-year-old Paul Runyan. He was a star—in the 1930s. Peter Thomson was in the field. He was a five-time British Open champion. He also was forty-eight, two years under the supposed fifty-year-old qualification age. The catch phrase for the event was that it was going to "turn back the clock."

Not in the field? Charlie Sifford.

"With the exception of one Japanese gentleman of uncertain credentials, the field will be as white as the 1949 Masters. Or the Confederate General Staff," Jim Murray wrote.

Sifford called for an explanation. He was told he wasn't "legendary." But who was? Bob Toski? Dale Morey? Ed Tutwiler? Pete Nakamura?

They were all at Onion Creek the final weekend of April 1978 while Charlie Sifford was home, in Ohio.

"I thought I had gotten past all that crap twenty years earlier, but it was coming back," he said. "And nobody at the PGA did anything about it."

And nobody called in 1979 for the second Legends event, also at Onion Creek, or the third or the fourth. Still waiting in 1980, Sifford started play on the new Seniors Tour, which, at the time, was for players fifty-five or older. There were only four events in that first season, including the first US Senior Open and the now-recognized-as-a-major PGA Seniors Championship.

In between them was an event in Melbourne, Florida, in November, called the Suntree Classic. Charlie Sifford won it. It would be his only victory on the Seniors Tour. He had finished sixth at the inaugural tournament in Atlantic City and third at the US Senior Open.

At the Suntree, Sifford blew past Don January with a hail of birdies on the final day, saying the victory "was just as thrilling for me as my victory in the LA Open." He pocketed $20,000. He finished the year in second place on the money list with nearly $35,000.

A new tour was starting up and Sifford was there, ready and waiting. He said the Senior Tour "gave me back some of some of those years that I lost and I thank God for it." Unfortunately for him, the next year, the PGA lowered the age eligibility to fifty, which allowed players like Arnold Palmer, Miller Barber, Billy Casper, and Gene Littler to join. Sifford ended up winning nearly three times as much money on the Senior Tour as he did on the PGA Tour and more than $1 million in total.

Some of those winnings came after he finally was allowed to enter the Legends tournament in 1981. The qualifications for admission had been changed to recognize past PGA Seniors Champions. So Sifford showed up at Onion Creek, played with Mike Souchak, and he finished tied for tenth and split $11,000.

Sifford was visibly upset after the round. He had desperately wanted to play well, maybe even win the tournament, to show his "legendary" bona fides. When he was done, he hurled his cigar to the ground in disgust and told a local reporter, "I've got nothing to say."

Things improved in Austin for Sifford later in the decade. A senior-senior division was added for players over sixty and Sifford teamed with Roberto De Vicenzo to win it three times and three more times with Joe Jimenez.

In March of 1986, Sifford showed up at the MountainGate Country Club in California for the Johnny Mathis Seniors Classic. He was in the tenth group of the day, starting on the tenth tee. Flyers had been posted noting that the first player to make a hole-in-one on the fifteenth hole would win $100,000 and a new Buick. Sifford aced the hole with a new Buick Riviera on display next to the tee box.

Sifford had a thing for Buicks. One of the perks of playing well in the Buick Open was the use of a Buick for a year. Sifford said that helped enormously with the transportation costs. When he was in his first full year on the PGA Tour, Sifford had aced a par-3 at the San Diego Open and won an Oldsmobile Toronado. He had just been given the keys when a man approached him, asking if Sifford would sell him the car. Sifford said he would, for $5,500. A deal was struck.

"The money I made allowed me to go out and buy a new Buick," Sifford said. "Buicks were lucky for me all through the 1960s."

But unlike in San Diego, they didn't give Sifford the keys to drive the car away. That $100,000 for the hole-in-one? He didn't get that either.

After Sifford aced the fifteenth hole, the sponsors claimed that there was no cash award.

The tournament's press department had sent out a release on Friday morning, before the first round of the three-day tournament, announcing the cash/car prize to the first professional to make a hole-in-one in tournament play. The *Los Angeles Times* received the same release in its office just before 9 a.m. on the first day of the tournament.

Sifford smelled a rat. He called his attorney in Connecticut, Gerard Roisman, who immediately flew out to Los Angeles.

It was clear to Roisman that Sifford was owed both the car and the cash. It took a while for the Buick to materialize. Eventually, Roisman and Sifford arranged for the new car to be picked up in Cleveland by Sifford's wife. Before driving away, however, Rose Sifford called Roisman. The dealer wanted her to sign some paperwork. When she read the fine print to Roisman, he told her not to sign. It was a Promissory Note, meaning at some point down the line, she would be responsible for paying back the car dealer. When that language was removed, Rose Sifford drove the new Buick home. Her husband was still short $100,000, though, and Roisman sued the sponsors and insurers to get it.

Sifford was so angry about the refusal to pay him what he knew he had won legitimately that he refused to play in the event in 1987, even though it had moved to a different location and offered a $1,100 guarantee. That December, Sifford's case against the insurers went to trial in Los Angeles before Judge John Davies, a Ronald Reagan appointee who, seven years later, would preside over the trial of two police officers charged in the beating of Rodney King.

Roisman showed the jury the flyers promoting the giveaway. He introduced evidence showing that the sponsors did not have the insurance to pay off the $100,000. It took the jury three and a half hours to decide unanimously for Sifford. He finally got his $100,000—it was actually $100,934 with interest—but it took twenty months and a three-day trial to get it.

It was the biggest payday of his career.

"It was like winning the LA Open five times with a Buick thrown in to boot," he said. "Not bad for one swing of the club."

Epilogue

Honors

In the days leading up to his death in 2001, Stanley Mosk was still thinking about Charlie Sifford, the PGA, and the Caucasian-only clause the two had worked so hard to eliminate forty years earlier. Mosk penned a short opinion piece for *Sports Illustrated* in what the magazine then called "My Shot." Mosk was again taking the PGA to task, this time citing the Americans with Disability Act (ADA).

The PGA had denied tour player Casey Martin the use of a cart in its tournaments. Martin, a teammate of Tiger Woods at Stanford, suffered from a birth defect in his right leg which made him unable to walk eighteen holes, denying him the chance to compete. He sued the PGA.

A local magistrate ruled in his favor, as did the Ninth Circuit Court of Appeals. Both found the PGA in violation of the ADA. The PGA appealed to the United States Supreme Court, and it ruled, too, in Martin's favor by a 7–2 vote announced on May 29, 2001. Justices Antonin Scalia and Clarence Thomas dissented. Scalia's dissent likened the situation to a Kurt Vonnegut short story where people in the future are forced to deal with physical handicaps.

Mosk applauded the high court but wrote that he was "disheartened by the reaction of Tour officials and players who fear that the Tour could be overrun by carts. The innate bigotry fueling these fears is the same bigotry that lay behind the Caucasian-only clause barring blacks from Tour events until 1961, when a fight I initiated forced the PGA of America to drop that offensive and illegal provision."

Mosk then reiterated the history of his meeting with Sifford, the decision by the PGA to stage its 1962 championship in Los Angeles, and how he and other attorneys general, along with the NAACP, finally forced the PGA to eliminate the clause in November 1961.

"Casey and Charlie's cases are similar in that both men faced rules attempting to bar them from golf because of irrelevant qualifications," Mosk wrote. "African-American and physically disabled athletes have the same desire to compete as other humans, and if their abilities are up to par, there's no reason they shouldn't have the opportunity to play at their sport's highest levels. Had it not been for Charlie Sifford, we might never have heard of Tiger Woods. Who knows? Maybe Casey Martin has opened the door for the next superstar."

Martin won one event on what is now known as the Korn-Ferry Tour, the feeder tour for the PGA. It came in 1998 in Lakeland, Florida. That same year he qualified for the US Open, finishing tied for twenty-third. The following year, he earned more than $122,000 playing on what was then called the Web.com Tour. This was all before he realized he could not continue as a professional golfer without the use of a cart.

He continued to play in events on the feeder tour through 2006, when he was named the head coach of the University of Oregon's men's golf team. Ten years later, he led the Ducks to the 2016 NCAA Division I Men's Golf Championship.

The article in the June 11, 2001, edition of *Sports Illustrated* turned out to be the last words published by Stanley Mosk. He was still working as a justice on the court but had come to the decision that it was time to retire. He had written his resignation letter and had prepared to deliver it to Governor Gray Davis the following morning. He died in his sleep of a heart attack at his Nob Hill home in San Francisco on the evening of June 18, after a full day at work, with the letter still in his shirt pocket. He was eighty-eight.

The tributes poured in after Mosk's death, from the floor of the United States House of Representatives to the governor's office in Sacramento to the pages of the once-hostile *Los Angeles Times*, which had enthusiastically endorsed his opponent in his first run for attorney general in 1958.

Soon, ceremonies would be held to dedicate state buildings in honor of the judge. A courthouse in Los Angeles. A state courts building in Sacramento. But in 2010, more than nine years after his death, a motion to rename Valley Region Elementary School No. 10 in Winnetka came before the board of the Los Angeles Unified School District to name the school in honor of the longest-serving Supreme Court justice in state history.

"How fabulous that we get to name a school for Stanley Mosk," said Monica Garcia, the board's president.

On the morning of October 12, 2010, Arthur Drye left his Pasadena home and made the drive into downtown Los Angeles for the afternoon meeting of the LAUSD. There were thirty-one items on the agenda that day, but number eighteen was the one that motivated the seventy-eight-year-old Drye to make the trip.

Drye was the third of four speakers who rose to endorse the renaming of the school. Appeals court judge Laurence Rubin, one of Mosk's former law clerks, spoke of the judge's passion for and belief in the importance of education. He cited the 1966 case *Manjares v. Newton*, in which Mosk, then in his third year on the California Supreme Court, wrote for the majority in a decision that required that a school district in Northern California provide transportation to school for the Manjares children. Without that transportation, they would not have been able to attend school.

Mosk wrote that "we indulge in no hyperbole to assert that society has a compelling interest in affording children an opportunity to attend school." He wrote that education was perhaps the most important function of state and local governments:

> Today, it is a principal instrument in awakening citizenship. Today it is a principal instrument in awakening the child to cultural values. In these days it is doubtful any child may reasonably be expected to succeed in life if he or she is denied the opportunity of an education. Such an opportunity when the state has undertaken to provide it, is a right which must be available to all on equal terms. In light of the public interest in conserving the resources of young minds, we must unsympathetically examine any action of a public body which has the effect of depriving children of the opportunity to obtain an education.

After Andrea Ordin spoke fondly of Judge Mosk and his visionary approach to guiding the attorney general's office, it was Arthur Drye's turn to speak. He briefly recited the facts of a case from sixty-three years earlier, when Judge Mosk had ruled that restrictive racial covenants were unenforceable, as well as reprehensible. His voice cracked as he remembered his father, a veteran of World War I and World War II and the main defendant in the case and how Mosk had supported their family's right to live in the home they had bought.

"I ask you to honor a real American, Stanley Mosk," Drye told the board. "Judge Mosk, more than any person in the Los Angeles area, was responsible for desegregating southern California housing. Judge Mosk assured my father, our family and others that housing equality under the law in 1947 Los Angeles was to be protected by the courts."

It was a powerful and moving speech. Here was a man whose life had been directly impacted by one of Mosk's decisions. He could speak to the struggle his family faced just to remain in their own house. He could speak to having to hire attorneys to represent his family and the families of two others in the neighborhood who were targeted because of their race.

"It would only seem appropriate that a school in Los Angeles be named in honor of Judge Mosk," Drye said, adding,

> His story of fighting prejudice and fighting for equality should be recognized by the district. Children of all ethnicities need to know who the pioneers of social and racial equality were. And a fitting way for this board to teach this lesson would be to name Elementary School Number 10 after a man who put his convictions in action and whose actions affected the entire region. It certainly affected me, and it affected my family.

The Stanley Mosk Elementary School is home to more than five hundred students, from kindergarten to fifth grade. It is a minority-majority school. Sandra Mosk, the judge's daughter-in-law, said without hesitation that of all the tributes to her father-in-law, the naming of an elementary school in his honor would have pleased him the most.

Before the LAUSD board moved onto other matters, one of its members, Marguerite LaMotte, asked to speak. She said she did not know Judge Mosk, but after hearing the speakers, "I certainly feel like I know him now." She suggested the students study the words of the man for whom the school was named. She called them, "a lesson for life."

In the summer of 2004, Charlie Sifford received a phone call he thought at first had to be a prank. On the line was Tim Finchem, the commissioner of the PGA Tour.

"What did I do now?" Sifford asked in jest.

He had done nothing to warrant any criticism from the commissioner. Finchem was calling to tell Sifford that he would be inducted into the World Golf Hall of Fame.

Sifford was thunderstruck. After hanging up, he yelled. He danced. He lit up a cigar and poured himself a drink. Finally, he broke down and cried.

"The images of the past would flash in my head: being turned away at tournaments, riding on dark highways with no motels to stay at, no restaurants to eat at and being jeered, heckled, cursed and called every name under the sun. A whirlwind of emotion came over me. Was this phone call real?"

It was. Tiger Woods had said earlier that there shouldn't even be a Hall of Fame if Sifford was not a member, and that apparently made an impact on the selection committee. Jim Thorpe, one of the few Black golfers to come after Sifford and enjoy success, mostly on the Senior Tour, was elated for the man he called "Dad."

Said Thorpe, "Charlie looked at it this way: somebody had to do it. Jackie Robinson had to do it. Althea Gibson had to do it. Someone had to do it."

In 2004, Jim Thorpe was fifty-five. He had grown up in Jim Crow North Carolina, just like Sifford, and was introduced to the game by his father, who was the greenskeeper at a local course in Roxboro. He was twelve when the PGA eliminated its Caucasian-only clause. By the time he turned pro in 1972, the racial barriers that had stood in Sifford's way were no longer there. Except, perhaps, for that tournament in Georgia every April.

"My father explained it to me years ago. Golf was a rich man's game, mostly a Caucasian game. We knew there were times we couldn't go out on the course and play. My dad explained all that. When they announced Charlie for the Hall of Fame, it was all well worth it.

"It had to be very, very difficult for him," Thorpe went on. "But Charlie was a mean character, man. Charlie wasn't backing down. He fought his way through the fires and the harsh words. Thank God there are people like Charlie who are willing to go out there and say, 'Okay, the only way you're going to get me out of here is to kill me.'"

By the time Sifford got the news from Finchem, all three legs from the stool that had propped him up and supported him throughout his life had gone. That was one of the reasons he broke down after receiving the news. The people most responsible for him making it in the world of professional golf would not be there to share it with him.

The first to go was Billy Eckstine, in 1993, at the age of seventy-eight. Sifford remembered Eckstine as "the catalyst that made it all happen," from bankrolling his golf career for a decade in the late 1940s and 1950s to introducing Sifford to Stanley Mosk at Hillcrest Country Club.

"He was the man with the celebrity, the fame, the money and the connections who opened doors for me and other Black golfers in the 1940s and 1950s," Sifford said. "Looking beyond music, he had the genius and the foresight to see that golf was a great game and that a Black man with enough talent and a fair chance could open the game for others to follow."

Eckstine died in Pittsburgh, his hometown, a year after suffering a stroke while on stage performing in Salinas, Kansas. According to his biographer, Eckstine's last word was "Basie."

"His style and technique have been extensively copied by some of the neocommercial singers, but despite their efforts, he remains out front to show how and what should have been done," Duke Ellington said of Eckstine in his autobiography, *Music Is My Mistress*.

Late in his career, Eckstine hosted a show on local television in Los Angeles called *The Jazz Show*. All the tapes from the show, however, were destroyed in the 1971 earthquake in the area. But his son, Ed, recalled his father welcoming a musician from West Virginia onto the show named Bill Withers. After hearing Withers perform, Billy Eckstine told his son, "This kid is good!" Withers, who wrote "Lean on Me," "Ain't No Sunshine," and "Just The Two of Us," won three Grammy Awards and was inducted into the Rock and Roll Hall of Fame in 2015.

Lionel Hampton called Eckstine "one of the greatest singers of all time. . . . He was our singer." Quincy Jones said, simply, "If he'd been white, the sky would have been the limit."

The same could be said for the man whom Eckstine hired in 1946 to be his driver, golf teacher, playing partner, and confidant.

Five years later, Sifford's wife, Rose, died, succumbing to leukemia. She had been at his side, physically and spiritually, throughout it all.

"Charlie was lucky," Gary Player said during his introductory speech for Sifford at the Hall of Fame enshrinement ceremony. "He had a lot of love in his wife, Rose. She had the most appropriate name for a woman because every time you saw her, she was like a rose. She was filled with positive thoughts and love, and she must have been a great inspiration to Charlie."

Added Dave Stockton, who played in Sifford's era, "When they enter him into the Hall, they'll be entering Rose with him."

She had worked in Philadelphia, raising Charles Jr., while her husband was touring the country and playing golf and making a living as Eckstine's Mr. Everything. She had been at her husband's side in Rancho Park in 1969 when he won the Los Angeles Open, having left her native Philadelphia a dozen years earlier. She had handled the bulk of the duties, along with her son, when the family moved to Cleveland in 1974 to do something they had no experience doing—running a golf course and pro shop. Her husband was not cut out for the job.

"The hardest thing for me was to be nice to people all the time," Sifford had said of the job. "I have a lot of patience, but those people practically wore me out."

The final loss came in 2001 with the death of Stanley Mosk. "This man was a legal giant," Sifford said. "I will always hold him in highest regard. What a wonderful man!"

When Sifford wrote his autobiography in 1992, he sent a copy to Mosk with a small note: "To Mr. Stanley Mosk, I would like to thank you for everything that you did for me and my family. I will never forget you. Best wishes and may God bless you all ways. Yours truly, Charles Sifford."

Mosk wrote back, thanking Sifford for the book and for the appreciative references to the work of the attorney general's office at that time. "One attitude that I have always considered to be contrary to the principles of American democracy is racial discrimination. It must be wiped out, and those of us in public life have a responsibility to do our best to rid society of that bias. I am pleased that some years back you were a beneficiary of my efforts. I wish you well in the days ahead. Sincerely, Stanley Mosk."

In retirement, Charlie Sifford received countless honors and awards in recognition not of his sterling play, but in his unwavering determination and perseverance. There was the honorary Doctor of Law degree conferred by the University of St. Andrews in 2006. There was the 2007 Old Tom Morris Award from the Golf Course Superintendents Association of America, a fitting honor for a former caddie. There was the establishment of the Charlie Sifford Exemption to what used to be known as the Los Angeles Open. There was the naming of the public golf course in Charlotte in his honor, a course he could play when he lived there. By 2014, Sifford was ninety-two and in a wheelchair, his body wracked by diabetes, congestive heart failure, and old age. But he still made it to the White House in 2014 to be given the Presidential Medal of Freedom by one of his heroes, President Barack Obama.

"In the final analysis," he said, "my story was one of survival."

It all came to an end on February 3, 2015, after Sifford suffered a fatal stroke.

But if there was one award Sifford treasured above all others, it was his induction to the World Golf Hall of Fame. The ceremony honoring Sifford was held on Monday, November 15, 2004, in St. Augustine, Florida, when he was still ambulatory and with a sense of humor. It was a ceremony of firsts. Sifford was the first Black to enter the Hall. Isao Aoki was the first Japanese man to enter the Hall (Hisako "Chako" Niguchi had been enshrined the year before) and amateur sensation Marlene Stewart Streit was the first Canadian to enter the Hall. The other honoree that year was Tom Kite.

In a video appearance, Tiger Woods told the gathering, "Not many people could have endured the indignities that he suffered in some very difficult times. That he persevered with grace and honor should inspire you when things aren't going your way. I know it inspires me." Player introduced Sifford, the final inductee of the ceremony. He talked about the abuse and indignities that Sifford endured and asked the audience to "imagine Tiger Woods and Vijay Singh, rated first and second in the world, and being told they couldn't play because they're not white. It's hard to comprehend what actually took place in our time. It's pleasing to know we've advanced in our thinking. Thank goodness."

Player recounted his rounds with Sifford, including one where a spectator kicked Sifford's ball into the woods.

"Persistence is an ingredient that is essential to success and Charlie had that persistence," Player said. "He handled adversity with great dignity. Some people said he was mean, and I said, 'If you went through what he went through, you'd understand.' He handled dignity in my eyes like President (Nelson) Mandela, who went to jail for 27 years and came out with love and appreciation of mankind."

Player then called Sifford to the podium to a standing ovation for the eighty-two-year-old.

Sifford then delivered a rambling but emotional fifteen-minute speech punctuated frequently by deep breaths to keep his composure. "You have to go along with me," he asked the crowd, breaking down. "This is tough. You're going to have to forgive me because this little old caddie from North Carolina is getting inducted into the World Golf Hall of Fame. How about that?"

After another round of applause, he said, "It makes me feel like I'm a worthwhile professional golfer and I did my best." Someone in the crowd yelled out, "We love you, Charlie."

Then, Sifford lost it for a bit when he started talking about his family. His two sons were there. Their spouses and children were there.

He paused again.

"The boss isn't here. I know without Rose . . ." He couldn't finish the sentence. But he made note of the wives of the Hall of Famers in front of him—Winnie Palmer and Barbara Nicklaus—and then observed, "who understood when their husbands left, they knew they were going to get some money and bring it home."

Sifford recognized Lee Elder in the audience. He saluted Gary Player, who he called "my man" for not buckling in the 1969 PGA in Dayton, Ohio, when protestors threw ice on him during the third round. Player always has said he thought that cost him the tournament; he finished one shot behind Raymond Floyd.

Sifford drew laughs when he said he wished he were younger and could still be playing. He recalled how he had to be careful to play by the rules and made sure his caddie did the same.

"And I had to be sure whoever came up and interfered with my game that I could be cool enough to brush him off. And I did that job," he said.

His final words were not for Stanley Mosk or Billy Eckstine, but an appeal to the Hall to recognize the Black golfers who paved the way for him—Teddy Rhodes and Bill Spiller—and to those he helped paved the way for—Lee Elder and Calvin Peete.

The PGA did grant posthumous memberships to Spiller, Rhodes, and John Shippen in 2009 and a posthumous honorary membership to Joe Louis. But the next Black golfer to get inducted was Tiger Woods in 2022.

Sifford ended the speech on a humorous note. He said the time between getting notified and the induction ceremony was the longest five months he had ever experienced. "I drove my car slow. I looked both ways before I crossed the street. I wanted to be damn sure I was here, tonight.

"I'm in the Hall of Fame! Don't forget that now. It don't get any better than this, please believe me."

Sifford was inducted for lifetime achievement on the golf course. But it was in changing that course that Charlie Sifford left his most lasting legacy.

Acknowledgments

$\mathscr{A}$fter appearing on a podcast with Connor T. Lewis to discuss my previous book, *The Open Question: Ben Hogan and Golf's Most Enduring Controversy*, he asked me what I had in mind for my next book. When I mentioned I had nothing cooking at that moment, he piqued my interest when he said I should write about the 1962 PGA Championship.

Why was that? I asked.

Because it had to be moved because of the Caucasian-only clause, he said.

I had no idea. At first, I thought it would be good to balance the PGA moving the 1962 championship for the wrong reason (racism) with the PGA moving the 2022 championship for the right reason (January 6 insurrection.) But the more I looked into it, the more it became clear to me that this was a story of two men whose unlikely meeting at a Los Angeles country club led to an alliance that ended codified racial discrimination in the last of the major American sports.

I knew of Charlie Sifford, of course, though not all the details of his incredible story. I was somewhat familiar with Stanley Mosk, who I soon discovered was most definitely an individual worth knowing. They were both believers in civil rights, both fighters, and their respective journeys and crusades led them to do what no one had been able to do for more than a quarter century. For his role alone, Mosk should be in the conversation for a place in the World Golf Hall of Fame. Sifford, rightfully, is already there.

This book would never have been written were it not for that brief conversation with Lewis three years ago. He hosts a terrific podcast called

Talking Golf History, and I can only hope to visit with him again to discuss the life stories of Charlie Sifford and Stanley Mosk.

I owe a huge debt of gratitude to two ladies who repeatedly fielded my sometimes challenging and off-the-wall inquiries with grace and professionalism. Laura Hibbler at Brandeis University was always available to unearth some obscure newspaper article from the 1940s. Marie Silva at the California Judicial Center Library patiently walked me through what was needed to read the Oral Histories and other materials on which so much of Mosk's life is based. I think they both nicknamed me "Bad Penny" because I kept popping up, asking questions.

Maggie Lagle at the USGA Library and Museum also was tremendously helpful, especially with the collection that focuses on the history of African Americans in golf. It's always worth a trip to the Museum. Bob Denney, who is the man to go to for PGA history, steered me in the right direction more than once. Liza Talbot at the LBJ Library helped me with the tapes of President Johnson and Pat Brown. Joseph Bree at Maryland Eastern-Shore allowed me to look over the Charlie Sifford Collection.

The generosity of Enid Gort cannot be overstated. She provided me with the transcripts of her interviews with Franklin Williams as he talked about his work fighting the PGA. My thanks also to the Schomburg Center for Research at the New York Public Library for assisting with Franklin Williams's personal papers.

I am grateful to Enrique Hervada, who is overseeing the restoration of Cobbs Creek golf course in Philadelphia. He drove me around the course, dodging holes in the ground and trees scattered all over the property while giving me a quick history of the venue. Mike Cirba helped with his exhaustive book on the history of Cobbs Creek. I can only imagine what the course and grounds will look like when everything is finished. It should be spectacular.

Billy Cleveland, the general manager of the Carolina Golf Club, helped with the history of the course, which is where Charlie Sifford caddied and learned how to play the game. Preston Buckman drove me around the public golf course in Charlotte named for Charlie Sifford.

Russ Crockett and Darryl Porter, who are managing partners of JLMP, LLC (Sifford Estate Branding) were quite helpful with questions about Charlie's life and struggles. Ed Eckstine generously gave me his time to talk about his famous father and one of his favorite people, the man he called "Horse." I even forgive him for being a Lakers fan.

I would have had a lot more difficulty piecing together Judge Mosk's life and contributions to California law and history without the help of

Laurence Rubin, an appeals court judge who clerked for Mosk in the early 1970s. He introduced me to Peter Weil, who took me to lunch at Hillcrest Country Club, and to Andrea Ordin, who shared her memories of Judge Mosk as a member of the attorney general's office.

Jay Coffin of Coffin Corner Media deserves a long and hearty shout-out. He was especially helpful with *The Open Question* and has been with me every step of the way in writing this book. I hope to rely on him once again.

My thanks also go out to the families of the two men who are the centerpieces of this story. Charles Sifford Jr. was extremely helpful, showing me the many articles and stories he has collected over the years. He even trusted me to take one scrapbook home for research purposes. (I returned it.)

Sandra Mosk and her children, Matthew and Julie, could not have been nicer in relating their memories of Stanley Mosk. Susan Mosk was equally accommodating in sharing stories of her late husband.

Family and friends get recognized here for sharing the whole experience with the author, which sometimes can prove to be a perilous exercise. Bill Nugent graciously offered to read the manuscript. Tom and Kathi Mullin checked in frequently during the process and Sue and Doug Noyes lived with the ongoing trials and tribulations of their neighbor writing another book.

My thanks to my literary agent, Colleen Mohyde, for helping to shepherd this project, and to Christen Karniski at Rowman & Littlefield for championing it. Jessica McCleary at Rowman & Littlefield proved to be a skillful and patient editor, for which the author is grateful.

Finally, thanks as always to the immediate family, most importantly Eileen McNamara. Her support and advice throughout were omnipresent, and she did an exemplary job of proofreading a manuscript as one would expect from a former Pulitzer Prize winner and writing professor. She even knows the difference between a birdie and an eagle. I think.

A Note on Sources

*W*hen writing about an event more than sixty years old, and with the main people involved in that event having passed away, the writer necessarily turns to secondary sources to recreate the situation for the reader as best he can.

In this case, most of the source material for information on Charlie Sifford came from his autobiography, *Just Let Me Play*, originally published in 1992. Virtually all of the quotations attributed to Charlie Sifford in this book are from that work. Other sources included two lengthy interviews he gave to the USGA and the World Golf Hall of Fame. Sifford was interviewed countless times by countless media over the years. But the story of his life and the hardships he overcame are revealed with heartfelt (and sometimes heartbreaking) authenticity in his autobiography.

Stanley Mosk is quoted extensively as well, and his remarks come from a variety of source materials. I relied on three oral histories provided by the judge as well as his letters to his brother during World War II and an unpublished manuscript. He also answered questions posed by author John H. Kennedy, who was gracious enough to share them with me. The *Los Angeles Times* proved to be an excellent source for its news coverage of the judge, from his campaigns for attorney general to his decisions from the bench on topics ranging from discrimination to capital punishment. *LA Weekly*'s detailed examination of the reasons behind Mosk's withdrawal from the 1964 US Senate race proved to be a huge help as well.

Author interviews with members of the families and with individuals such as Gary Player, Ed Eckstine, Larry Rubin, and others helped to complete a portrait of the men and the times in which they worked.

This is a story about golf history. It is also a story about civil rights. In retelling the stories of Charlie Sifford and Stanley Mosk, I hope the reader has a better understanding of the issues these men dealt with amid the times in which they lived. Stanley Mosk saw wrong and tried to right it. So did Charlie Sifford. Their alliance changed golf and the world of professional sports—for the good.

Bibliography

BOOKS

Barkow, Al. *Gettin' to the Dance Floor*. New York: Atheneum, 1986.

Barrett, David. *Miracle at Merion: The Inspiring Story of Ben Hogan's Amazing Comeback and Victory at the 1950 U.S. Open*. New York: Skyhorse, 2010.

Bolden, Abraham. *The Echo from Dealey Plaza: The True Story of the First African-American on the White House Secret Service Detail and His Quest for Justice after the Assassination of JFK*. New York: Three Rivers Press, 2008.

Braitman, Jacqueline, and Gerald Uelmen. *Justice Stanley Mosk: A Life at the Center of California Politics and Justice*. Jefferson, NC: McFarland & Co, 2013.

Brown, Edmund G., and Dick Adler. *Public Justice, Private Mercy: A Governor's Education on Death Row*. New York: Weidenfeld & Nicolson, 1989.

Darsie, Darsie L. *My Greatest Day in Golf*. New York: A.S. Barnes, 1950.

Demas, Lane. *Game of Privilege: An African American History of Golf*. Chapel Hill: University of North Carolina Press, 2017.

Eubanks, Steve. *Augusta: Home of the Masters Tournament. A Revealing Look Inside America's Most Intriguing Golf Club*. Nashville, TN: Rutledge Hill Press, 1997.

Frommer, Myrna Katz, and Harvey Frommer. *It Happened in the Catskills: An Oral History in the Words of Busboys, Bellhops, Guests, Proprietors, Comedians, Agents and Others Who Lived It*. New York: Harcourt Brace Jovanovich, 1991.

Gabler, Neal. *An Empire of Their Own: How the Jews Invented Hollywood*. New York: Anchor, 1988.

Ginell, Cary. *Mr. B: The Life and Music of Billy Eckstine*. Milwaukee, WI: Hal Leonard Books, 2013.

Gort, Enid, and John M. Caher. *A Bridge to Justice: The Life of Franklin H. Williams*. New York: Fordham University Press, 2022.

Graffis, Herb. *The PGA. The Official History of the Professional Golfers Association of America*. New York: Thomas Y. Crowell, 1975.

Kennedy, John H. *A Course of Their Own. A History of African American Golfers.* Lincoln: University of Nebraska Press, 2000.

Louis, Joe, Edna Rust, and Art Rust. *My Life.* New York: Harcourt Brace Jovanovich, 1978.

McDaniel, Pete. *Uneven Lies: The Heroic Story of African-Americans in Golf.* Greenwich, CT: The American Golfer, 2000.

Mills, James R. *A Disorderly House: The Brown-Unruh Years in Sacramento.* Berkeley, CA: Heyday Books, 1987.

Mosk, Stanley. Unpublished manuscript at California Judicial Center Library Special Collections and Archives.

Owen, David. *The Making of the Masters: Clifford Roberts, Augusta National, and Golf's Most Prestigious Tournament.* New York: Simon & Schuster, 1999.

Rampersand, Arnold. *Ralph Ellison: A Biography.* New York: Alfred A Knopf, 2007.

Rapaport, Ron. *The Immortal Bobby: Bobby Jones and the Golden Age of Golf.* Hoboken, NJ: John Wiley & Sons, 2005.

Sampson, Curt. *The Masters: Golf, Money and Power in Augusta, Georgia.* New York: Villard, 1998.

Sifford, Charlie, and James Gullo. *Just Let Me Play. The Story of Charlie Sifford.* Latham, NY: British-American Publishing, 1992.

ORAL HISTORIES AND PERSONAL PAPERS

Alexander, William Sutton. A Widows Will. Carolina Golf Club. Date Unknown.

Belton, Peter. Interview by Germaine LaBerge. California Regional Oral History Office, 2003.

Lytton, Bart. Interview by Ronald J. Grele. John F. Kennedy Library Oral History Program, 1966.

McEnery, John. Interview by James Fuchs. Harry S. Truman Library, 1970.

Mosk, Richard M. Interview by Matthew Mosk. California Supreme Court Historical Society, 2001.

Mosk, Stanley. Interview by Amelia Fry. California Governmental History Documentation Project. 1979.

———. Interview by Germaine LaBerge. State Government Oral History Program. 1998.

———. Interview by Margaret Levy and Gordon Bakken. California Supreme Court Historical Society. 1996.

Roberts, Clifford. Interviews by John T. Mason. Columbia Center for Oral History. The Eisenhower Administration Project. 1972.

Williams, Franklin H. Schomburg Center for Research in Black Culture, Manuscripts, Archives and Rare Books Division, New York Public Library

PODCASTS

Lewis, Connor T. (host). TalkinGolf. "The Caucasian Clause." May 15, 2022. https://talkingolf.fireside.fm/83https://talkingolf.fireside.fm/83.

ARCHIVES AND MUSEUMS

The Homestead Museum, Los Angeles, California.
The Lyndon B. Johnson Presidential Library, Austin, Texas.
The Office of Military Personnel Records, St. Louis, Missouri.
The Charlie Sifford Collection, Maryland Eastern Shore University, Princess Anne, Maryland.
The United States Golf Association Museum and Library, Far Hills, New Jersey.

PRIMARY NEWSPAPERS

Akron Beacon-Journal
Austin American-Statesman
Chicago American
Chicago Defender
Chicago Sun-Times
Chicago Tribune
Daily Mirror
Los Angeles Sentinel
Los Angeles Times
Los Angeles Weekly
Pittsburgh Courier
New York Times
San Diego Union

MAGAZINES

American Heritage
Cigar Aficionado
Golf Digest
Golf World
Sports Illustrated
Town & Country

Index

About the Author

Peter May has spent the last four decades covering sports for the *Boston Globe*, the *New York Times*, ESPN, the *Hartford Courant*, and United Press International. He is the author of three books about the Boston Celtics—*The Big Three*, *The Last Banner*, and *Top of the World*—and helped craft the narrative for the autobiography of Hall of Fame basketball coach Kim Mulkey, *Won't Back Down*. His latest book, *The Open Question: Ben Hogan and Golf's Most Enduring Controversy*, was nominated for the Herbert Warren Wind Award. He lives in New Hampshire with his wife, the journalist Eileen McNamara, and his miniature schnauzer, Fauci.